COMBAT

CHARTWELL
BOOKS, INC.

CONTENTS

Editor: Len Cacutt
Designer: John Fitzmaurice

Published by Chartwell Books, Inc.
A division of Booksales Inc.
110 Enterprise Avenue
Secaucus, New Jersey 07094

ISBN 1-55521-240-9

© Aerospace Publishing Ltd 1988
This edition © Marshall Cavendish Limited 1988

Reprinted 1989

Printed and bound in Italy

INTRODUCTION

The most successful of all early armies were the Roman legions and they were successful because their soldiers were tough, well-trained and disciplined. There were thirty legions, each having some 5,300 legionnaires who formed the troops of ten cohorts. The Roman soldier went into battle with a clear view of his objective and his tactics and he was skilled in the use of his weapons, a big, double-bladed sword, a dagger and two throwing spears. Important, too, was the fact that he was well led by officers he respected. So what was the secret of the Legions' successes, when they conquered most of the then known world? Good weapons, training and discipline.

Nothing has changed. Today's fighting man, if he is to be a winner, must have the same criteria. Unfortunately, the eventual fall of the Roman Empire – not the fault of its soldiery – was the beginning of a long period of confused and ill-led warfare.

The human race in one respect has little to boast about. While priding himself on being lord of the Earth, man is the only animal that makes war in its own species for religious or political purposes, and predictably has brought science and technology into use for his military needs. No longer do fanfares and trumpets proclaim battle as the kings and princes take up their arms and go out to face their enemies in personal combat for one to defeat the other. Our fate is no longer in the hands of our rulers, it lies in the verbal manoeuvring of our politicians, who are the last people to do physical combat, using words with which to instill a national fervour into their people. Swords, we have been told, can be turned into ploughshares – but what do you do when someone steals your plough and turns it into a weapon?

When sheer physical strength and skilled swordplay meant face-to-face combat wars lasted no longer than the time it took to disarm or kill the other. But it was not long before great armies of followers were employed, some nothing but slaves forced to take up primitive arms on behalf of their owners. But one way or another, they in their massed hundreds would charge and counter charge leaving piles of dead and dying as evidence of their supremacy – or otherwise. In the Middle Ages and later those armies were composed of men and boys armed with nothing but steel and wood and fortified by fear, and they were facing an enemy with the same limited means.

Sometimes, the battles would be decided on numbers given that other things were equal. If your army had thousands and your opponent only hundreds all you had to do was advance upon him and absorb the losses of x-numbers of your men in eliminating the other side. The victors then walked across and took over as the remains of the enemy fled.

In some cases, early battles were fought on the premise that when it was obvious one side was going to win the principals shook hands and that was that, except in holy wars of course when under one or other of the banners of divine guidance it was perfectly in order to massacre the unbelievers.

The invention of gunpowder made it possible to kill one's enemy at long range, even longer than the formidable British longbow. This was a formidable weapon, with its pull of 50lb. A battle report written in 1188 said of a casualty: 'An arrow shot by a Welshman went right through his thigh, high up, where it was protected outside and inside the leg by his iron thigh armour, and then through the skirt of his leather tunic; next it penetrated that part of the saddle which is called the alva or seat; and finally it lodged in his horse, driving in so deep that it killed the animal'. Some of today's small-arms ammunition might not be as effective.

Later, the crossbow, with a pull of 1200 lb, gave more penetrative power to the missile, enabling it to pierce the body armour of the day. When steel was used in its manufacture the crossbow was reported to have a range of 500 yards. Wars were becoming more 'effective' in terms of eliminating the opponent.

In fairly recent years the well-worn phrase 'Wait until you see the whites of his eyes!' was a standard order to the infantryman and was good advice, but for reasons not connected with bravery or fighting prowess. The order was given simply because the weapons of the day were so inaccurate that a hit was quite unlikely at any range beyond the point when those 'whites' could be distinguished.

The battlefields of World War One soaked up more than enough blood to put mankind off wars, because the generals responsible for the unnecessary slaughter were still practising the tactics and combat skills they had learned from military college manuals written by soldiers who knew all about the Boer War but who were not aware of the domination of the machine-gun across open ground. And even in the war that followed the war-to-end-wars, the one that began in 1939, Polish cavalry were still sent to face certain annihilation in front of the tanks of the German panzers.

Combat in late Twentieth Century style is now so sophisticated that the time is not far off when we will be sending robot armies to laser each other to pools of molten metal, but what the political outcome will be will not be left to those who press the buttons controlling the tin troops. Today's battlefields are still likely to be populated by human soldiers, but their frail bodies, so vulnerable when faced with modern weaponry and the various means of detection employed by all the major powers, need very special protective measures and their training takes this into consideration. Much of this is discussed in the following pages.

Today's soldier is never invisible to the enemy. The heat his body and his equipment generates can be 'seen' by special thermal detectors and homed-in on by weapons that follow his every movement, weapons that use lasers to calculate his range, take into consideration the wind speed and direction, humidity, select the appropriate ammunition and open fire. The means of long-range offence and defence are virtually out of the hands of man. But for all that, the infantryman is still needed and, to quote a World War Two soldier: 'You'll still have to have the little guy with a rifle and bayonet to winkle the other out of his foxhole and get him to sign the peace treaty!'

This book, broadly entitled COMBAT, covers a number of subjects which affect the infantryman at war. The professional soldier today is a highly trained technician, not the maligned cannon fodder of not so long ago. His means and methods if he is to be an effective member of a fighting team are described, and while it is not a pleasant thought there is useful comment on the possibility of capture and what this entails. He will obviously consider escape, and for some it is the only possible attitude. This is why it is a subject in which only the properly prepared escapee has any chance.

If there is to be another global war where will its battlefields be? The armies of today are extremely mobile and large numbers of troops can be moved quickly to the far corners of the world. A soldier might find himself slogging across arctic wastes, through snow and ice-covered mountain passes or, at the other extreme, over burning desert or through the cloying humidity of dense jungle. In all these extremes of terrain today's infantryman must not only survive but he must retain full fighting mobility and also feed himself. There are sections here that will help to know the problems.

The Editor in the course of his work has had the privilege of visiting British and foreign military units in many parts of the world and has had first-hand experience of a number of modern weapons. During the conversations he has been able to hold with soldiers, sailors and airmen one fascinating thing has emerged. Each was asked what was the most effective way to fight a battle. The answer, whether from infantryman, fighter or bomber pilot, submarine captain, MBT crewman, was 'My way!'

This conviction that his chosen career was the right one indicates that he has enormous confidence in his weaponry, his tactics and, most importantly, himself. That is why he will prevail.

CHAPTER ONE

INFANTRYMAN

Even today, the basic human element of all land warfare is still the class of soldier known as the infantryman, and that old P.B.I. label – 'Poor Bloody Infantry' – has often been a very true and accurate description. But cannon-fodder today he certainly is not, for the infantryman has to have a wide range of skills and military disciplines and be able to act decisively on his own initiative when faced with a sudden development or an offensive movement. And because he is likely to be the first one to know what is happening his re-actions can be vital.

Military textbooks all agree on one thing, that inescapable fact that any territory which has been taken by armed force must then be occupied by troops in sufficient number and of suitable calibre to keep control of the resi-dent, and probably seething, population. Hitler found this out after his soldiers over-ran most of Europe in 1939-40. Anyone who has driven the length and breadth of France will understand the extreme problems that faced the German Wehrmacht after the capit-ulation of the French Army at that time.

To hold such a vast country under strict military occupation demanded large num-bers of German soldiers and the planned invasion of Britain and then Russia meant that massive reinforcements of troops would be needed. The way that Hitler chose to hold France (and all the other countries he had invaded) was cruel subjugation, fear and ter-ror by recruiting as many collaborators as he could enlist. As the world knows the method failed as it had to do in the long run. But even though it is a truism that only the victor will write the history of the war, the archives tell the story.

The title of this chapter, opening COM-BAT, is Infantryman. It introduces the way properly planned patrols must be made by infantry from their home base. The reasons for such patrols and the techniques that ensure that they are as safe and successful as possible are outlined. Information must be obtained about the enemy's strength and positions, the type of units along the front, his strength of armour and defensive arrange-ments, all these are of great importance if operations against him are to succeed.

Since today's highly trained infantryman is likely to find himself in an aircraft and on his way anywhere from tropical jungle to a remote icecap, we describe some of the prob-lems that may face a four-man team. In this case, our chapter puts the operation in the jungle, where the hazards are of a particular nature.

The chapter continues with the patrols having been made. They have seen, logged and estimated the enemy's strength, and the intelligence gained has been processed so that the plans for the forthcoming offensive are based on known facts. If these were well-founded and accurate, and the strength of the forces needed to attack and destroy the enemy were right, in go the infantry, sup-ported by the required amount of armour and air support.

We continue with the sniper's role. It is lonely, hazardous and demands of its wearer of the badge the ability to work in sometimes frighteningly isolated places close to the enemy. He needs very special expertise in handling his weapons and it goes without saying that he must have an exceptionally good eye. This is one of the most demanding ranks for any soldier. Two articles describe how the sniper operates, where best be can do his job and how he applies his craft to obtain the necessary result.

In all battles and skirmishes there are advances and retreats, attacks and times of desperate defence. The last of the features in Chapter One deals with how to prepare a defensive position and hold it with deter-mined and disciplined methods until the time comes to move forward on the offensive again.

RECCE THE ENEMY

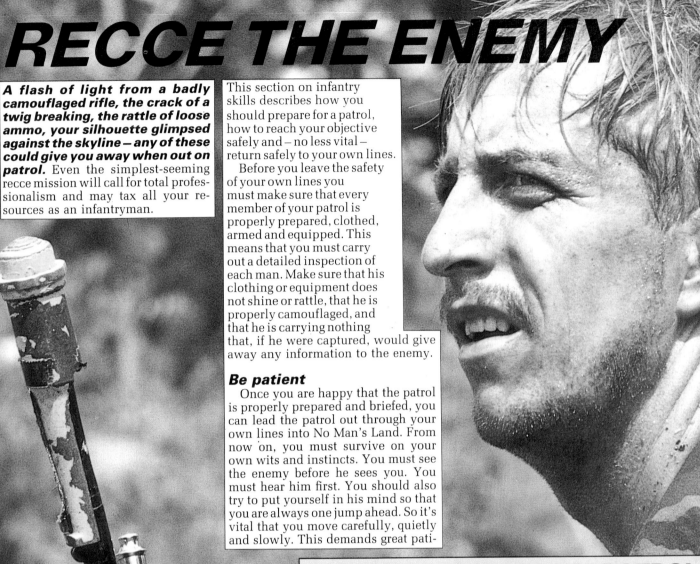

A flash of light from a badly camouflaged rifle, the crack of a twig breaking, the rattle of loose ammo, your silhouette glimpsed against the skyline – any of these could give you away when out on patrol. Even the simplest-seeming recce mission will call for total professionalism and may tax all your resources as an infantryman.

This section on infantry skills describes how you should prepare for a patrol, how to reach your objective safely and – no less vital – return safely to your own lines.

Before you leave the safety of your own lines you must make sure that every member of your patrol is properly prepared, clothed, armed and equipped. This means that you must carry out a detailed inspection of each man. Make sure that his clothing or equipment does not shine or rattle, that he is properly camouflaged, and that he is carrying nothing that, if he were captured, would give away any information to the enemy.

Be patient

Once you are happy that the patrol is properly prepared and briefed, you can lead the patrol out through your own lines into No Man's Land. From now on, you must survive on your own wits and instincts. You must see the enemy before he sees you. You must hear him first. You should also try to put yourself in his mind so that you are always one jump ahead. So it's vital that you move carefully, quietly and slowly. This demands great pati-

On patrol your team is on its own. Here the lead scout scans a jungle clearing before skirting round the edge of it. Your mission on a recce patrol is to return with the information and avoid combat with large groups of the enemy

CARRYING OUT A RECCE PATROL

1. The combat team commander briefs the patrol commander during the afternoon, ready for a night patrol. The recce patrol must know:

a) All information about the positions of friendly and enemy forces.

b) Anything affecting the route such as wire, minefields and areas known to be under observation by the enemy.

c) Time in and time out.

d) What action to take on meeting the enemy.

e) Passwords and recognition signals in use tonight.

ACTION UNDER FLARES

ence. You will also need to make frequent halts to listen for any sign of enemy activity.

Every time you halt, everyone must lie down, to take advantage of the sky-line. That way you will see the enemy's silhouette first, and he will not see you. When you are lying down, scan the landscape around you with an individual weapon sight (IWS) or binoculars. You should also listen for any sounds of movement. Don't move again until you are sure that no one is nearby.

When you are moving, you should do so positively and at best possible speed – but not so fast that you make any unnecessary noise. The formation that you use will depend on the size of your patrol and the type of ground you are crossing. The formations you'll use most often are file, single file, and diamond. Individuals need to keep about five metres apart, although on a dark night you may have to reduce this distance to one metre.

There and back

You will need to work out the route to your objective very carefully – and be sure to choose a different route for the return journey. Break your route down into 'legs', or sections, each having a magnetic bearing and a measured distance. Ideally, each leg of the journey should be not more than 1,000 metres long. When you are actually following the bearing of a particular leg on your compass, you should nominate the man behind you

1 The enemy may have set trip flares in front of their position. It is worth probing ahead with a small stick to find the wires if you are crossing an obvious position. If you set one off, move out of the area as fast as you can; do not go to ground in the area lit up by the flare.

2 You must have a pre-arranged plan of action in case the enemy attack your patrol. If you need to withdraw, you should

to count the paces and at least one other man to check his accuracy.

Each leg should end at a feature that you can recognise easily at night – though it shouldn't be so obvious that the enemy might choose to ambush it. At the end of each leg, designate a rendezvous (RV) should the patrol get dispersed or any individual get lost. On the outward journey the patrol reorganises at the last RV, on the return journey at the next RV – in other words, the RV nearest your own lines.

What to avoid

Keep clear of obvious approaches to an enemy position such as prominent tracks or deep defiles – they are likely locations for enemy standing patrols. Rather than walk along the edge of a wood, walk parallel to the edge,

perhaps five metres into the wood. Avoid skylines but, if you have to cross one, order the patrol to crawl and make use of any available cover.

Patrolling by day is much more difficult than at night, and it is even more important that you take advantage of any available cover. In the jungle it is so dark that you will find it's impossible to patrol at night without using artificial light. This would obviously betray your presence at once, so jungle patrols normally go out by day, when visibility is in any case probably only 20 to 30 metres.

Tackling obstacles

Patrols are particularly vulnerable when they are crossing obstacles. The sort of obstacle that you might come across will vary from a stream or a wire fence to an enemy wire emplacement. Even a road or a track, that you have to cross and that the enemy are likely to be using, has to be regarded as an obstacle. Plan how you intend to get your patrol over or across an obstacle and rehearse your plan.

Essentially, you should stop when

2 (Below) The patrol commander studies the ground from a frontline trench, planning the route the recce team will take and thinking out a plan for the operation.

3 (Right) The next step is the preparation of orders. If you are leading a patrol you should study maps of the area, any available aerial photos, and previous recce reports.

4 (Below) The patrol commander meets the soldiers he will lead on the patrol and explains the nature of their mission and his plan.

retreat as shown, two men providing covering fire while the other half of the patrol falls back a set distance. Then the process is repeated until you are out of contact.

3 The exact arrangements for doubling back in pairs must be rehearsed before you go on patrol: making it up as you go while under fire at night is a recipe for disaster. Smoke grenades are useful for masking your escape. If your patrol suffers casualties you should make every effort to bring them back, not just for morale purposes but to deny any useful information to the enemy.

you reach an obstacle and put your patrol into a position of all-round defence. Next, listen and look for any sign of the enemy. Then inspect the obstacle if you can, to check there are no unforeseen complications – for instance, the level of a stream may have risen higher than wading depth.

Reading the other side

Your next step is to get a footing on the far side of the obstacle. At this stage, apply the rules of fire and manoeuvre – no member of your patrol should move unless he is covered by fire from the remainder of the patrol. While the others are ready to give covering fire, two members of the patrol must negotiate the obstacle and 'go firm' on the other side. Then it's their turn to cover the next two across, and so on, until finally you have all established yourselves in a position of all round defence on the far side of the obstacle. You should then take a further brief pause to check everyone is across, and to listen and look again for signs of the enemy before moving on.

Signs and signals

During a patrol it is obviously important that you maintain silence. The British Army has worked out a series of hand signals that you can pass down the line of the patrol. It is vital that you keep every member of the patrol informed all the time of what is happening and what is going to happen next. Then, everyone will know when you have reached an obstacle (a cross, formed by covering both arms or one arm and a rifle) or if you need to change formations (one arm in the air for single file, two for file), and so on.

This sign language grows and adapts in different theatres of war. In past jungle campaigns it has become increasingly sophisticated. The order for the patrol to take a five-minute smoke break, while the platoon commander questioned a local native woman became: five fingers held up, two fingers put to the mouth as if smoking a cigarette, two fingers on the shoulder (to indicate the two 'pips' on the platoon commander's shoulder epaulettes), followed by a movement with both hands as if cupping two female breasts!

Rehearsals

The most important part of any patrol is clearly the action on the objective. In so far as you can, you must rehearse this in minute detail so that every man knows his part. In the case of a recce patrol this may be simply every man watching and listening in order to bring back every possible strand of information; if you are taking a fighting patrol, the task may be more complex and dangerous and could involve capturing a prisoner or destroying an outpost.

The other action that you must rehearse is what you will do if you bump into the enemy. You will

5 (Above) Ideally the patrol should have time to practise the recce mission during daylight. Here the patrol commander informs the soldiers in the front-line trenches when and where to expect the patrol during the night.

6 Once past the front-line, the patrol will move slowly and silently in single file. Exact distance between men will depend on the terrain and the visibility.

7 (Above) The route is divided into 'legs' each with a magnetic bearing and distance and near a feature you can recognise at night. At each halt, the patrol forms up for all-round defence.

usually have several alternatives; the one you choose will depend on the precise circumstances, but include: an immediate assault on the enemy if they are very close; getting down and returning fire, to give your platoon commander a breathing space to decide upon the next course of action; or you can throw grenades in the direction of the enemy (including smoke grenades, to cover your withdrawal), and then run in a pre-arranged direction or in the direction you indicate at the time.

If your patrol is unfortunate enough to receive casualties, you must at all costs bring them back, not only for reasons of morale but also to deny the enemy information. You may have to leave a man wounded on the outward journey at an RV, probably with another man to look after him, and then collect him on the way back. A casualty can be carried between two

Your ears are more useful than your eyes when on night patrol, so make frequent stops to listen for the enemy. Lie down so that enemy troops will be visible against the skyline and put your left leg over the leg of the man to your left. This enables you to communicate in complete silence by touching each other's boots. Inset: Remember the thumbs down signal means enemy in sight.

men sitting on a rifle or, if he is more seriously wounded, you can make an improvised stretcher using rifle slings, pieces of wood or other material.

8 The patrol commander takes the patrol through a full rehearsal in daylight and must make sure that everyone knows what is expected and what their role will be.

9 A small stream like this offers cover and concealment but your patrol should avoid obvious approaches like tracks or the edges of woods. The enemy may well expect your patrol to pass.

10 In a close reconnaissance two men will crawl right up to the enemy position while the other two wait about 50 metres behind ready to cover the retreat of their comrades.

The safe way back

The return journey may be more dangerous than the outward, since the enemy may have been alerted to your presence and could warn its own patrols to watch out for you as you return.

The enemy could put up flares. When a flare is fired there is normally time to fall flat before it is fully effective. But if you are caught in the open the next best thing to do is freeze. At night it is movement that will give your presence away. It is also a good idea to close one eye so that night blindness does not result from looking at the light.

Watch for tripflares

Much more dangerous are tripflares, which are virtually impossible to detect unless you move very slowly, waving a stick at ankle height, trying to feel for the trip wire. Trip flares consist of a pot containing a magnesium flare attached to and set off by a long wire, which can be stretched for 10 or 15 metres across likely approaches or tracks. They are very sensitive and easily set off. They are usually sited around a defensive position to give early warning of an enemy approach, and you can expect them to be covered by fire. If you do set off a trip flare, get out of the area as soon as possible so as not to be silhouetted against the light and smoke.

Patrolling is a demanding and complex business. Patrols can only be undertaken successfully by highly professional soldiers. Know the art of patrolling, and you are a long way towards knowing how to win your campaign.

The Individual Weapon Sight is a valuable item of equipment on night patrol; it gives a good view at up to 1,000 metres under starlight, although it is rather bulky and weighs nearly 3 kg. Its use is completely undetectable by the enemy.

11 The last stage of the approach must be very cautious; the slightest sound could betray you to the enemy sentries.

12 Having crept as close as you dare, observe the enemy position carefully and make a mental note of everything of military significance.

13 Once back in your own lines you must make a patrol report immediately while your memory is fresh. The combat team commander will probably want you to explain personally what you have seen.

On patrol, the thermal imager will pick out hidden
enemy troops.

PATROL INTO NO-MAN'S LAND

Successful patrolling techniques lie at the heart of all forms of modern warfare. For an army to keep its information about the enemy up-to-date, to dominate the area between opposing front lines, or to destroy or disrupt enemy forces, an efficient system of patrols is vital.

And it's essential that every soldier should be intimately familiar with the art of patrolling and its purposes. This is one of the combat techniques which outlines the basic kinds of patrol and the weapons, clothing and equipment that you will need.

Time-honoured tradition

Conventional warfare has always involved the protagonists patrolling between their respective front lines in order to gain information about each other and to dominate 'No Man's Land'.

In so-called 'limited' warfare, patrolling is arguably even more important. In the Falklands campaign, for instance, a comprehensive programme of patrolling preceded every set piece attack. These patrols mapped out routes, found gaps in minefields, tested the best approaches to enemy positions and even carried out close inspections of the dispositions of the Argentine troops. By carrying out hit-and-run attacks on isolated Argentine positions, British patrols kept their adversaries awake, tired, worried and on the defensive.

In counter-insurgency warfare, patrolling from established bases is the main way in which the security forces dominate the countryside, keep in touch with the population and maintain the initiative.

Why patrols?

You cannot plan a successful operation without accurate and up-to-date information. Despite the many sophisticated means of gaining information such as satellite and aerial photography, drones, remotely piloted vehicles, night surveillance devices and many other systems, patrolling is still the most reliable way in which you can obtain detailed and verifiable information.

You must dominate No Man's Land if you are to maintain this flow of in-

SIX POINTS FOR A SUCCESSFUL PATROL

1. Always vary your route out and back from patrol.
2. Don't tire the patrol out: this is when mistakes will happen.
3. Call a complete halt every now and then and listen for enemy activity.
4. Be familiar with the sights, sounds, and smells of the area.
5. Make sure your equipment is packed correctly and does not rattle or squeak.
6. Try to look through, rather than at, thick bushes and vegetation.

FIGHTING PATROL

Aggressive fighting patrols take the battle to the enemy, raiding command posts, heavy weapons positions and important installations. Not knowing where you will strike next, the enemy is kept off balance and thinks defensively. The Falklands war was very much a war of patrols: small teams of British troops scouted all over the islands, gathering information about the enemy and preventing the Argentines from doing the same.

In the bleak and open terrain of the Falklands, patrols often made contact with the enemy at over 300 metres. In this situation a General Purpose Machine Gun is ideal, enabling you to withdraw safely under covering fire from the gunner.

Accurate fire
Naval gunnery can be very accurate, but real precision is only possible with a man on the ground, observing the fall of shot. At Pebble Island careful direction by a member of the patrol allowed HMS *Glamorgan* to shell part of the airstrip and wreck the Argentine aircraft parked there.

formation. This will make it harder for the enemy to gain information about your positions. Therefore, patrolling has a positive and a negative aspect: while most patrols may be mounted in order to gain information, it may be equally important to deny the enemy the information that he requires.

Successful patrolling calls for a high degree of professionalism. You will need meticulous planning, a high standard of individual training, good team work and determined leadership. In many ways, patrolling asks more of you as an infantryman than any other facet of your training.

There are three types of patrol: the reconnaissance patrol; the standing patrol; and the fighting patrol.

Reconnaissance patrols

Reconnaissance patrols gain information by observation and operate by stealth. On such patrols you should avoid combat, except for self defence or to take advantage of a most unusual opportunity. On 'recce' patrols you can carry out a number of tasks, which include:

1 Locating enemy positions and approaches to them.
2 Obtaining as much detail as possible about the extent, strength and layout of enemy positions including details of minefields, wire and sentry positions.
3 Collecting information about the lie of the land, to aid future operations.
4 Monitoring enemy patrol activity.
5 Checking that your own wire and minefields have not been tampered with.

Standing patrols

Standing patrols are static by nature but, unlike recce patrols, their role can be active as well as passive. They occupy a position forward of your main positions, to give warning of any enemy movement and to prevent or disrupt enemy infiltration. The minimum size of such a patrol should be between three and four men. On a standing patrol, your tasks are to:
1 Watch and listen for likely enemy approaches
2 Watch ground in front of and between defended locations that you cannot see from the main position.
3 Cover minefields and obstacles that you cannot cover from the main position.

On standing patrol, you normally move into position at night and aim to remain concealed throughout daylight hours. You must be in radio contact with the position you are protecting, so that you can call down and control artillery, mortar and machine-gun fire. By controlling other fire and withholding your own fire, you are more likely to maintain the security of your own position. If you fight, it is likely you would have to withdraw.

Fighting patrols

Fighting patrols are offensive. For them, you are organised for a particular task with enough weapons and firepower to fight. The sort of tasks for which you might use fighting patrols include:
1 Carrying out raids on enemy positions.
2 Capturing prisoners or equipment for intelligence purposes.
3 Laying ambushes, including tank ambushes.
4 Taking offensive action against enemy patrols.

Fighting patrols are normally led by an officer and should be between nine or ten men strong. You must have sufficient strength to look after yourselves if you bump into an enemy

Harder than it looks

A night raid looks easy on TV but the reality is very different. Fighting among enemy positions at night, the situation is utterly confusing: only good training and thorough planning will enable you to win. Argentine reaction at Pebble Island was unplanned, unco-ordinated and unsuccessful; those who tried to block the raiders were shot down.

Detailed planning

Fighting patrols are organised for a specific task and are armed and equipped according to the nature of the mission. Proper planning is essential to the success of a raid; the attack on Pebble Island was worked out, rehearsed and ready to go in just five days. In advance of the raid a small patrol spent three days ashore studying the enemy positions.

Propaganda tactics

Aggressive patrolling can sap the morale of the enemy: after the Pebble Island raid a British radio station broadcast to the Argentine forces on the Falklands in Spanish. It announced that the raid had been carried out by the SAS and that this elite force would attack again soon. The morale of the gloomy conscripts sank lower.

Air strike alternative

The easiest way to take out the Argentine aircraft at Pebble Island would have been to organise a massive naval bombardment and an air strike, but the civilian settlement was too close to the airstrip. A raid by a fighting patrol was the only option.

GPMG

Patrols need a lot of automatic firepower even if on a recce mission, avoiding contact with the enemy. The GPMG is heavy, but well worth including in a patrol's armament. Some British patrols used captured Argentinian FNs, which can fire fully automatic, unlike the SLR.

Cold-weather kit

If you are part of a fighting patrol engaged on a raid you normally do not need to take much more than ammunition and rations with you. But if you are operating in a cold and hostile environment like the Falklands you will need to take enough kit to survive alone if you are cut off from the rest of the patrol.

THE PEBBLE ISLAND RAID

A fighting patrol from 'D' Squadron SAS raided the Argentine airstrip at Pebble Island on 14 May 1982. The area was reconnoitred beforehand by a small patrol which landed by canoe. During the night Sea King helicopters brought ashore some 45 SAS men and an artillery observation team. Their objective: the Argentine Pucará ground attack aircraft, which had to be taken out before British forces could attempt a landing on the Falklands.

The SAS men arrived at the airstrip undetected and were among the aircraft before the Argentines realised what was happening. All six Pucarás at Pebble Island were destroyed by small demolition charges placed in the cockpit; other Argentine aircraft on the strip were shot up with M16s and GPMGs, and after the patrol withdrew the artillery observers directed HMS *Glamorgan*'s gunfire on to the area.

The Argentine defenders mounted a half-hearted counterattack which melted away in the face of heavy automatic fire from the SAS men, and the whole patrol was picked up by Sea King helicopters shortly afterwards.

DANGER AND WIRE

patrol, yet not have more men than one man can control at night.

The other factors that might affect the size of a fighting patrol are the likely strengths of enemy patrols and the mission of the patrol. For instance, the SAS night raid on Pebble Island during the Falklands Campaign, in which a large number of Argentine aircraft were destroyed on the ground, involved over 40 men because the mission required a relatively strong force.

Good planning

A fighting, recce or standing patrol requires an immense amount of preparation, planning and rehearsal. You will need to know exactly the formations you will use, the methods for crossing obstacles, the action you will take on meeting the enemy and the objective, the way you will evaluate a casualty or escort a prisoner.

When patrolling in the jungle you must move very carefully: the enemy may have an ambush prepared. Noise is the most common giveaway in the jungle, so use hand signals rather than shouting.

1 A four-man patrol probes forward towards the enemy front line under cover of darkness. You have to move quietly, so communication must be by silent signalling.

2 The lead scout encounters an obstacle: he signals this to the rest of the team, who stop moving and go to ground.

Then you must give careful consideration to the weapons, clothing, equipment, and even footwear that you will take.

Fighting patrols should carry a high proportion of weapons capable of automatic fire, so that you can produce the maximum rate of fire quickly. The new British Army SA80 has an automatic facility and is therefore highly suitable. If you need a weapon with more punch, you can carry GPMGs as long as they are not too cumbersome for the task in question. Grenades can be a highly effective method of extricating a patrol in trouble at night and of causing casualties to the enemy in an offensive action.

Clothing

The clothing you take depends on the climate, but in all circumstances it should be comfortable and enable you to move silently.

Except in Arctic conditions, when you may have to take special precautions, your face and ears should be unencumbered so that you can remain alert and aware, and hear and see without any problems.

One of the abiding images of the Falklands Campaign is of Argentine soldiers with large hoods on their big padded parka jackets up around their heads, so that they could not see or hear. The British soldiers, on the other hand, despite the cold and wet, merely wore berets.

Before you set out on a patrol make a thorough check that your clothing does not rustle, rattle or shine. Water-

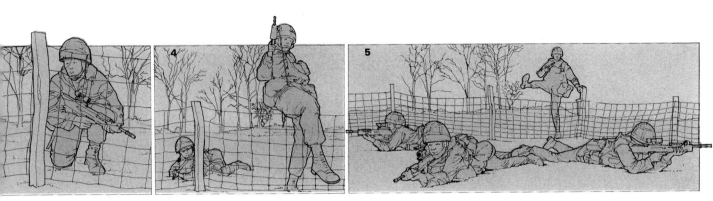

3 Check the fence for booby traps and watch out for trip flares or even simple devices like tin cans on a wire, which will rattle when you cross over, alerting the enemy.

4 Having thoroughly checked the area, the lead scout crosses over, covered by the rest of the patrol. He goes to ground on the other side.

5 One by one the rest of the patrol crosses the fence and assumes an all-round defensive position. When everyone is over, the patrol continues to advance.

proofs tend to do this and are not suitable.

The task of your patrol affects the equipment you will wear. In a north-western European setting, it is normal to wear webbing and carry an NBC suit and respirator, but in other theatres it is unlikely you will need either. Clearly, you will need a luminous compass with which to navigate, since on dark, moonless nights map reading may not be possible. You should also take binoculars (which aid night vision), a torch, a watch with a luminous face, and morphine in case any member of your patrol is wounded.

Don't forget the food

Take rations, too. Even though it may be your intention to complete your task between last and first light, for instance, you may have to lie up through daylight hours if an unexpected delay is met.

Surveillance equipment will be needed if you are going on a recce patrol to carry out the patrol mission. On a fighting patrol you will also need this to see and engage the enemy in the event of a contact. The British

Army's current night sight, the Individual Weapon Sight (IWS), may be used as a surveillance device as well. It works by multiplying, several hundred times, the natural light available from the stars and moon. However, the IWS is heavy, and it may not be practicable or desirable for every member of your patrol to carry one.

Strong, silent shoes

In the days of the old leather-soled ammunition boot it used to be fashionable to wear PT shoes for quiet movement at night. However, with the new rubber-soled high combat boots this is completely unnecessary – indeed, counter-productive. PT shoes do not support or protect your ankles, and anyone wearing them is likely to turn an ankle on rough ground in the dark.

On patrol you must be capable of rapid movement, be self-sufficient for relatively long periods of time, be equipped for any likely eventuality and be capable of producing a high and intense rate of fire. You must give orders precisely and brief every man comprehensively. Rehearse and practice any complex or dangerous stages

of the patrol. Patrolling is an intensively demanding business, and you will need to achieve the highest standards of infantry training to complete your mission successfully.

On patrol in the Falklands, 1986. If a patrol is to operate away from friendly forces for any length of time it has to carry so much kit that mobility can be reduced. The best solution is helicopter re-supply.

How not to do it: this patrol illustrates the danger of being skylined. Each figure is perfectly silhouetted and presents a clear target for the enemy. Always make sure that you blend into the background, avoid ridges wherever possible and crawl over any crest that you cannot avoid.

SETTING UP A PATROL BASE

You have to take a four-man team through miles of jungle, well beyond your own lines, to check whether a suspected enemy base is operational or not. It's vital to move swiftly, stealthily, and relay your intelligence without being discovered. So why do you go storming out with an entire platoon of 30 men?

The answer is that an operation at this range would be all but impossible for four men on their own. They are the key to the mission, but the rest of the platoon is there to create a patrol base – an advance post, totally concealed and easily defended, which will guarantee the success of the mission, giving it support, security, and a

crucial ability to surprise the enemy if need be.

As one of the basic infantry skills, we explain how to set up a patrol. base on operations like this – whether they're recce patrols, prolonged ambushing missions or hit-and-run affairs to disrupt enemy communications – and how it should operate.

5 POINTS FOR SITING YOUR PATROL BASE

1. **You must be able to defend it from all directions, but if discovered your aim is to melt away, not stand your ground.**
2. **The position must be easy to conceal and off the beaten track.**
3. **You need to be near a supply of fresh water.**
4. **The terrain must not interfere with your radio communications; you must be able to contact friendly forces.**
5. **. The base should be close enough to the objective so that you can support the four-man recce team.**

Planning the final patrol: a four-man recce team could not be expected to report on an enemy position that might be 20 miles away. Instead, a 30-man platoon supports the recce team by advancing into the jungle and setting up a secret base near the objective.

On the way to the site planned for the patrol base you must move forward slowly and quietly, remembering that the enemy could come on you from any direction.

When you reach the site, part of the platoon deploys for all-round defence while patrols probe into the surrounding jungle to check that there are no enemy lurking nearby.

The next stage is to dig shell scrapes and clear vegetation that blocks your immediate field of fire. But don't cut too much, or your position will be obvious to the enemy.

Essentially, you'll need to establish a patrol base whenever a patrol halts for an extended period. It can be used to send out smaller units into more exposed ground, or as a concealed supply post for larger operations nearby, such as an ambush in platoon strength. From the base you can plan, feed, rest, maintain weapons and equipment, and direct a number of smaller operations.

You can set up a patrol base in any terrain, in any type of warfare. But it is most effective in counter-insurgency operations in the jungle.

You can select a suitable site for a patrol base from a map, by reconnaissance in person before the patrol, or on the spot, as your patrol proceeds. However you choose your position, bear in mind that you will have to secure it before you take up occupation.

Keep it secret

Look for an area that you can defend easily but remember that secrecy is vital. You don't want to get involved in a defensive firefight unless there's no alternative, so try to put your base where the vegetation is dense enough

While part of the platoon stands watch, you build your basha next to your shell scrape or trench. By overlapping thick jungle leaves on a simple framework you can build a very effective and fairly waterproof shelter.

As always, your personal camouflage must match your surroundings and be replaced as it begins to wither. It is especially vital for a small patrol trying to avoid contact.

for the patrol to melt away. It should also be near a supply of fresh water and where the terrain doesn't obscure your radio communications.

Setting up the base

The British Army has a tried and tested drill for occupying a patrol base. You can learn the routine easily enough.

Assuming that the patrol is at platoon strength, the patrol commander deploys the sections around the site like this. Meeting the section commanders at the six o'clock position of the base area, he gives the arc from 10 to two o'clock to section one, the arc from six to 10 o'clock to section two, and remaining two to six o'clock arc to section three.

The patrol commander then sets up the platoon HQ at the centre of the base area. From here you must be able to see your section commanders. They in turn must be able to see their machine-gun groups. Next, you should check the base perimeter by walking round it and meeting each section commander.

Securing the area

Your next job is to send out patrols from each section to clear the surrounding area. These patrols must move quickly, and in all directions at the same time. If they don't, the

The patrol base must be near a source of water, but the whole area must be carefully explored before settling down: you have to be sure that the enemy did not see you arrive.

HOW IT WORKED IN BORNEO

During the Borneo War of 1962-66, we had to reconnoitre a distant kampong to determine whether or not Indonesian troops were using it as a base from which to mount attacks on British troops.

It would not have been safe or sensible to cover the entire distance through 13 miles of jungle with the four-man patrol that would actually 'recce' the kampong, so the whole platoon of 30 men went in order to set up a secure and powerful patrol base very close to the objective, from which the small 'recce' patrol could operate.

Logistic back-up

The patrol base provided logistic back-up, acted as a radio relay station and provided a source of reinforcements should the small four-man patrol get into trouble. The existence of a radio relay station allowed contact with

Company HQ (and supporting artillery) to be maintained, but at the same time meant that the large radio set needed for this purpose could be operated from the patrol base while the recce patrol could take a smaller and less cumbersome set to maintain contact with the patrol base.

The enemy location was carefully located by the four men, who were able to creep to the very perimeter of the Indonesian kampong. The rest of the platoon waited in a secure platoon base about 500 metres away in a thick and inaccessible piece of jungle where they were most unlikely to be discovered. If the close recce group run into trouble we would have been able to withdraw to the patrol base for help and support, but in the event we were able to return to it when our mission had been accomplished and without being discovered.

Above and left: the same leaves that serve for your basha can also be made into a water-collecting device. A platoon obviously needs a proper water source, but collected fresh rainwater is likely to taste better and harbour fewer bugs than a jungle stream.

enemy could slip from one section's area to another, playing cat-and-mouse with the clearing patrols.

It's important that these patrols don't mistakenly clash with one another. Make sure that each patrol moves out of the patrol base through the left of the rifle group, sweeps its sector, and re-enters the base through the gun group position.

The patrol should consist of the section commander and one man from each group in the section. The distance they will need to clear out depends on the terrain and on the range of noise and smell. This could be as much as 300 metres.

Building the base

Once the area is secure, you can set about digging shell scrapes or even trenches, laying out obstacles and sensors and clearing fields of fire against possible enemy approach, and digging refuse pits and latrines. You should also clear a perimeter track,

and possibly tracks between sections and HQ, to keep down noise at night and stop anyone getting lost when moving from one section to another. Once all this is done, you can erect shelters.

Routine in the base

You must organise the base meticulously: you need to post sentries, set up water patrols, prepare alarm positions, place equipment ready for a quick move.

Keep movement inside the base to a minimum. In the jungle you may not even be able to cook, smoke, shave or wash if contact with the enemy is at all likely. Cooking can be smelled hundreds of yards away, and cigarette smoke carries perhaps 25 yards. In Borneo, British patrols often went 10 days at a time without washing or smoking, and ate all rations cold.

Security is vital

The most important thing to remember about a patrol base is its security. It is a secret place and a safe place. You will need sentries and listening posts to cover approaches to the base area. Put them beyond the range of noise and smell during the day, closer in at night. And keep everyone as silent as possible. Set up communication cords between sentries and section commanders, and between sections and the patrol HQ, and use pre-arranged signals to cut down the need for talking.

The real value of a patrol base lies in its remaining undiscovered. This is the place from which you mount operations, and those operations will be really successful only if the enemy has no warning of them.

Clearing patrols

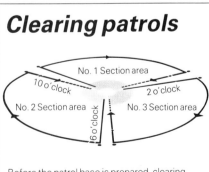

Before the patrol base is prepared, clearing patrols circle the area to make sure there are no enemy close enough to hear or smell the presence of the platoon, i.e. about 300 metres. They consist of the Section Commander and one man from each group.

A PATROL HARBOUR

The patrol base must remain hidden from the enemy, so communication between each section is by hand signal during the day and by runner at night. Each section commander must be in sight of the platoon commander, and the perimeter gun scout and rifle groups must be in sight of their section commander.

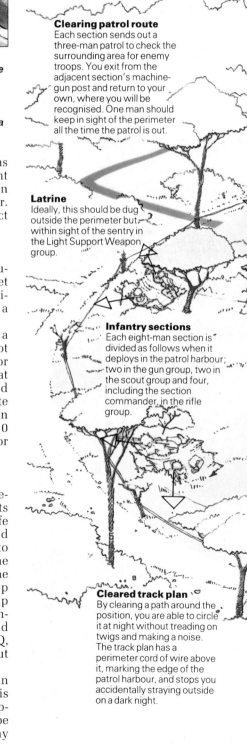

Clearing patrol route
Each section sends out a three-man patrol to check the surrounding area for enemy troops. You exit from the adjacent section's machine-gun post and return to your own, where you will be recognised. One man should keep in sight of the perimeter all the time the patrol is out.

Latrine
Ideally, this should be dug outside the perimeter but within sight of the sentry in the Light Support Weapon group.

Infantry sections
Each eight-man section is divided as follows when it deploys in the patrol harbour: two in the gun group, two in the scout group and four, including the section commander, in the rifle group.

Cleared track plan
By clearing a path around the position, you are able to circle it at night without treading on twigs and making a noise. The track plan has a perimeter cord of wire above it, marking the edge of the patrol harbour, and stops you accidentally straying outside on a dark night.

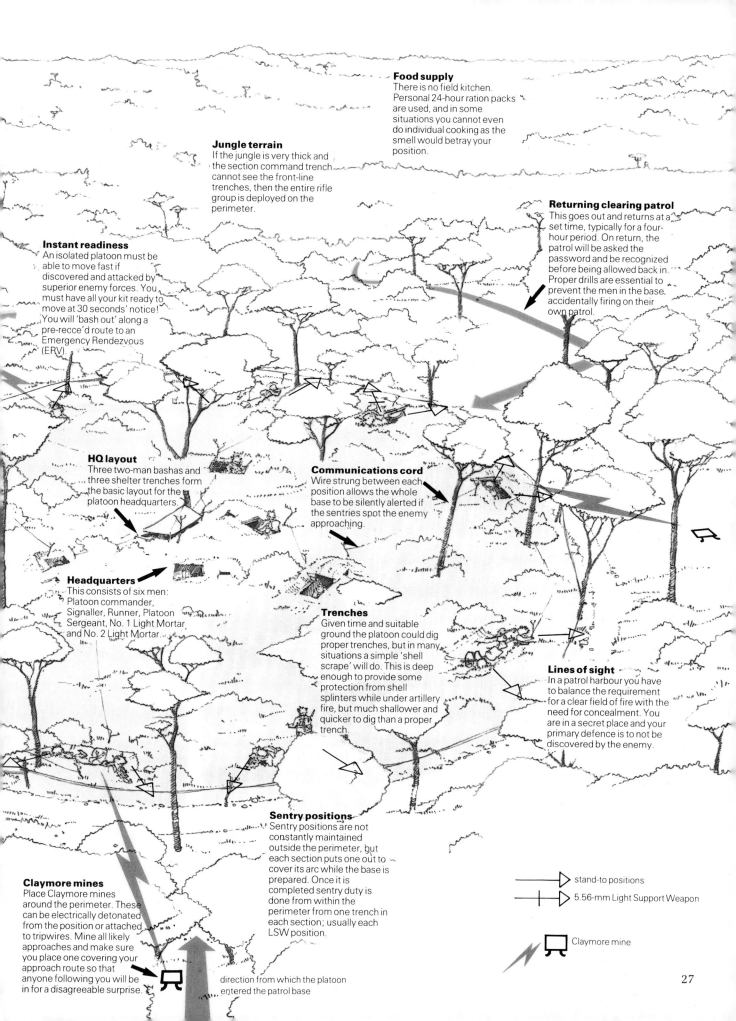

Food supply
There is no field kitchen. Personal 24-hour ration packs are used, and in some situations you cannot even do individual cooking as the smell would betray your position.

Jungle terrain
If the jungle is very thick and the section command trench cannot see the front-line trenches, then the entire rifle group is deployed on the perimeter.

Returning clearing patrol
This goes out and returns at a set time, typically for a four-hour period. On return, the patrol will be asked the password and be recognized before being allowed back in. Proper drills are essential to prevent the men in the base accidentally firing on their own patrol.

Instant readiness
An isolated platoon must be able to move fast if discovered and attacked by superior enemy forces. You must have all your kit ready to move at 30 seconds' notice! You will 'bash out' along a pre-recce'd route to an Emergency Rendezvous (ERV).

HQ layout
Three two-man bashas and three shelter trenches form the basic layout for the platoon headquarters.

Communications cord
Wire strung between each position allows the whole base to be silently alerted if the sentries spot the enemy approaching.

Headquarters
This consists of six men: Platoon commander, Signaller, Runner, Platoon Sergeant, No. 1 Light Mortar, and No. 2 Light Mortar.

Trenches
Given time and suitable ground the platoon could dig proper trenches, but in many situations a simple 'shell scrape' will do. This is deep enough to provide some protection from shell splinters while under artillery fire, but much shallower and quicker to dig than a proper trench.

Lines of sight
In a patrol harbour you have to balance the requirement for a clear field of fire with the need for concealment. You are in a secret place and your primary defence is to not be discovered by the enemy.

Sentry positions
Sentry positions are not constantly maintained outside the perimeter, but each section puts one out to cover its arc while the base is prepared. Once it is completed sentry duty is done from within the perimeter from one trench in each section; usually each LSW position.

Claymore mines
Place Claymore mines around the perimeter. These can be electrically detonated from the position or attached to tripwires. Mine all likely approaches and make sure you place one covering your approach route so that anyone following you will be in for a disagreeable surprise.

direction from which the platoon entered the patrol base

stand-to positions

5.56-mm Light Support Weapon

Claymore mine

PREPARE FOR BATTLE

Faced with the task of leading a section out through hostile country and taking out an enemy position, what do you do? How should you prepare for the mission? How will you react to enemy fire, or even find the enemy in the first place? And how will you mount a successful assault?

There are, in fact, six logical steps – 'battle drills' – that you are trained to follow on such an operation. In the heat of battle it's not always possible to stick slavishly to the rules, but the six drills for a section likely to come under enemy fire give you a tried and tested framework on which to hang your plan of action.

1: Preparing for battle

Before advancing to contact you must first check that your personal camouflage is correct. It should break up the outline of the helmet, equipment and the outline of your body by using scrim, faceveil and suitable foliage representative of the ground over which the section is about to

6 SECTION DRILLS

1. **Prepare weapons and equipment.**
2. **React quickly to enemy fire.**
3. **Locate the enemy's position.**
4. **Win the firefight.**
5. **Assault under covering fire.**
6. **Re-organise the section.**

Before battle you must prepare your personal camouflage and check your weapon and ammunition. This American soldier needs to add plenty of local foliage to break up his shape.

Opening fire with a Self-Loading Rifle: it is difficult to control the shooting of a 10-man section, but your firepower must be co-ordinated if it is to be effective. British soldiers practise fighting in pairs, one providing covering fire as the other advances. Conducted with live ammunition, it fosters confidence and teamwork, as well as good shooting.

GETTING ON TARGET

One of the biggest problems in controlling the firepower of the section is getting everyone to fire at the correct target. When indicating a target to the rest of the section, shout out the range (e.g. '300'); the direction (e.g. ¾ left); and any obvious point of reference (e.g. 'gate') – so the call is '300 – ¾ left – gate'.

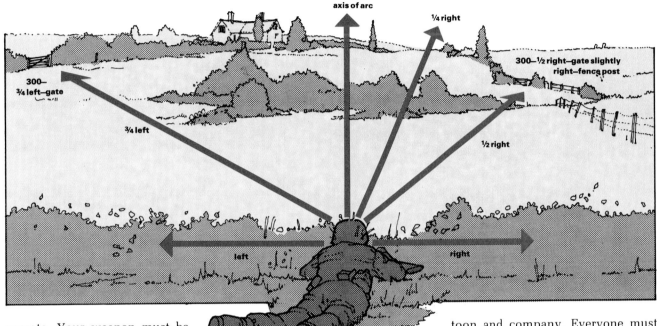

axis of arc

¼ right

300 – ½ right – gate slightly right – fence post

300 – ¾ left – gate

¾ left

½ right

left

right

operate. Your weapon must be clean, serviceable and well oiled. Ammunition must be clean and magazines and grenades properly distributed throughout the section. The radio operator must ensure that he is properly in touch with platoon headquarters.

As section commander you must prepare and deliver your orders before the section starts out on the operation. Those orders should ensure that all members of the section know as much as possible about the nature of the ground they are about to cross, the likely weapons and dispositions of the enemy, and the location, intentions and tasks of the rest of the platoon and company. Everyone must know what his mission is and how he is going to carry it out.

You will give everyone details of the route, the formations the section will be using, which flank the machine gun group should go on and any other relevant details. As the sec-

The firepower of the section must be controlled by the commander. Here a US squad leader directs the fire of an M203 grenade-launcher mounted on an M16A1.

tion advances to contact, you will give your anticipatory fire orders: "If we come under fire go to ground along that bank," and so on. All the details come under the heading of 'Preparation for Battle'.

2: Reacting to effective enemy fire

Sections must be trained to carry on advancing regardless of the noise of fire directed at someone else and re-gardless of stray rounds. Effective enemy fire, on the other hand, is fire that would cause heavy casualties if the section continued on its course.

The immediate reaction to effective fire must be for the whole section to get off the killing ground immediately. If you have been able to give anticipatory orders, the section will know exactly where to take cover. If not, they must listen to orders and crawl into the nearest available cover. Every

If you come under fire, get out of the killing ground immediately; go to ground and return fire. You must understand the importance of fire control and avoid unnecessary expenditure of ammunition.

man must try to establish where the enemy fire is coming from – and return it.

The drill for getting off the killing ground is:
1 Dash
2 Down
3 Crawl
4 Observe
5 Sights
6 Fire!

3: Locating the enemy

Locating the position from which someone is firing at you can be very difficult, particularly in a built-up area. Clearly, you have to locate the enemy as soon as possible, in order both to continue to advance and to prevent casualties. There are three methods of finding the enemy:
1 By observation If you look in the direction from which you think the sound of the fire came, you may see movement, smoke, muzzle flashes, or something glinting. There are two components to the sound of a shot: a 'crack', which is the round passing you; and a 'thump', which is the explosion in the chamber of the rifle.

The time between the crack and the thump gives an indication of range – each second represents about 600 metres.

CLOCK RAY METHOD

To identify more difficult targets to the rest of the section you can use the Clock Ray method. Give the same reference as before, but refer to an imaginary clock over one of the reference points. To refer to the hedges to the left of the house in the diagram you shout: '300-half left-7 o'clock-hedge'. If someone is pointing out a target to you, shout 'Seen' or 'Not seen' as appropriate.

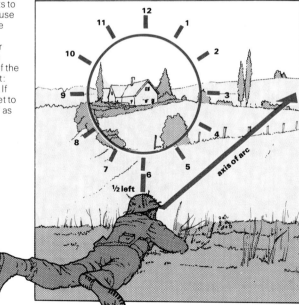

It is not always possible to give a rapid indication of the enemy position. Here a soldier fires a tracer round at the enemy – a quick way of identifying an area, but it tends to give away your own position.

2 By fire You can try to draw the enemy's fire by instructing perhaps two riflemen to fire into likely cover.
3 By movement If the enemy has still not been spotted, you will have to order two men to get up and run forward about 10 metres to a different position. This will almost certainly draw enemy fire, but don't worry. A man getting up and dashing 10 metres is a very hard target to hit.

Finally, if there is still no enemy reaction, you must continue to advance.

Anyone who spots the enemy must indicate the position to his comrades by firing a round of tracer at the enemy position.

4: Winning the fire fight

As soon as the enemy has been firmly located, you must bring down a sufficient weight of fire on the enemy to neutralise him. Having won the fire fight, you must maintain a sufficient weight of fire with the machine gun group to allow your rifle group to move to a position from which it can assault the enemy.

5: The attack

The attack consists of four stages:
1 Orders The section commander issues brief orders so that each rifleman knows exactly what he is to do. Moreover, the machine gun group, which will usually stay behind to provide covering fire, must be clear about precisely what is going to happen *before* the rifle group departs on its flanking attack.
2 The advance The aim of this stage is to move from the position where the section first came under fire to a suitable position from which to assault the enemy. In order to make an angle as near 90 degrees as possible between the supporting fire of the gun group and the assault position of the rifle group, most advances will be to a flank.

In certain circumstances, it might be best to move the gun group to a flank and advance forward on the same axis – if, for instance, there is some 'dead ground' directly in front of the enemy.
3 The assault Attacking troops normally need a superiority in the region of three to one. Therefore a section, by definition, is capable of attacking only a single trench, a sniper or a pill box. If

JUDGING DISTANCE: THE 100-METRE METHOD

The range is the first detail you must give when identifying a target to the section, and you should practise judging distances so that you can do so quickly and confidently. A full-size football pitch is about 100 metres long. Once you can visualise this distance, use it as a unit of measurement between you and the target.

Things seem further away
1 When you have the sun in your eyes.
2 In bad light.
3 When you are looking down a street or over a valley.
4 When they are smaller than their surroundings.
5 If you are lying down.

Things seem closer
1 In bright sunshine.
2 If they are bigger than their surroundings.
3 If they are higher than you.
4 If there is dead ground between you and them.

Familiar objects
Learn what familiar objects like trucks or houses look like at different ranges. This will help you judge the distance.

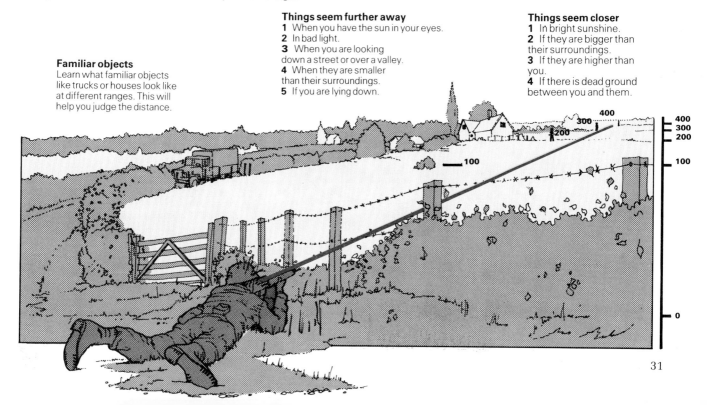

you find that you are faced with opposition much stronger than this, call in any available reinforcements.

The assault is the final stage of the advance on the enemy position. The maximum fire must be brought to bear at this stage from both the assaulting rifle group and the supporting machine gun group. Fragmentation grenades can be thrown, or you can fire the section's light or medium anti-tank weapon to create the maximum shock. Smoke grenades can be thrown to cover the assaulting riflemen over the last few yards.

This is the most difficult part of an attack for the section commander: you have to coax your men to get up from a

A captured Argentine position. If possible, reorganise a little way off as the enemy may have pre-registered artillery on the position.

secure fire position and charge, with bayonets fixed, across probably open ground to close with and kill the enemy. It is no mean task.

4 Fighting through The position may be sited in depth. Once committed, the section must maintain the momentum by using fire and man-oeuvre to capture the whole position, or the assault may collapse.

6: Reorganising your section

As soon as you have neutralised the enemy position, you must organise your section as quickly as possible, to

You are very vulnerable in the moments after taking the enemy position, and immediate re-organisation is essential. Deal with casualties, check ammo state and dig in if necessary.

be ready for a possible counter-attack.

You must allot arcs of fire to each man, deal with casualties, redistribute ammunition and, if necessary, dig trenches or shell-scrapes. The gun group must regroup on the position as quickly as possible.

White phosphorus grenades are horribly effective in close-quarter fighting. Lighter than a fragmentation grenade, you can throw them further and more accurately.

FIRE AND MOVEMENT

You run forward with the rest of the eight-man rifle group while the machine-gun team is covering you. The mass of vegetation in your webbing must be secured so that it does not fall off once you are on the move.

You may be fighting on a broad front, part of an engagement involving several divisions — or you may be on patrol at no more than platoon strength. However large or small the operation, the infantry-man's response to events on the battlefield is centred on his Section, the most basic fighting unit in any regular army.

This fire-and-movement feature details your tasks as a member of an Infantry Section – known in the US Army as the squad – and describes the principles of Section tactics.

The Section

In most armies this basic unit consists of between eight and 10 men (in the British Army it is eight men), one of whom is a full Corporal, the Section Commander. The section is divided

When you have reached the spot indicated by your section commander, you and the rifle group go to ground and cover the advance of the machine-gun team.

FIRE AND MOVEMENT: THE TECHNIQUE

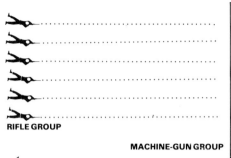

RIFLE GROUP

MACHINE-GUN GROUP

1 The gun group of two or three men advances towards the enemy under covering fire from the six to eight men in the rifle group.

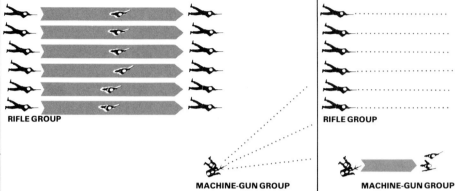

RIFLE GROUP

MACHINE-GUN GROUP

2 The machine-gun group goes to ground and opens fire: a GPMG provides enough firepower to cover the advance of the riflemen. The same principle of one unit firing while the other advances is used for pairs of riflemen, sections and whole platoons.

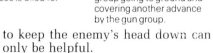

RIFLE GROUP

MACHINE-GUN GROUP

3 The movement is completed by the rifle group going to ground and covering another advance by the gun group.

into a Rifle Group and Machine Gun Group. The rifle group consists of up to six riflemen, who can act in pairs or in two groups of four and two men each. The machine gun group consists of the Gunner and the Lance-Corporal in charge of the group. He is also the second-in-command of the section.

Weight of fire

There are many variations on this theme: if, for instance, a greater weight of fire is required to support an attack the machine gun group could be boosted by two extra riflemen, leaving four men to carry out the attack.

Section tactics are based on the principle of simultaneous fire and movement. Thus, if the rifle group is moving, the machine gun group should be static and ready to support – or, if necessary, actually supporting with fire – the rifle group. Clearly, the rifle group is vulnerable while on the move, and anything that can be done to keep the enemy's head down can only be helpful.

Likewise, particularly during the final stages of an assault, fire and manoeuvre will often be necessary within the rifle group itself. At the very lowest level, one member of a 'battle pair' will engage the enemy while the

Single file is the most basic formation: excellent for moving along hedges and the edges of woods, but you are vulnerable to fire from the front and few men in the section can shoot forwards.

SECTION FORMATIONS

These are the six basic formations used by an infantry section. **Single File** and **File** are easy to control but vulnerable from the front; **Arrowhead** and **Extended Line** are difficult to control, but effective against enemy in front of you. When moving in formation remember to watch your section commander for hand signals.

Arrowhead The machine-gunner is on the flank from which attack is most likely.

Single File Good for moving along the edges of woods or hedges or at night.

Extended Line Used when assaulting enemy positions.

Spearhead A variation of Arrowhead, where you don't need the machine-gun on a flank.

File Easy to control and good for night movement, but makes a good target.

Diamond For crossing open ground at night; gives all round firepower.

other member is moving forward.

'Fire and manoeuvre' is the term given to the combined use of weapons, movement and ground. The object of fire and manoeuvre is to move with the minimum of casualties when in contact with the enemy. Suitable ground is used to protect your section from enemy fire when on the move, while fire from the static element of the section or platoon suppresses enemy fire directed at the moving element.

Supporting fire

Fire and manoeuvre is practised at all levels so that, in a major attack involving a company or battalion, a combination of supporting fire from artillery, mortar, tanks, anti-tank guided weapons (ATGW) and aircraft are used to get dismounted infantry

The General Purpose Machine Gun provides more firepower than the rest of the section put together. Everyone must be trained on both rifle and machine gun so that they can take over the GPMG if the gunner is killed or wounded.

On your feet and forward again, this time covered by one other rifleman: the members of the rifle group are paired off and work closely together. A two-man team also uses fire and movement, with one man covering the advance of the other.

onto an objective.

At a much lower level, fire and manoeuvre will be used within a platoon by using one section as the fire section and the other two sections as manoeuvre groups. Similarly, fire and manoeuvre can be used within a section between individual riflemen for fighting through the enemy position.

Riflemen within a section are paired off not just so that they can fire and manoeuvre, but also so that they can help each other in a number of other practical ways. For instance, while one member of a pair is on sentry duty, the other could be preparing a meal; or if one is wounded, the other can apply first aid.

Section formations

The basic section formations are **Single File, File, Arrowhead** or **Spearhead, Diamond** and **Extended Line.** The formation that you should adopt depends on six factors:
1 The country you are moving in.
2 The likely direction of enemy fire.
3 How far you can see.
4 How the Section can best be controlled.
5 The need to produce the maximum fire effect.
6 Who has control of the air.

Single File is the most basic form of military formation, and may be the only one possible in jungle. It is excellent for moving along hedges or the edge of a wood, and ideal for moving through a narrow gap in, for instance, a minefield. It is easy to control, particularly at night, and it is least vulnerable to fire from a flank. However, you are very vulnerable to frontal fire, and it is difficult to fire to your front.

Concentrated target

You can use **File** when you are moving along a path or a track that is wide enough to permit men to move on both sides of the track. Again, this formation is easy to control and useful at night, but it makes a concentrated target for enemy fire.

Arrowhead is probably the most widely used formation for moving across country. The machine gun group is put on the flank from which an attack is most likely. **Spearhead** is a variation of Arrowhead, and can be used when you don't need to deploy the gun group to one particular flank. The gun group is kept in the centre,

FIELD SIGNALS ON FOOT

Hand signals are very important: it is an impossible job to shout above the noise of automatic weapons or shell fire. These signals will often be the only way your section commander can tell you something; their purpose is to get you in the right place at the right time and in the right formation. The NCO below is telling you that there is no enemy in sight.

Halt

Advance or Follow me

Close on me

Double

forming the shaft of the 'spear', ready to deploy to either flank depending on the threat. Both Arrowhead and Spearhead are good for producing effective fire against frontal attack. However, both formations are difficult to control, particularly when engaged by flanking fire.

Night movement

Diamond is often used when crossing open ground at night. It is easy to control and affords good all round observation and protection. Fire can be returned in any direction. However, it can present a concentrated target.

Extended Line can be used as an assault formation, but it is difficult to control.

Whatever formation you choose, the gun group should normally be on the open flank, or the flank that provides the best potential fire positions, such as undulating or high ground. The degree to which members of the section should be spaced out depends on the ground but, as a general rule, they should be within voice control of the section commander.

The General Purpose Machine Gun can be slung across the chest when moving and even fired from the hip in close-range firefights. But forget 'Rambo': you need to position the gun on the sling and use both hands!

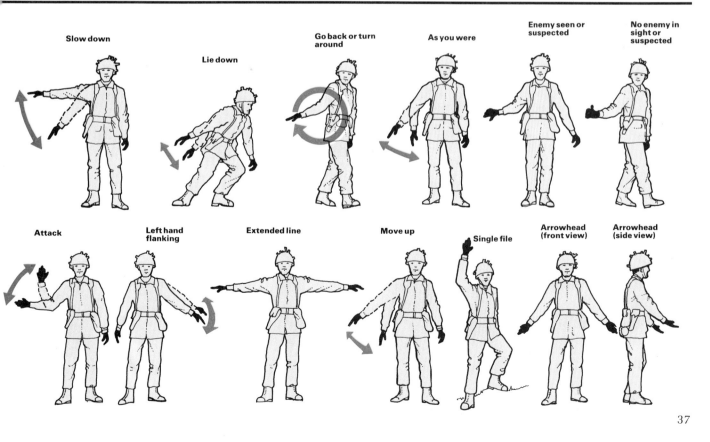

Slow down

Lie down

Go back or turn around

As you were

Enemy seen or suspected

No enemy in sight or suspected

Attack

Left hand flanking

Extended line

Move up

Single file

Arrowhead (front view)

Arrowhead (side view)

STALKING THE TARGET

One highly-trained man can dominate the battlefield by taking out officers, radio operators and other specialists. Using modern sniper rifles such as the M76 seen here, the sniper has a formidably long reach: no-one is safe.

The sniper is the most feared man on the battlefield. Slipping elusively from cover to cover, he deals death without warning. A lone sniper can pin down whole units of enemy troops or take out high-value, strategically vital single targets. But, just as the military rewards are high, so are the risks. As a sniper, you'll spend days at a time in constant danger, surrounded by enemies all too eager to stop you short. So, besides being an expert marksman, you have to be highly skilled in the arts of concealment and stealth.

The following article is based on the United States Marine Corps sniper training manual, and shows how the USMC keeps this most valuable of all infantrymen on the move at the least risk to himself.

Calculating the risks

As a sniper you are constantly seeking the most effective position from which to do your work. But reaching the best firing point involves a calculated risk. You have to measure the advantage gained against the danger of attracting enemy attention and drawing fire as you move, and weigh the importance of your target against the risk involved. A general is worth a high risk; the squaddies cleaning his car are not.

Using Sights

Ideally you should adjust the setting of the sight according to the range of the target; otherwise the bullet will not strike where the crosshairs of the sight are centred. This is fine in theory, but not always possible while in action: set the sights for 500 yards and if there is not time to change the setting, aim as follows.

Aiming point 600 yards
If the target is at a greater range than you have set the sights for, you must aim above it.

Aiming point 500 yards
If the target happens to appear 500 yards away, the bullet will strike dead centre where you are pointing the sight.

Aiming point 100 yards and 400 yards
When the target is at these ranges, aim low. It is difficult to place the shot accurately when aiming off, but you should manage a disabling body hit.

Aiming point 200 yards and 300 yards
Due to the trajectory of the bullet you must aim slightly lower if the target is at these middle distances.

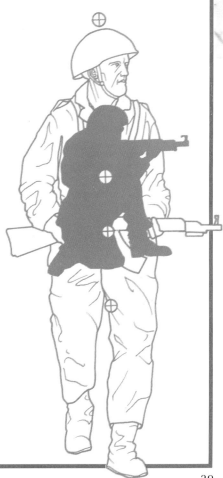

Preparing for the move

Before making any significant movement, take the following precautions:

1 Check and optimise all camouflage, of yourself, your clothing, and your equipment.

2 Ensure your equipment will not rattle or snag. Tape loose items such as dog-tags. Tape or pad all free-hanging or slack equipment without impeding its efficiency.

3 Check that all clothing is soft, flexible and snug. A starched uniform makes a noise. Baggy clothes are easily snagged by undergrowth and branches. Use ties to secure field trousers at thigh and ankle to reduce slack. Use no other ties, as they could impair circulation, leading to frostbite or injury.

4 Wear a soft cap, giving a blurred head-outline. Snipers should not wear helmets. They are distinctive in shape, and muffle or distort sounds, particularly in wind.

5 Pare down all equipment to the minimum necessary for the mission. Weight reduces speed.

Cover

Whenever possible make your move in conditions that will obscure your presence, such as darkness, fog, smoke or haze. Your first rule of safety is to assume that your area of opera-

Above and left: One of the most important functions of camouflage is to blur the shape of the sniper and his equipment; there are few straight lines in nature. A sniper should not wear a helmet; it spoils his hearing and looks very familiar.

Movement techniques

THE RUSH

The rush is the fastest way to move, and you start it from the prone position.

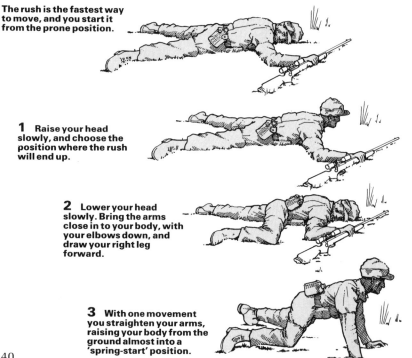

1 Raise your head slowly, and choose the position where the rush will end up.

2 Lower your head slowly. Bring the arms close in to your body, with your elbows down, and draw your right leg forward.

3 With one movement you straighten your arms, raising your body from the ground almost into a 'spring-start' position.

4 Spring into action, leading off with the left foot, and run directly to the new position.

THE CRAWL

If you need to move without exposing yourself by rising to your feet, use the low or high crawl according to visibility, available cover and concealment, and how fast you need to move.

THE LOW CRAWL

When you need to move over terrain with poor cover, or where the enemy is likely to spot you, and when speed is not essential, you should use the low crawl.

1 Lying flat, and keeping your head down all the time, hold the rifle sling with one hand at the upper sling swivel, with the balance on top of the fore-arm, and the butt dragging on the ground.

2 Push your arms and right leg forward, then cover ground by pulling with the arms and pushing with the right leg. Keep the whole body flat, and change the pushing leg frequently to avoid fatigue.

tion is constantly under enemy observation.

Modes of movement
Use the specially explained techniques of the rush, the walk, and the crawl (see below).

Pre-planning
1 While still in a safe position, carefully select your next operating location. Survey minutely for signs of enemy presence, and for risks of exposure to enemy observation.
2 Before making any move, methodically work out and memorise the entire route to your new position.
3 Once at the new position, halt, listen, and observe. Animal and bird movements may give you away, so keep as still as possible.

Terrain problems
1 Tall grass. Travelling in a straight line through tall grass attracts attention, as the grass will wave unnaturally. Therefore, change direction frequently, and if possible move only when the wind is blowing the grass.
2 Roads. These are dangerously exposed; never travel along a road. Cross roads and trails where possible via culverts. Otherwise opt for low spots or curves where exposure is limited. Move quickly and quietly.
3 Ploughed fields. Crawl parallel to

Above: When you need to look past a linear obstacle such as a wall, do not look over the top: lie down and observe from ground level at a corner.

Above: Scrim netting is used to break up the shape of head, shoulders and rifle. Having moved back 18 inches, he will still see you, but you won't see him.

Right and wrong: the uncamouflaged man has his back to the light, silhouetting himself. By paying attention to what is behind him, the camouflaged sniper is well concealed. A successful sniper needs all the skills of a poacher.

THE HIGH CRAWL

In more favourable conditions, with adequate cover, and concealment, poor visibility in your favour, and where increased speed is needed, use the high crawl.

1 Rest your weight on your forearms and lower legs so that your trunk is clear of the ground. Cradle your rifle on top of your arms, with the muzzle off the ground.

2 Proceed by alternately advancing right elbow and left knee, then left elbow and right knee. Use short movements, keeping your knees well behind your buttocks. Keep your head and your buttocks low.

THE SILENT CRAWL

When you are close to the enemy, the low and high crawls are too noisy. Crawling on hands and knees is carried out extremely slowly, and in almost complete silence.

1 Lay your weapon on the ground. Use your right hand to feel for or clear a place for the right knee.

2 Keeping your hand in place, bring your knee forward until it touches the hand. Repeat the process with your left hand and knee.

3 As you progress, move your weapon by feeling for and clearing a place, then lifting the weapon slowly and carefully into position. Make all movements in slow motion.

THE SILENT WALK

Silent walking is done with extreme care and deliberation, and is needed mainly at night or in heavy cover.

1 Balance solidly on one foot, then lift the other foot high enough to clear grass or brush.

2 Keeping your weight on the back foot, gently let the forward foot down, feeling with the toe for a solid place before lowering your forward heel.

3 Shift your weight forward, find the balance, and then repeat the action. Use short steps so that you do not lose your balance by over-reaching.

4 At night, or in very poor visibility, hold your weapon in one hand, holding the other out in front of you to feel for obstructions.

5 To assume the prone position from the walk, crouch down slowly, holding your weapon under your arm, and feeling for a clear spot with your free hand. Rest your weight on your free hand and the opposite knee, then extend the free leg backwards, keeping it clear of the ground until the toe finds a clear spot. Then roll gently into the prone position. At any indication of discovery by the enemy, go rapidly into the prone position.

5 As you drop to the ground, plant the feet apart, land on your knees, and slide your right hand down to the heel of your rifle butt.

6 Fall forward and break your fall with the rifle butt, taking care not to damage the scope.

7 Shifting your weight to your left side, pull the rifle butt into your right shoulder-hollow, then roll back into the firing position.

8 Lie flat to the ground, and move quickly to any cover on either side if you have reason to believe that your rush has been seen by the enemy.

Estimating Range

The range card is a handy reference which allows you to accurately judge the range of the target. If you have time to observe the field of fire from your position, estimate the range of each significant terrain feature and mark it on the range card. You can note the appropriate sight settings in the boxes along the base of the card so that, when a target appears, you can quickly determine its range, set the sights and fire. The bottom row of boxes show where to shoot if your sights are set for 500 yards and there is not time to adjust them.

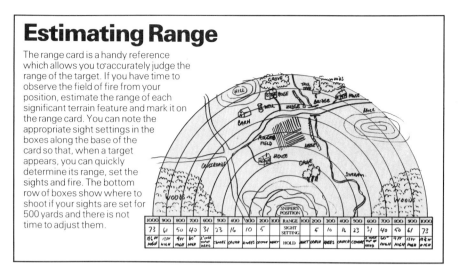

1000	900	800	700	600	500	400	300	200	100	RANGE	100	200	300	400	500	600	700	800	900	1000
73	61	50	40	31	23	16	10	5		SIGHT SETTING		5	10	16	23	31	40	50	61	73
16½ ft HIGH	12 ft HIGH	9 ft HIGH	60" HIGH	2' OVER TOP OF HEAD	CHEST	CROTCH	KNEES	CROTCH	WAIST	HOLD	WAIST	CROTCH	KNEES	CROTCH	CHEST	2' OVER TOP OF HEAD	60" HIGH	9 ft HIGH	12 ft HIGH	16½ ft HIGH

furrows wherever possible. Otherwise cross them at the lowest part of the field.

Avoid

1 Steep slopes and loose, stoney areas. You will be in constant danger of causing inadvertent movements or sounds that may reveal your position.
2 Ridge lines, and areas cleared of cover, which will reveal your outline even when you are camouflaged. Remember, enemy snipers are looking for your silhouette.

Distractions

Loud noises such as overhead aircraft, artillery barrages, and tank or truck engines all distract the enemy's atten-

Selecting priority targets

The sniper is able to pin down a large force of soldiers by killing leaders and communications specialists. Without command and control, the enemy advance grinds to a halt, individual soldiers now aware that somewhere out there is a highly-trained individual able to place his shots with phenomenal accuracy.

Using a first-class rifle with high-resolution optical sights and firing specially-selected top quality match ammunition, the sniper is able to shoot people at ranges far greater than the ordinary infantryman. The sniper's reach often comes as a disagreeable surprise, particularly for officers. The American General Sedgewick's last words were 'Don't worry men, they couldn't hit an elephant at this dist . . .'

Colouring
Mud, charcoal, burnt cork and charred coffee grounds can all serve in place of military issue camouflage cream, but avoid using fuel, oil or grease, which all have a strong smell.

Weapon care
Obviously your rifle must be well maintained but it is important not to use too much oil, especially in the barrel. Excessive oil will make the gun produce a telltale puff of smoke when you fire.

Rubber bands
In most cases it is preferable to use natural foliage for camouflage rather than artificial scrub. However, real material can be difficult to attach to your body. Rubber bands cut from discarded truck, jeep or bicycle tyres are a handy solution.

Camouflage
You must blend with the local environment but do not tailor your camouflage to suit only one type of background.

tion. Take advantage of noise to cover your own movements.

Action under flares

You have a split second to hit the ground if overhead flares catch you out in the open. You may recognise the distinctive sound of the flare gun, and get down before the light explodes above you. The sudden light may also temporarily blind enemy observers. Move on the moment the flare burns out. If you are caught in the light of a ground flare, move rapidly and silently out of the lighted area. If the flare catches you while you are crossing an obstacle such as barbed wire, crouch low and remain motionless until the flare has burnt out.

However good your firing position, the crosshairs will move slightly. Apply trigger pressure steadily until you are just short of firing, wait until you have the crosshairs exactly placed, and then gently apply final pressure to fire the weapon.

5 points for successful concealment

1 Silhouette
However good your camouflage you will be spotted if the light is behind you. It is vital to blend in with your surroundings. Remember that the sun moves, so what seems a wonderful position this morning may be a dead giveaway in the afternoon.

2 Shape
The first thing the enemy will be looking for is a familiar shape: a human figure, a helmet, a rifle etc. A wide variety of kit is available to blur your shape, but do not overdo it. The 'walking bush' might look good but you must not generate a lot of rustling noises when you move off.

3 Shine
Shiny objects must be either removed or dulled. This means watches, rings, and metal on your webbing in addition to your barrel.

4 Shadow
You must always remember to check what sort of shadow you are casting; perfect positions can be totally compromised by shadow. As for silhouette, do remember that the sun moves round.

5 Movement
Any movement can betray you; even working the action on your rifle. If your location is suspected you will be under observation through binoculars.

Radio operator
Modern armies depend n their ommunications; king out a radio perator and/or his kit will create serious roblems for the nemy. Look for telltale erials – some radio en curl the aerial into loop to make hemselves less bvious.

Officer
Leaders often carry rifles and conceal anything which gives away their rank. This man is betrayed by an old problem: sunlight glinting off his binoculars.

Anti-tank gunner
Weighed down by heavy kit, anti-tank men are a good target, and their loss renders their unit vulnerable to armoured attack, demoralising the whole force.

Machine-gunner
He provides most of an infantry section's fire power Machine-gunners often hold the weapon down against their body to make them look like another rifleman. Observe an enemy section carefully to identify the machine-gunner.

A German sniper giving his position away – his weapon's barrel will be visible.

MARKSMANSHIP

The sniper's job is to kill with a single shot. Calmly and deliberately he takes out his target from the rough security of his hiding place, even moving off in pursuit when his prey is highly valued. He is a master of fieldcraft and, above all, of the art of marksmanship. This section, drawn from the US Marine Corps' Sniper's Manual, reveals the secrets of the sniper's success and tells you how he prepares for his lone expeditions into enemy territory.

The sniper has to prepare two things before he sets out to do his job: himself and his weapon. His own preparations may have taken years of training: first and foremost is the position he takes up when it comes to firing a round.

The four basic firing positions are: prone, sitting, kneeling, and standing. Which one you adopt depends on the individual circumstances, but your aim is to adopt the steadiest firing position in a location which gives you an adequate field of fire and good cover.

There are five elements involved in taking up a good shooting position.

Modern night sights can penetrate the cover of darkness, giving the sniper a clear view of his target. This amphibious landing took place on a dark night with little moonlight but is clearly visible through the scope.

The soldier is using a Starlight Scope fitted to an M16A1 rifle. The eyepiece is positioned firmly against the eye, otherwise light would 'leak' around the eyepiece, illuminating his face. So long as this is remembered, hostile forces cannot detect a Starlight Scope.

Natural point of aim

The first point is to ensure that you have a natural point of aim.

The secret of achieving a natural point of aim is to make the rifle an extension of your own body, so that you point it at the target without thinking, just as you would your finger. You can test yourself like this: with the rifle to your shoulder, take aim at a target, then close your eyes and relax. If the rifle is still pointing at the target when you open your eyes again five or 10 seconds later, then you have a natural point of aim.

Bone support

A steady, reliable shooting position needs support from your bones, not from your muscles. When lying prone, your left hand is forward, palm up. The wrist is straight and locked, the rifle lying across the relaxed palm of the hand; the left forearm and elbow are directly below the barrel.

If the elbow is not directly underneath the barrel, the arm muscles will have to work to hold the rifle and it will not be steady. The rifle butt is held firmly into the shoulder, the right arm and elbow out at an angle to help form the 'shoulder pocket' and to give balanced support.

Right-hand grip

Your right hand must hold the stock firmly, thumb over the top, and forming a 'spot weld' against your cheek. The trigger finger should just touch the trigger, so that it can come straight back without itself touching the stock and perhaps spoiling the aim. Don't slacken your hold on the trigger. A loose grip may make you jerk the trigger at the last moment.

The point of contact between the thumb and the cheekbone is called

Prone shooting po

Offering the lowest silhouette, this position is well adapted both for cover and for a stable firing posture. To assume the correct firing position, stand facing the target with the left hand well forward and the right hand grasping the stock at the heel of the butt. Spread your

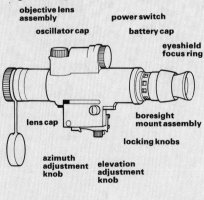

Shadow Effects

If you are not looking directly through the telescope you will see shadows in the field of vision. If crescent-shaped shadows like these appear in the sight, the bullet will strike to the side away from them.

The bullet strikes left — The bullet strikes right

The bullet strikes high — The bullet strikes low

Using the Starlight Scope

The Starlight Scope increases the weight of a rifle by 2.7 kg which makes it doubly important to adopt a steady firing position.

The AN/PVS-2 Starlight Scope allows you to shoot accurately even in the dark. It is battery-powered and uses whatever natural light is available (moonlight or the light of the stars) and amplifies it, allowing you to see targets which would be invisible otherwise.

Unlike infra-red sights, the Starlight Scope cannot be detected by the enemy unless you are careless and fail to keep your eye pressed firmly against the rubber eyepiece. If you do leave a gap, some of the light emitted by the eyepiece will shine out around the eyeshield and onto your face.

The Starlight Scope increases the weight of the rifle by 2.7 kg, so it is very important to have a good firing position and steady hold technique. If at all possible, adopt a supported firing position such as from the lip of a foxhole or the prone position. If the sky is overcast and there is little moonlight or starlight available, then the scope will not give you such a good view, but its capabilities are much increased if it is possible to illuminate the target area with flares or starshell.

Under artificial illumination the Starlight Scope is far superior to the naked eye and gives you excellent depth and clarity of vision. Fog, sleet or snow all reduce the usefulness of the scope, and so does dense vegetation, but the view in lightly wooded country on a moonlit night is very good.

Looking across a body of water such as a stream or lake increases the capabilities of the scope, too.

The Starlight Scope is a valuable item of equipment and must not be allowed to fall into enemy hands. If it seems likely that the sight could be captured, it must be evacuated or, failing that, destroyed. If it is necessary to destroy the scope two methods are possible:
1 Place the scope on end, preferably in a hole, with the objective lens face up. Place a thermite grenade on top and pull the pin. Make certain the optics, image intensifier tube and oscillator are destroyed.
2 Place it in a hole as above, and fire a couple of rounds straight through the objective lens.

range focus ring

objective lens assembly

oscillator cap

power switch

battery cap

eyeshield focus ring

boresight mount assembly

lens cap

locking knobs

azimuth adjustment knob

elevation adjustment knob

the spot weld. Keep the cheek pressed firmly against the thumb so that head, arm, hand and weapon all act as a single unit, keeping the eye still in relation to the sight both before and after firing.

Breathing

If you breathe normally while you're aiming, the rise and fall of your chest will spoil the shot. Instead, breathe in as usual, release part of it and then hold the rest while you aim and fire. Don't try and hold the breath for too long – more than 10 seconds, and you'll produce muscular tension and involuntary movement.

Squeezing the trigger

How you control the trigger is probably the single most important aspect of marksmanship. It is the key to firing off the round without disturbing the way the weapon is lined up with the target.

Your finger should touch the trigger somewhere between the tip and the second joint – the exact position is up to you; it depends on the size of your hand, the size of the rifle's stock and the way you hold your hand. It's very difficult to hold a rifle perfectly still and, instead of trying, the sniper concentrates on getting perfect hand/eye co-ordination.

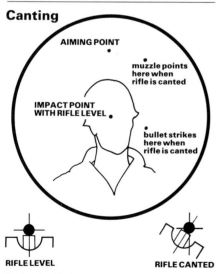

feet comfortably apart and drop to your knees, grounding the toe of the rifle butt well forward on a line between the right knee and the target.

Roll down on your left side, placing the left elbow well forward on the same line. Use your right hand to force the butt of the rifle into your right shoulder, grip the small of the stock with the right hand, and lower your right elbow to the ground so your shoulders are now level.

Secure a spot weld and use your left elbow as a pivot when adjusting your position to find a natural aiming position. You have a well-balanced position if the crosshairs of the target move between 6 o'clock and 12 o'clock as you breathe.

CHECK LIST:

1 The crosshairs are level
2 Rifle rests in a 'V' formed by the left thumb and forefinger and is supported by the palm, not the fingers
3 Left elbow is well under the receiver
4 The rifle butt is close to the neck, in the shoulder pocket
5 Shoulders are level to prevent canting
6 Body is well behind the rifle to absorb the recoil
7 Face is firmly fixed on the thumb or stock (spot weld)
8 There is space between trigger finger and stock

Breathing effects

CORRECT

Take in breath; the crosshairs move straight down through the centre of the target between 12 o'clock and 6 o'clock.

INCORRECT

If the crosshairs move down at an angle, your elbow is not properly supporting the barrel.

INCORRECT

To achieve the correct position, move your body to the right by pivoting around your left elbow.

Unless the round is fired at the precise moment that the cross-hairs are over the target, it will probably miss. That may sound obvious, but is actually all there is to say about marksmanship. The best shots are

Canting

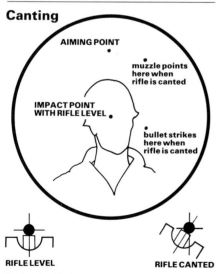

AIMING POINT

muzzle points here when rifle is canted

IMPACT POINT WITH RIFLE LEVEL

bullet strikes here when rifle is canted

RIFLE LEVEL   **RIFLE CANTED**

Tipping the rifle from side to side, so that the muzzle is no longer directly vertical with the sights, is known as canting. All the calculations involved in setting up the rifle's geometry are useless if you don't maintain this vertical alignment, as you can see from the illustration.

Gravity causes the round to fall vertically in the course of its flight – it won't compensate for you canting the rifle!

Zeroing and trajectory

Zeroing a rifle means setting up its sights so that a round fired in perfect conditions will go through the centre of the target.

Bullets do not travel in straight lines between muzzle and target. In the vertical plane they travel in an arc called the trajectory. The further a bullet has to travel on its way to the target, the higher trajectory it must make.

That's why sights have to be re-set to take range into account. The line from your eye to the target is a straight line, and it intersects the trajectory of the bullet at just two places: somewhere close to the end of the muzzle, and at the target.

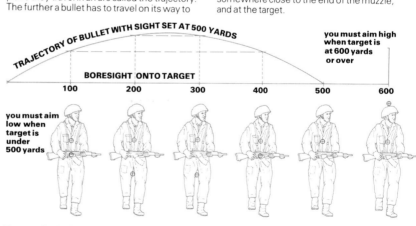

TRAJECTORY OF BULLET WITH SIGHT SET AT 500 YARDS

you must aim high when target is at 600 yards or over

BORESIGHT ONTO TARGET

100   200   300   400   500   600

you must aim low when target is under 500 yards

Boresighting

One way to zero the rifle is to boresight it. Remove the bolt, and support the rifle on a bed of sandbags. Look through the breech and down the barrel, adjusting the rifle's position until you can see the centre of the target through the centre of the bore.

Without moving the rifle, look through the telescopic sight and see where the cross-hairs fall, adjusting windage and elevation until they coincide with the view down the rifle's barrel.

Now all that remains to be done is to adjust the elevation by the standard amount for the range you're covering – three and a half minutes for two hundred yards, nine minutes for four hundred yards, and so on.

You can zero your weapon by firing it on the range under test conditions, too. Fire a three-round group, and observe where it falls. Make corrections to the setting of the sights and try again, repeating the procedure until the three rounds are falling on target.

Using the Redfield telescopic sight

US Marine Corps snipers use the Redfield telescopic sight fitted to the M40 7.62-mm sniper rifle. Used correctly, it enables the sniper to hit targets barely visible to the naked eye. It magnifies the image by a minimum of three times and a maximum of nine adjusted with the power selector ring. The selection of the correct power of magnification is a matter of fine judgement: generally you need lower power in poor light conditions because low power gives a wider field of view, and allows the sight to gather more of the available light. The higher the power, the more pronounced the movement of the crosshairs, though high powers do enable you to see further into heavy foliage and shadowed areas. Always try to shoot using the lowest power magnification possible. The crosshairs are centred and become finer as the magnification power is increased, so as not to obscure the target.

The Redfield sight also enables you to estimate accurately the range to a target and to aim at a precise part of the body. All you need to decide is whether the target is within 600 yards or not. The telescope has two parallel horizontal reference lines in addition to the crosshairs, and at ranges of up to 600 yards the distance between them corresponds to a distance of about 18 inches: the distance between a target's shoulders and belt. At over 600 yards the distance corresponds to about 36 inches – the average distance between the shoulders and knees of a standing figure. Engagement sequence is as follows:

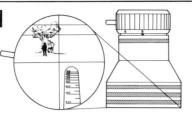

1 Locate the enemy by setting the sight to '3', which gives the widest field of vision. Scan the area until the target is spotted.

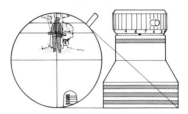

2 Adjust the magnification power until the difference between the two horizontal lines corresponds to an 18-inch distance: the typical distance between a man's shoulders and his belt. Read the scale in the lower right quadrant and set the sight for the range shown.

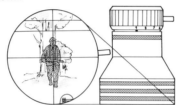

3 Having determined the range and set the sight accordingly, increase magnification to give you a clearer view of the target.

Optical system

A good telescopic sight is essential for sniping missions. The Redfield sight used by the US Marine Corps has variable magnifying power, and its lenses are coated with magnesium fluoride for maximum light transmission.

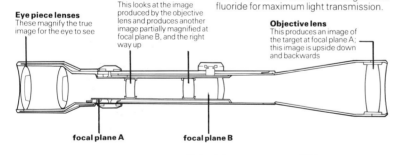

Eye piece lenses
These magnify the true image for the eye to see

Erector lens
This looks at the image produced by the objective lens and produces another image partially magnified at focal plane B, and the right way up

Objective lens
This produces an image of the target at focal plane A; this image is upside down and backwards

focal plane A   focal plane B

Humidity and temperature

Damp, humid air is thicker than dry air, so will resist the passage of the bullet more when it's on its way to the target. This slowing down will cause it to drop faster than normal, so your shot will strike low.

High temperature has the reverse effect. Hot air is thinner than cold air, so offers less resistance to the bullet, sending it high.

You should also make sure that your rifle doesn't stand in the sun. One side getting hotter than the other will cause it to warp – not much, but enough to throw your aim off by a long way at three or four hundred yards.

Keep your weapon and ammunition dry. Wet ammo is colder than dry. Warmer ammuniton works more efficiently than cold, making the round go high. If some is dry and some wet, you'll get different results from different rounds, so if you can't keep your ammo dry you are better off making sure it is all thoroughly wet and reduce elevation when shooting.

Wind

Winds are classified by the clock system according to the direction from which they are blowing in relation to the firer. A wind blowing from right to left across your front is called a 3 o'clock wind; one from the left front is an 11 o'clock wind. The different directions are assigned fractional values depending on how much they affect the bullet.

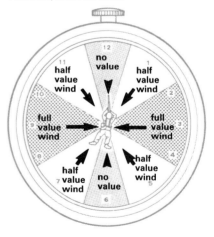

Windage adjustment

The stronger the wind, the more you will need to alter the windage on your sight to compensate. The basic formula to remember is: R × V ÷ 15 = the number of minutes of windage to be placed on the sight for a full value of wind. 'R' is the range in hundreds of yards; 'V' is the wind velocity in miles per hour. One way to estimate wind velocity is by observation:

1 A wind of under 3 mph can hardly be felt, but causes smoke to drift.
2 A 3-5 mph wind is felt lightly on the face.
3 A 5-6 mph wind keeps tree leaves in constant motion.
4 A 8-12 mph wind raises dust and loose paper.
5 A 12-15 mph wind causes small trees to sway.

---

generally quick ones, where everything comes together straight away, and there's no time to drift off. But even so, it's most important not to snatch at the trigger. A good exercise is to balance a small coin on the muzzle and see how still it stays when you squeeze off a dry shot.

Wind and weather

The wind and other weather conditions can make a very great difference to where the bullet strikes the target, and also has an effect on the sniper unless he's lying in the prone position. The wind direction is referred to by the clock system.

Light conditions

The light effects how you see the target. In general it seems that people shoot low on bright, clear days and high when it's gloomy and overcast. But this may not apply to you! The answer is to keep a logbook that details the weather conditions on each day of shooting as well as recording your performance.

The sniper's rifle

The US Marine Corps snipers use the M40 sniping rifle, a commercial model bolt-action 7.62-mm weapon with a medium heavy barrel for improved accuracy. It has a five-round internal magazine, and with scope fitted it weighs 4.2 kg.

Telescopic sight
This is matched with the rifle at the factory, and is numbered to correspond with the serial of the gun.

Heavy barrel
This provides greater strength and accuracy than standard commercial barrels.

Elevation turret
This is used to give the bullet an appropriate trajectory according to the range of the target. A half-minute adjustment moves the strike of the bullet half an inch for each 100 yards of range.

Internal magazine
Situated immediately in front of the trigger guard, this is opened by depressing a latch in the front end of the trigger guard.

Bipod
The bipod is not fitted as standard but can be a useful addition to the sniper's kit.

Trigger
The pressure needed to fire the gun can be varied from 1.3 kg to 2.2 kg, to suit your preference.

Camouflaged case
The stock of a sniper rifle can be manufactured in different camouflage schemes or by a camouflage case fitted over the body of the weapon.

Moving targets: calculating leads

Moving targets are very difficult to hit, and it is almost impossible to obtain consistent results at over 300 yards.

If the target is moving across your front from left to right, you should aim at a point approximately four inches ahead of the target at 300 yards and about eight inches ahead at 500 yards; this distance is known as the lead.

If it is moving at an angle of about 45 degrees towards or away from your, allow half as much lead, but if it is travelling from right to left, and you are right-handed, allow twice as much since you will be slower at tracking a target against your firing shoulder.

Holding this lead, you fire and follow through with the movement after the shot in case another one is needed or in case the enemy suddenly stops or changes direction.

Shooting a moving target with the sights set for 500 yards
This assumes that the target is moving directly across your front; the crosshairs show approximate aiming points for different ranges.

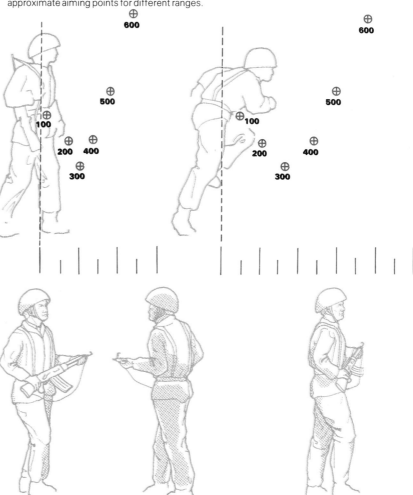

If the target is not moving directly across your front, you must modify your lead accordingly.

No lead
If you can see both arms and either the whole front or the whole back, no lead is required.

Half lead
When one arm and two-thirds of the front and back are visible, the target is moving at roughly a 45° angle. Use half the lead required by a target moving at 90°.

Full lead
When the target is moving across your front, perpendicular to the path of the bullet, use a full-value lead.

DIGGING IN FOR DEFENCE

Success in combat involves more than daring feats of arms on a shifting battlefield. It's part of every soldier's trade to know how to dig himself in, so that he can survive to win the next battle.

In this section we show how to construct defensive positions for two or four men.

An effective defensive position makes the best possible use of your available firepower. Whether at platoon or section level, you need to site and arrange your trenches so that the approaches to your position are all covered by at least two arcs of fire. Then, before they can reach you, enemy forces will always have to enter a potential killing ground.

An effective defence depends on these basic principles:

1 Defend ground of tactical importance

You must deny the enemy any ground of tactical importance. You can do this by holding and defending the ground, or you can cover the approaches to it.

2 Defend your position in depth

You need depth to your defence to absorb an attack and slow its momentum. A 'thin red line' can be easily breached.

3 Individual positions provide mutual support

Mutual support within a section means that each trench must be able to support adjacent trenches by producing fire to the front, flanks or rear of them. Within a platoon each section should be able to support the other two in such a way that machine gun and rifle arcs of fire overlap.

4 Conceal your position

Trenches must be carefully concealed from observation from both the

Defensive positions should be arranged so that the long fields of fire of the General Purpose Machine Guns can overlap, catching the enemy in a cross-fire and breaking up the attack.

6 points for successful defence

1. Select a position of tactical importance.
2. Defend your position in depth.
3. Individual positions mutually support each other.
4. Conceal your positions.
5. Prepare for all-round defence.
6. Keep stock of your ammo state, food and water and medical kit.

Fields of Fire

Section positions should be sited so that enemy troops attacking one position can be engaged with rifle and machine-gun fire from at least one other. Range cards should be prepared and all likely target areas recorded. In the diagram the rifles are firing to the limit of their effective range so their arcs of fire meet. The GPMGs' longer range allows their arcs to overlap.

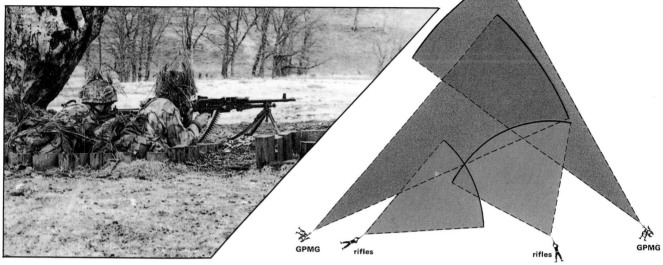

GPMG **rifles** **rifles** **GPMG**

air and the ground. This is partly achieved by effective camouflage, but mainly by careful siting. The ground can be used so that an enemy suddenly comes upon a defensive position without warning. One way of achieving this is to site defensive positions on a 'reverse slope', that is to say behind the crest of a hill so that the enemy only comes across your position and can only bring direct fire to bear upon it after crossing the skyline and when he is within range of your direct fire weapons.

5 Defend all approaches

All defensive positions must be sited so that they can meet an attack from any direction. Although sections and platoons will be given a primary direction in which to concentrate their fire, your lines can be penetrated – especially at night – and they must be prepared to face an attack from any direction.

6 Keep your supply lines open

As in any other phase of war, a successful defence depends upon reliable logistic support. However well sited a position, it is unlikely to be held if the ammunition runs out.

Always follow these six principles

In the worst cases you will have to organise your defences while in contact with the enemy. In Vietnam, combat ranges were so short that this could be very difficult indeed.

when constructing your defensive position. Your individual fire trench will have been sited with these principles in mind and will be part of a bigger plan.

Siting your trenches

The following factors, some of which may conflict, should be considered in designing trenches. Any design will involve a degree of compromise.

1 Use of weapons: you must site your trench to allow you a good field of fire and of view. You must construct it so that your weapon can be fired without hindrance.

2 Protection: the main threat to dug-in infantrymen is from artillery fire, and especially from air-burst projectiles. For maximum protection trenches should not be more than half a metre wide. Overhead protection in the shelter trench should be at least 45 cm thick.

3 Speed of construction: hand held power tools can be used instead of spades or pickaxes, or you can prepare the ground with explosives. The best solution is a light mobile digger.

Below: Just below the parapet of a four-man fire team's defensive position, the notebook gives the stag (sentry duty) rota. The range card is on the back of a ration pack and shows the approximate distances judged by observation.

This can scoop out fire trenches, command posts or larger weapon pits very quickly.

4 Concealment: the trench should, obviously, be as well concealed as possible.

The basic fire trench

The two-man fire trench, the four-man fire trench and the GPMG fire trench are the three basic types you

Together with the GPMG, the 84-mm MAW (Medium Anti-Tank Weapon) forms the cornerstone of the defence. These weapons should be sited first when laying out your defensive position and their arcs of fire clearly defined.

will encounter. The two-man trench is a metre deep, half a metre wide and two metres long. The depth can be varied according to the height of the tallest man in the fire trench; as a

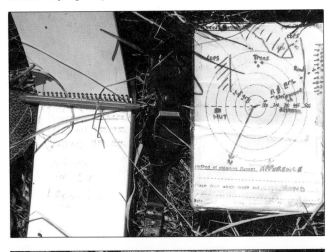

Left: The sentry keeps watch with all the tactical information at his fingertips: a sketch of the ground within his arc of fire, the map, notebook and upright torch.

Above: Prepared for a long stay – mug, mess tin and hexamine stove, kept in a specially-excavated cubbyhole.

general rule it should be as deep as armpits of the tallest man.

Fire trenches should be provided with overhead protection. This should not be more than a third to half a metre above the height of the ground. If overhead protection is added to a fire trench, a gap must be left uncovered for access, to fire anti-tank weapons with a backblast, and to throw grenades.

Taking shelter

Once the fire trench is complete, the next stage is to dig the shelter trench. This is a continuation of the fire trench and should be one and a half metres long, and covered with 45 cm of spoil. This spoil can be supported either by struts or logs or, more easily, by the so-called 'Kip sheet' – the Kit Individual Protection. This is a tough tarpaulin sheet with anchor points and attached cords that secure and tighten it. Incredibly, it supports 45 cm of overhead cover and even the weight of a tank moving over the

US Marines in a hastily improvised perimeter in the so-called De-Militarized Zone between North and South Vietnam. If there is no time to prepare a proper trench, you can take advantage of terrain features such as folds in the ground.

trench. The shelter trench is for you to sleep in.

A four-man trench is quite simply twice the length of a two-man fire trench and will incorporate a shelter trench at each end.

It will take you approximately one to two hours to dig a two-man fire trench in relatively soft soil. This time can be doubled in harder soil. It will take a further hour to add overhead

Camouflage nets should be used to help conceal positions. If foliage is employed you must collect it from outside the position and change it every day.

protection, and a further three to five hours in soft soil (up to nine hours in the hardest soil) to complete the shelter trench.

Obviously, all these times can be drastically reduced if you use mecha-

nical methods. Ideally, allow yourself approximately 24 hours to prepare a defensive position.

Extra defence

When the trench is complete, you need to add further defences. Wire obstacles can be constructed in front of your position, though these are no good unless they are covered by fire. Mines can also be laid. Well-sited and carefully concealed minefields covered by fire can prove a highly effective obstacle to both men and vehicles.

Last, you should have a comprehensive fire plan, tying in supporting artillery and tanks, mortars, machine-guns and anti-tank weapons, to provide the cement to keep the defensive position intact.

The two- and four-man defensive position is at the heart of all effective defence. The only way that an infantryman will survive a coordinated enemy attack is by constructing a sound and strong fire and shelter

trench – if possible with overhead cover. If he can survive enemy artillery bombardment, he can emerge to blunt and defeat the enemy infantry attack that will surely follow.

While digging in you should leave your kit near at hand and your rifle pointing down the middle of your arc of fire: if the enemy arrives early you must be ready. This is especially important in case you are attacked after dark.

HOW TO DIG IN

These are the stages in the construction of defensive positions. The time to prepare them varies enormously. Those given here assume fairly easy soil; harder ground at least doubles the time.

1 Dig survival hole: time ½-2 hours
It should come up to the armpits of the tallest man in the group.

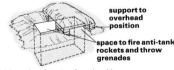

support to overhead position

space to fire anti-tank rockets and throw grenades

2 Add overhead protection: time 1 hour
Leave a space clear for firing anti-tank weapons and throwing grenades.

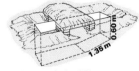

3 Dig shelter trench: time 3-5 hours
This is an extension of the fire trench for sleeping in and for storing everyone's kit.

4 Add overhead protection to the shelter trench

A two-man fighting position with overhead cover: the turf has been re-laid over the parapet, as a heap of chalky soil will instantly betray your position to the enemy.

Leave a lip between 30 and 60 cms above the ground around the trench with gaps for firing your rifle. Note the sloping floor of the shelter to drain water out of the sleeping/storage area.

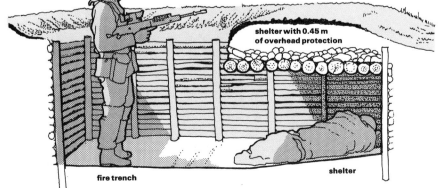

shelter with 0.45 m of overhead protection

fire trench   shelter

*Infantry in **CBW** gear firing the **Gustav AT** weapon at enemy armour.*

CHAPTER TWO

MECHANISED INFANTRY

No longer does the infantryman assemble, form into column with colours flying, then with bands playing bravely march into battle to fight a war he knows little about other than that it was likely to be his last day on earth. While his army approached, drums clattering, the enemy would stand and wait patiently. That is how it used to be. But not today. For one thing, the enemy of today would not sit idly by while all this was going on. Such a noisy and heralded approach would soon be spotted and it is likely that the army would never reach the intended battlefield.

The modern soldier now knows a good deal about the reasons for the battle about to take place. His unit assembles, climbs into a squadron of Armoured Personnel Carriers (APCs) and is transported to the fighting zone in company with all the other armoured fighting vehicles and back-up units. The APC is lightly armoured but has weapons for defence. Its plate armour will stop small-arms fire but could not prevent penetration by any of the sophisticated armour-piercing projectiles now available, rounds which can penetrate some of the toughest and thickest Main Battle Tank (MBT) frontal armour.

This chapter is concerned with the role of mobile armoured vehicles engaged in transporting infantry and other troops into the fighting zone so that they can alight safely and go straight into action. Much of this chapter is devoted to the problems involved in operating the APC. When tanks first appeared, rattling and clanking over the muddy and shell-cratered No Man's Land in World War One, they were crude, clumsy and unreliable and driven and handled by soldiers inexperienced in them. These strange armoured monsters created an impression of invincibility when seen for the first time by an incredulous enemy.

Today's formidable AFVs bear no resemblance to these early models. They have very strong frontal armour, tough enough to withstand all but the most sophisticated AT weapons, and are armed with anything from 150mm artillery to MGs and the crew's handguns. Their motive power is very reliable and they can move over, past or through obstacles which would have beaten the old original models. Their guns do not use shell cases, so more ammunition can be carried. All the ballistic problems are evaluated by the modern AFV's instrumentation. Laser rangefinders feed exact distance, humidity and the motion of the AFV itself into the inboard computer and this in turn produces the data to lay the gun accurately on target.

Their crews can live for days in their own airtight compartment with its atmospheric pressure raised above that outside and so keep out toxic gases. But AFVs do have vulnerable points and some of these are described, with the way infantry can best deal with them. Putting a 60-ton AFV out of action as it clatters towards you would appear unlikely, but it is something that really can be done. The man on the ground can also call-up hedge-hopping anti-tank helicopters armed with missiles.

The infantry can call on special AT artillery as well as aircraft but the man on the ground can surprisingly do quite a lot to knock out enemy tanks. The sight of a 70-ton steel monster clanking towards one must be a testing moment, certainly one for keeping one's hand down. But once the tracks of a main battle tank, for example, are broken an AFV is immobilised, it is a heavily armed and armoured sitting duck.

RIDING INTO BATTLE

Modern armoured forces are a combined team, with tanks and infantry fighting in close co-operation. The infantrymen ride into action in Armoured Personnel Carriers which can keep pace with the tanks; sometimes you will fight from the vehicle, but in most situations you dismount to fight on foot. Certainly, the mechanised infantry platoon with its four APCs has far greater freedom of movement and can respond far quicker than 'leg' infantry. This section, taken from the US Army Field Manual FM 7-7, introduces you to mechanized warfare in the M113 APC, the combat vehicle of the US infantry.

Built from a special aluminium alloy that keeps the all-up weight down to less than 11 tonnes fully loaded, the APC gives its occupants protection from most small-arms fire and from grenade and shell fragments, but not from anti-tank guns, missiles and rockets. This means that the in-fantry leader must think very hard about when and how to dismount his troops and use them in the traditional foot soldiers' role.

In attack, the leader will try to fight from the vehicles for as long as possible, using the tactics worked out in advance for just this sort of situation, and will only get his men out of the protection of the APCs when he gets into close terrain like trees and bushes or comes up against obstacles or a strong anti-tank force.

This flexibility – to fight from vehicles with armour strong enough to deflect small-arms fire or to dismount

An Armoured Personnel Carrier enables you to move swiftly, keeping up with tanks. These US M113s carry the increased machine-gun armament adopted during the Vietnam War: a .50-cal Browning at the front, and an M60 7.62-mm machine-gun on each side.

6 BASIC RULES OF MOVEMENT

1. Make use of terrain that hides you from enemy observation or fire.
2. Avoid silhouetting your vehicle by crossing a skyline or moving directly forward from a hull-down position.
3. Cross open areas of ground as fast as you can.
4. Use your smoke grenade-launchers to cover disengagement or to protect a halted APC.
5. Move with a small force scouting ahead and with the rest of your team following behind.
6. Make sure your leading team can be covered by the vehicles behind.

fire, the whole operation will be a great deal safer. If the vehicles can move in the hull-down position as well – along roads or tracks with hedges and banks on each side, for example – then they are very difficult to detect, even when moving. This adds very considerably to their effectiveness, but gives them less room to deploy in case of attack.

Unit commanders must consider all these points when using the APC in attack. The extra speed of the vehicle gives you every chance of over-running enemy positions – especially if they've been careless in their anti-armour preparations – but it also means that it's easy to over-extend, to get so far in front that the advance becomes a series of isolated fire-fights that do little or nothing to really gain ground, and where you're in every danger of being surrounded and cut off.

On foot, infantrymen can fire and move as the need arises. In vehicles, the whole operation has to have a little more planning involved in it, though the excellent specification of the M113 Armoured Personnel carrier does make it surprisingly flexible. It can span trenches and ditches nearly two metres wide, and climb up 60-degree slopes.

Keep in touch

Communications between vehicles often require a radio net. As well as the sets fixed into the APC, the platoon commander, the platoon sergeant and each team leader will have personal radio transceivers. This means that communications are usually better between members of a mounted infantry unit than between foot soldiers in a squad, again making for better mobility and quicker response times.

It does make for one added danger, however – the enemy may be able to listen in to your transmissions. If he does he will not only gain intelligence, but also be able to pin-point your position.

As well as sophisticated radios, APC-mounted troops also have a wide range of STANO (Surveillance, Target Acquisition, Night Observation) devices available – Binoculars and AN/PAS-6 Metascopes for general observation, the M19 Infra-red Periscope for the driver, and AN/PVS and AN/TVS sights for the various different weapons.

Sustaining the attack

Because APCs are at risk from even hand-held anti-tank weapons, it's

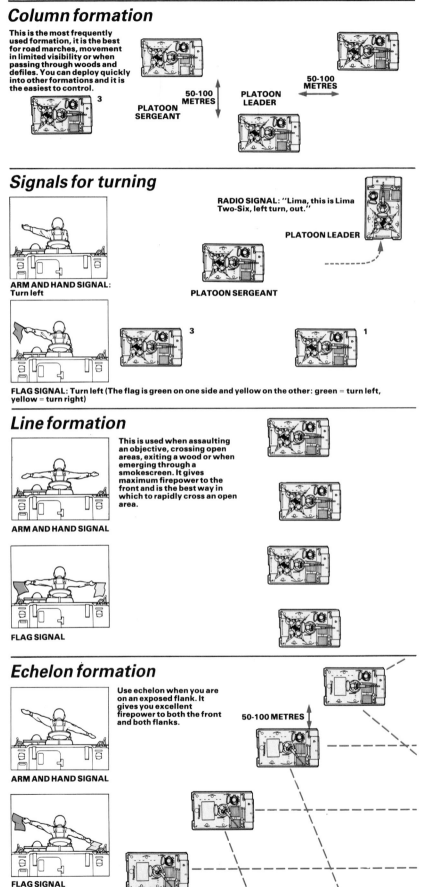

PLATOON FORMATIONS

Column formation

This is the most frequently used formation, it is the best for road marches, movement in limited visibility or when passing through woods and defiles. You can deploy quickly into other formations and it is the easiest to control.

PLATOON SERGEANT
50-100 METRES
PLATOON LEADER
50-100 METRES

Signals for turning

ARM AND HAND SIGNAL: Turn left

FLAG SIGNAL: Turn left (The flag is green on one side and yellow on the other: green = turn left, yellow = turn right)

RADIO SIGNAL: "Lima, this is Lima Two-Six, left turn, out."

PLATOON LEADER

PLATOON SERGEANT

Line formation

ARM AND HAND SIGNAL

FLAG SIGNAL

This is used when assaulting an objective, crossing open areas, exiting a wood or when emerging through a smokescreen. It gives maximum firepower to the front and is the best way in which to rapidly cross an open area.

Echelon formation

ARM AND HAND SIGNAL

FLAG SIGNAL

Use echelon when you are on an exposed flank. It gives you excellent firepower to both the front and both flanks.

50-100 METRES

Vee formation

Use this when the situation is unclear and you want the unit concentrated with all-round firepower.

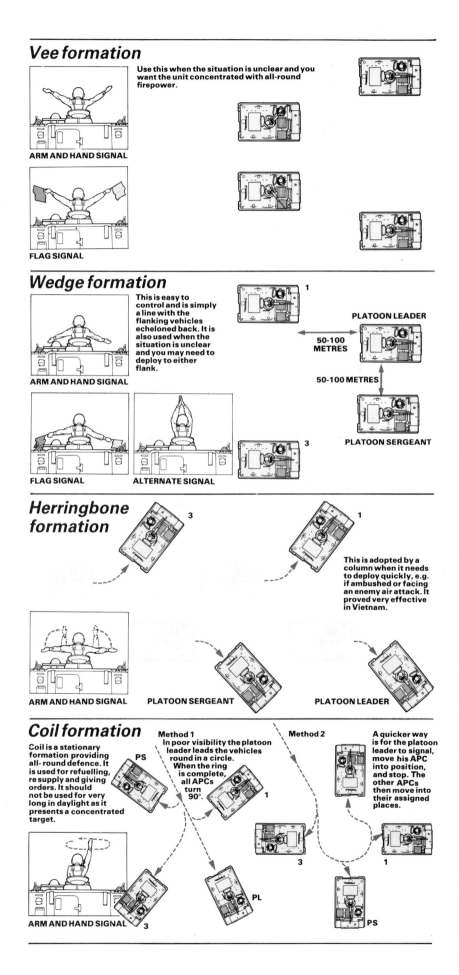

ARM AND HAND SIGNAL

FLAG SIGNAL

Wedge formation

This is easy to control and is simply a line with the flanking vehicles echeloned back. It is also used when the situation is unclear and you may need to deploy to either flank.

ARM AND HAND SIGNAL

FLAG SIGNAL

ALTERNATE SIGNAL

1

PLATOON LEADER

50-100 METRES

50-100 METRES

3

PLATOON SERGEANT

Herringbone formation

3

1

This is adopted by a column when it needs to deploy quickly, e.g. if ambushed or facing an enemy air attack. It proved very effective in Vietnam.

ARM AND HAND SIGNAL

PLATOON SERGEANT

PLATOON LEADER

Coil formation

Coil is a stationary formation providing all-round defence. It is used for refuelling, re supply and giving orders. It should not be used for very long in daylight as it presents a concentrated target.

Method 1
In poor visibility the platoon leader leads the vehicles round in a circle. When the ring is complete, all APCs turn 90°.

PS

1

3

PL

Method 2
A quicker way is for the platoon leader to signal, move his APC into position, and stop. The other APCs then move into their assigned places.

3

1

PS

ARM AND HAND SIGNAL

3

If an M113 strikes an anti-tank mine anyone inside is likely to be injured. These Australian troops are riding on top where they are safer from mines, but of course more vulnerable to enemy rifles.

most important to allow the enemy no time to re-group and get its anti-armour specialists into the fire-fight. The speed at which the M113 can move cross-country gives the mounted infantry unit commander an advantage here, but he is still just as concerned to keep a high rate of fire concentrated on enemy positions. Getting from place to place quickly is important, but it's still weight of fire that wins fire-fights.

New supplies

He has to think about re-supply, too – ammunition, food and one new factor: fuel for the vehicles. Get too far away from a supply point, and you could suddenly find yourself helpless, with your carriers out of fuel. At that point, all the advantages you've had suddenly turn into liabilities.

Though the M113 can carry 12 men, including its driver, the normal load is nine. When the infantry squad is mounted in the vehicle, offensive operations involve the .50 calibre machine-gun plus four members of the squad positioned in the open well at the back of the vehicle and armed with automatic weapons and grenade launchers – though the Platoon Commander may have changed the weapons mix to include TOW and LAW anti-armour missiles, depending on intelligence reports of the enemy strengths he's likely to meet.

As well as the heavy machine-gun (which may be taken off and used as a dismounted support weapon if necessary), there are vehicle mounts for the squad's own 7.62-mm calibre M60 machine-gun and for anti-tank weapons.

Where the troops dismount for a

59

short 'mopping up' operation, close to the vehicle, these heavier weapons are often left with the APC, their operators arming themselves with more appropriate semi-automatic weapons instead.

Deadly missiles

The APC's worst enemy is the Anti-Tank Guided Missile (ATGM), now so light and compact that you must expect even small units of enemy troops to be equipped with them. Missiles such as these have one big weakness: they don't work well if there are obstacles – trees, for example, or even wire fences – between the launcher and the target. In open country, though, they're deadly.

It is the APC's driver who is the vehicle's first line of defence against ATGMs. His skill at using the shape of the country to keep the vehicle out of the sight-line of enemy troops, and his ability to keep the vehicle moving through difficult patches instead of cutting across open country, make all the difference.

Terrain driving, as it is called, is

practised over and over until it becomes second nature following four very basic guidelines:
1 Use all available cover.
2 Avoid the skyline.
3 Cross even small open areas fast.
4 Don't move straight forward out of a hull-down firing position.

Even though all but the last of these are basic skills that every infantryman learns, the way they're put into prac-

A combined arms team of M48 tanks and M113 APCs halts at the edge of a forest and the dismount teams prepare to assault on foot. In Vietnam armoured forces proved more effective than expected in jungle.

tice is changed a lot by the size and speed of the vehicles. Reading the terrain, whether from the map or from looking directly at the ground, becomes even more important than ever before.

DISMOUNTED OPERATIONS

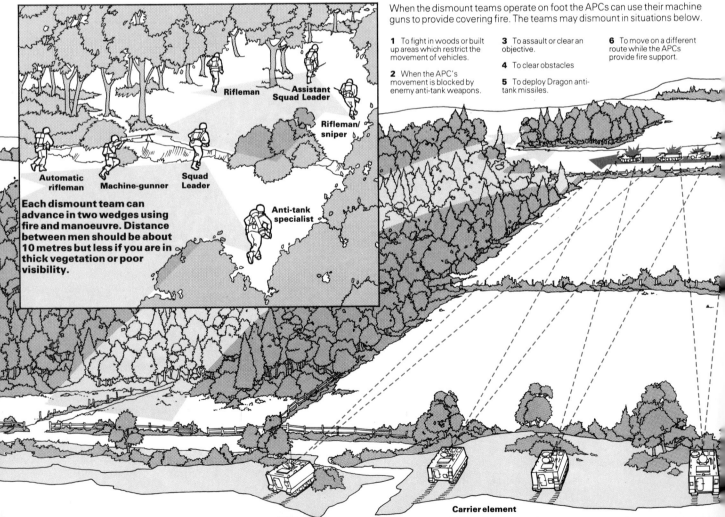

When the dismount teams operate on foot the APCs can use their machine guns to provide covering fire. The teams may dismount in situations below.

1 To fight in woods or built up areas which restrict the movement of vehicles.

2 When the APC's movement is blocked by enemy anti-tank weapons.

3 To assault or clear an objective.

4 To clear obstacles

5 To deploy Dragon anti-tank missiles.

6 To move on a different route while the APCs provide fire support.

Rifleman

Assistant Squad Leader

Rifleman/ sniper

Automatic rifleman

Machine-gunner

Squad Leader

Anti-tank specialist

Each dismount team can advance in two wedges using fire and manoeuvre. Distance between men should be about 10 metres but less if you are in thick vegetation or poor visibility.

Carrier element

ADVANCE! ATTACK! ASSAULT!

The M113 Armoured Personnel Carrier, fast, agile and heavily armed, is a frightening weapon. Working together in company strength, just a dozen of them can deliver more than 100 fighting men into the thick of an attack quickly and in relative safety and support them with their own devastating fire power.

We can now look at the way APCs are used in attack, to assault enemy positions and destroy them in the shortest possible time. It is taken from the US Army's FM 7-7 Field Manual.

An attack can be split into two separate parts:
1 Movement to contact.
2 The assault itself.

Intelligence from patrols, airborne surveillance and perhaps interrogation of enemy prisoners will give the attack commander an idea of the positions the enemy is occupying, but things happen so quickly in battle that this information is only ever a starting point. Moving towards contact with the enemy, the attack commander wants to achieve two things: update his information, and get his troops into position safely and without giving away too much of his plan.

Clearing obstacles

Moving forward using the technique called Bounding Overwatch, the company's armoured vehicles support each other and the much heavier armour of the tank platoon, dismounting their infantrymen to clear obstacles and possible ambush sites and whenever they encounter difficult terrain such as woodland and buildings that can't be by-passed, and when visibility is poor. Their speed and manoeuvrability allows them to get in, dispose of the obstacle, and get on with the advance with the least possible delay.

Movement to contact

The moment the leading element of the patrol or advance makes contact with the enemy it must react quickly and aggressively. The platoon's action in the first few seconds of the engage-

An APC platoon of the Israeli army prepares to move out: the squad commander joins the .50-calibre machine-gunner on top of the vehicle and other soldiers sit up to maintain all-round vision. Extra machine-guns are mounted on the vehicle sides; these are particularly valuable in disturbing the aim of an enemy anti-tank guided missile operator.

Your squad's M60 general-purpose machine-gun can be used either on its bipod or fixed to a tripod and used to provide sustained fire to cover an attack.

ment may well determine whether the battle is lost or won.

The Platoon Commander has three objectives now:
1 Suppress enemy fire.
2 Deploy his forces.
3 Report the contact.

His first step is to assess the situation and make an estimate of the enemy's strength.

Quick attack

If enemy resistance is light, a hasty attack without further planning or reinforcement may be the best way to deal with it. Troops should be mounted in the vehicles wherever possible, so that they can be moved or redeployed quickly.

It may be, though, that the enemy doesn't present a real threat, and can be safely by-passed. It's important to keep the forward movement going, and so the company commander will probably use this option whenever he can, mopping up the enemy pocket later when there's more time.

Enemy contained

If there is strong enough enemy resistance to stop the lead platoon's forward movement, then they will have to be contained and suppressed. If this is the case, it may require the attention of the whole company together with

whatever support units, such as combat engineers, are available.

The assault

An attack generally has one of two objectives – to destroy or capture enemy troops or material, or to secure a key territorial feature. Accurate intelligence, training and equipment, and troop morale are all vitally important, but so is effective leadership – to assess the situation, organise the tactical plan, and communicate it to the men who are going to carry it out.

At a minimum, the plan has to cover five headings:

ADVANCING ALONG ROADS

A column of APCs moving down a road is very vulnerable to enemy anti-tank weapons, particularly where the road bends. When advancing to contact, send the dismount teams ahead to check out each corner.

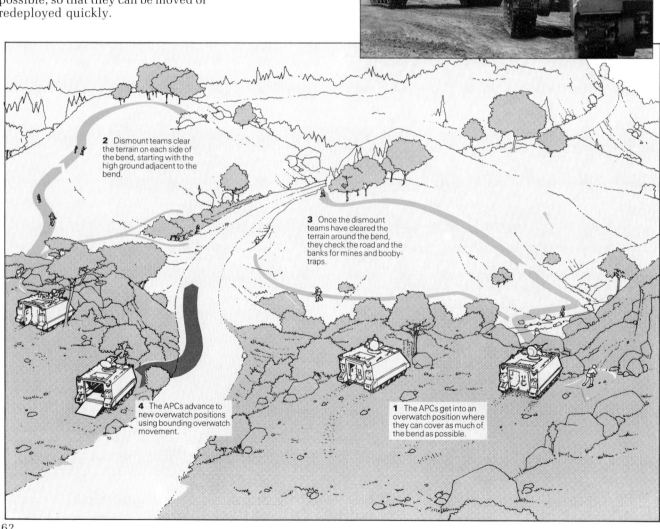

2 Dismount teams clear the terrain on each side of the bend, starting with the high ground adjacent to the bend.

3 Once the dismount teams have cleared the terrain around the bend, they check the road and the banks for mines and booby-traps.

4 The APCs advance to new overwatch positions using bounding overwatch movement.

1 The APCs get into an overwatch position where they can cover as much of the bend as possible.

HOW THE PLATOON CROSSES A BRIDGE

Approach a bridge as a possible ambush site and clear it before crossing. Remember, the enemy may have weapons ranged in on the bridge, or may have booby-trapped the approaches or wired the whole structure for demolition.

2 If a fording site is available the dismount teams cross the river and secure the far side, occupying overwatch positions.

3 A carrier and its dismount team advance to the bridge and carefully examine the approaches and the bridge itself in case the enemy has mined them.

1 The APCs move into an overwatch position where they can cover the terrain on both flanks of the bridge and the far side.

1 Situation
2 Mission
3 Execution
4 Support
5 Communications

Nothing must be left to chance – or even assumed – at this point. The troops involved in the operation must all know their starting point, timetable and objectives, and there must be enough flexibility to take account of changes in the way enemy forces are deployed and the inevitable problems of troops sticking to the timetable as a result of resistance being more forceful than was anticipated.

Where enemy resistance is light, anti-armour weapons can be dealt with and the terrain allows easy movement, then the infantry will stay mounted in the vehicles.

Heavy armour

If a tank force is available, then the heavy armour will take the lead, laying down as dense a volume of fire as possible on to the enemy positions, with the APCs following two to four hundred metres behind, covering the flanks and rear of the tanks with heavy machine-gun fire.

If a stop order comes, the vehicles commander chooses a covered position with a good field of fire and continues to engage specific targets or lay down general suppressing fire.

Any halt at this stage will be short, so troops do not dismount to establish security for the vehicles, but should there be real danger from enemy anti-armour teams, the dismount order will come before the final assault is begun. It would be suicidal to stop the transport in the full face of enemy fire and dismount troops then.

As in any other circumstances, the dismount option is used during the final assault when enemy anti-tank weapons can't be suppressed, or when there are obstacles that will slow or halt the APCs. And, just as

before, the carrier element will be placed to give the best possible covering and suppressing fire, moving to an overwatching position from the point where the troops have been dropped if necessary.

The object of the final phase of the attack – the assault proper – is to lay down ferocious firepower into the enemy positions and then take them

The M113 armoured personnel carrier is fully amphibious, its tracks propelling it through the water. Before taking the plunge, switch on the two bilge pumps and set up the trim vane at the front.

physically if necessary, killing and capturing as many enemy personnel as possible and securing the maximum amount of equipment and material. The assault is not a mindless charge. It is a cautious yet bold and aggressive action, using all the principles of cover and concealment and fire and movement.

Resistant positions

The most hastily-prepared defensive positions can be surprisingly resistant to vehicles, even to tracked vehicles such as M113 APCs and tanks, and the attack commander must always be ready to dismount his troops and fight them as regular infantry. Even then, the heavy weapons and ammunition load that the APCs can carry can have a significant effect on the outcome of the assault.

The carrier element, now empty of all troops except for the driver and gunner and in one case the team leader, maintains heavy covering fire. This supporting fire needs to be close in to the dismount element, especially in the last stage of the assault, and so the gunners responsible must be very careful when selecting their aiming points so as not to endanger friendly forces.

The carrier element leader will mark the borders of fire zones, perhaps with tracer rounds, and also order smoke grenades where necessary. The dismount element will generate their own smoke as well, of course, and the dismount element leader will vary the colour of smoke used – yellow, green, red, for example – to signal to the carrier element that certain pre-arranged points have been reached so that supporting fire can be redirected.

Flexible overwatch

The overwatching position of the carrier element need not be firmly fixed. In fact, there will probably come a time during the assault when the vehicles will have to cease their supporting fire for fear of hitting their own dismounted men.

At that point they are free to move to a secondary overwatch position, from which they have a clearer view of the target and can re-start their support activity. In this way it may be

ASSAULTING THE OBJECTIVE

The assault is the last phase of the attack when the attacking force closes on the enemy position. It is not a 'charge' in the old-fashioned sense; you must use all available cover and concealment and the techniques of fire and movement. Using mutually supporting covering fire, you move on to and across the objective, destroying or capturing the enemy.

Mounted attack
If the enemy has had little time to prepare his defences or is short of anti-tank weapons, you can overrun them with a mounted attack. Each APC uses its machine-guns to suppress individual enemy positions, and the soldiers manning the cargo hatch in the top of the vehicle must be especially alert.

Clearing positions on foot
Whether you attack mounted or dismounted, the dismount teams must complete the assult by clearing the enemy positions on foot. Use supporting fire from the APCs to assist attacks on any pockets of resistance.

Move to support
If the dismount teams make the final assault on foot, the APCs must move up to support them as soon as possible. As soon as their fire is masked by the dismount teams arriving on the objective, the APCs drive forward and occupy hull-down positions near them.

Dismount in covered position
If you have to make the assault on foot, dismount from your armoured personnel carriers in a covered position as close to the objective as possible. While you deploy for the assault the enemy position must be attacked with artillery or tank gun fire to keep enemy anti-tank gunners at the bottom of their trenches.

DODGING ENEMY ANTI-TANK MISSILES

1 Look out for the tell-tale flash as the enemy anti-tank guided missile operator launches his missile.

2 Immediately fire all your machine guns at the enemy gunner: if it does not hit him it will at least disturb his aim.

4 Head for the nearest cover: a hollow or ridge is ideal, but trees, bushes or even telegraph poles can obstruct the missile's flight.

3 Drive in an erratic zig-zag to make it hard for the enemy to keep you in his sights.

1 Anti-tank missile operators need to keep the crosshairs of their sight centred on your vehicle. You must do everything you can to put them off.

2 Obstacles like bushes and small trees may not actually detonate the missile but they can snag its control wires, causing it to miss.

3 If all else fails you can try a sudden turn to right or left in the last seconds of the missile's flight.

---

possible to hit the enemy defensive position from both sides at once.

As soon as enemy resistance has been suppressed, the assault force must consolidate and reorganize, either to continue the attack or to prepare to repel a counterattack. When the troops have remained mounted on the vehicles right through the attack, it's often possible to push on and make much more significant gains in the relatively soft and ill-defended rear echelons.

Rear gains

In fact, gains made in the rear, which will contain command posts and assembly areas, may be considerably more important than taking the front line defensive positions, especially from an intelligence point of view.

Even though the fighting may be over at this point, the operation isn't. The captured areas have to be scoured for hidden dangers, both human and in the form of mines and booby traps; defensive positions have to be prepared; essential troops lost in the action – TOW and GPMG crews, for example – have to be replaced; resupply organized; casualties and prisoners evacuated; and a detailed report of the operation made to higher command.

And even when all these follow-up tasks have been completed, still there's no time to relax. There's never time to relax on the battlefield.

Signal progress
As the dismount teams arrive on the objective they must signal their progress so that supporting fire can be shifted ahead of them. It's a good idea to have a pre-arranged visual signal such as coloured smoke grenades in case radio communication is not available at the vital moment.

Leading by example
In the assault, dismount team leaders must lead by example because it is practically impossible to shout orders above the noise of battle. 'Follow me and do as I do' is the way to lead.

Accurate shooting
Everyone's shooting must be properly directed for maximum effect. Since the squad leader is at the centre of the dismount team he fires his rifle at the centre of each target. He can also get the squad grenadier to use his M203 grenade launcher to mark targets with a smoke grenade.

TAKING THE HIGH GROUND

Your armoured personnel carrier is bullet-proof and protects you from shell splinters, but an anti-tank missile will smash through its thin armour with horrific consequences. When on the move you must scan the ground ahead for possible killing grounds where enemy anti-tank teams are lying in wait and use the principles of fire and movement, one APC covering another.

The US Army's Field Manual FM 7-7 gives three standard strategies for APC movement. The one you select depends on the strength of your chances of making contact with the enemy.

Although this 'contact status' determines which of the three movement strategies will be used, you as platoon commander must consider the terrain and the job to be done when deciding which of the five movement formations the mounted infantry unit will adopt.

In theory, any one of them can be used in any of the three contact statuses, though in Conditions Two and Three this can be done only by splitting the platoon into two parts or by joining up with another of the Company's platoons.

1 Travelling: single-unit movement

When contact with the enemy is thought to be unlikely, your APC formation moves as a single unit, without splitting up into two elements that protect and cover each other. Because speed across the ground and control are the two most important factors, the column movement formation is used most often.

The unit is not likely to have to go into action, and it's important to keep moving as fast as possible, so the platoon commander will generally take the point position. You will use hand and arm signals to indicate the direction that the unit is to take, and also to signal changes of formation.

The APC's rear door is left open, and one member of the squad is detailed to maintain a watch on the vehicle following, reporting to you if he loses contact.

Travelling in this way, each of the

Because of the range and power of modern weapons, a moving unit needs to have a scout element well ahead of the main body of vehicles to detect the enemy before the whole unit is in range of their weapons. Here a squad of the US 11th Armored Cavalry scans the ground ahead in Vietnam.

---

3 MOVEMENT STRATEGIES

1. Travelling
Used when contact with the enemy is unlikely.

2. Travelling Overwatch
Used when there is a possibility of contact with the enemy.

3. Bounding Overwatch
Used when contact with the enemy is expected or likely.

BOUNDING OVERWATCH

This is the most cautious movement technique, used when you expect to contact the enemy. One team advances towards a specified terrain feature while another positions itself to provide covering fire.

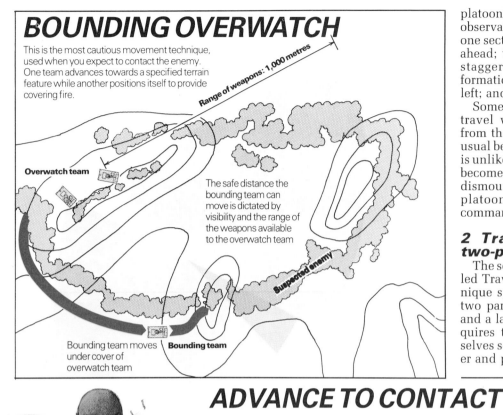

Range of weapons: 1,000 metres

Overwatch team

The safe distance the bounding team can move is dictated by visibility and the range of the weapons available to the overwatch team

Suspected enemy

Bounding team moves under cover of overwatch team

Bounding team

platoon's vehicles is responsible for observation and first-line security in one sector. The lead vehicle looks out ahead; the second vehicle, which is staggered to the right in column formation, to the right; the third to the left; and the fourth to the rear.

Sometimes it becomes necessary to travel with the troops dismounted from the vehicles, though this is unusual because contact with the enemy is unlikely in Condition One. If it does become necessary, you will generally dismount with your men while the platoon sergeant, your second-in-command, stays with the vehicles.

2 Travelling Overwatch: two-part movement

The second stage of readiness is called Travelling Overwatch. This technique splits the travelling force into two parts, a small spear-head group and a larger overwatch force, and requires them both to position themselves so that the larger force can cover and protect the other all the time.

ADVANCE TO CONTACT

Your job as platoon leader is to make certain that everyone knows what to do before the movement begins. You need to make clear: (**1**) What is known about the enemy situation; (**2**) The next overwatch position: this is where the bounding team will halt; (**3**) The route of the bounding team to the next overwatch position; (**4**) What you intend to do when they have got there; (**5**) Target reference points and sectors of fire.

The bounding element travels towards the objective under covering fire from the overwatch force. As it approaches the objective the supporting fire shifts to engage targets further ahead.

The overwatch force will deploy its dismount teams in some circumstances. This enables them to make full use of all squad weapons, including the Dragon anti-tank missile.

The lie of the land, together with whatever information about enemy positions and strengths that's available, will decide which movement formation your unit will take up. By definition, it won't be the line formation, but any one of the other four may be used.

Moving into country that may conceal enemy forces is part normal advance and part patrol activity. It's important to keep the forward movement going, but at the same time you must present the enemy with as small a target as possible – if he can be persuaded to attack a single vehicle, he gives away his position without being able to do much good for himself in the process.

Because you must be in a position to control all four of your vehicles, you drop back to number two position in the movement formation in Travelling Overwatch, and send the lead vehicle out 400 to 600 metres ahead, staying in visual and radio contact all the time.

Because its armour will withstand anything less than an Anti-Tank Guided Missile, the APC is well suited to this decoy role. If he does succeed in drawing enemy fire, the heavy .50 calibre machine-guns mounted on the platoon's vehicles will stand a very good chance of winning a fire-fight even at ranges of up to 1,000 metres, and the distance involved will give them every chance to reform into the most effective grouping possible in order to mount an assault.

Moving while dismounted

Even though the object of the exercise is to move forward as fast as possible, it may sometimes be necessary to move using the Travelling Overwatch technique with the platoon dismounted from the vehicles, especially if you suspect that the enemy forces may have their anti-armour specialists deployed.

In this case the lead section will take the place of the lead vehicle, and will stay in closer contact with the rest of the platoon – perhaps 100 metres in front. The vehicles must keep to positions where they can cover both the lead section and the rest of the dismounted element.

Remember, both these techniques – Travelling and Travelling Overwatch – have the same objective: to advance on an objective as fast as possible. Separating the men from their vehicles takes away the speed advantage that is the main part of the difference between Mounted Infantry and ordinary footsoldiers. Keep the men in the carriers. Dismount only when it's absolutely necessary.

Distance between vehicles varies according to the terrain. In this Vietnamese jungle, the APCs have to keep very close indeed to be able to see each other and thus provide covering fire.

The Browning .50-cal machine-gun provides effective long-range firepower: you can hit an individual target at up to 500 metres, a vehicle at up to 800 and an area target at up to 1000 metres.

When firing the Browning .50-cal from the APC, hold it tightly to the chest. Aim slightly low of the target and 'walk' the rounds on to it. Cease fire when the rounds go high and repeat the process.

The APC driver manoeuvres the vehicle under the direction of the vehicle commander, but it is his job to make the best use of the ground when on the move.

In heavily forested or urban areas or when an enemy ambush appears likely, the dismounted teams will work ahead of the APCs. However, dismounted operations should be kept to a minimum because they dramatically reduce the movement rate.

HULL DOWN TO ENEMY FIRE

Occupying a hull-down position simply means positioning the vehicle so that its hull is behind cover and cannot be hit by enemy weapons. However, the vehicle's own weapons are above the cover and able to fire at the enemy.

DAY SIGNALS

Arm and hand signals are the basic way of communicating within squads and platoons in conditions of good visibility. Because of the dangers of misunderstood signals it is important that everyone practises these signal techniques regularly. The bottom row of signals is performed by the vehicle's crew members.

I am ready

I do not understand

Assemble

Disregard previous command

Enemy in sight

Attention

Commence firing

Cease firing

Cover our move

Move out

Form line

Enemy in sight

3 Bounding Overwatch: fire and move

The third movement technique, called Bounding Overwatch, is used when contact with the enemy is expected. The attacking force is split into two equal parts, the bounding force and the overwatch force, and are used in a way very similar to the traditional infantryman's fire-and-move tactics.

Bounding overwatch is the most deliberate and cautious of the three movement techniques. While the other two assume that the enemy may be about, and arrange the unit to counter any move he may make, Bounding Overwatch assumes that the enemy is definitely there waiting to attack.

Approaching the enemy

The overwatch force covers the bounding force from a static position that offers a good field of fire against possible enemy operations. How far the bounding force will go is decided in advance. The sort of things that you will look for when selecting a target site depends on which of two types of movement you use at the time. These could be:

1 Successive advance, where the overwatch force moves up to the positions that the bounding force has just established, takes them over and covers the next movement of the bounding force.

2 Alternate advance, where the overwatch force moves forward through and past the area where the bounding force has come to a halt, and takes on the job of the bounding force itself.

STREET FIGHT

In built-up areas the dismount teams lead the way in a modified column formation, clearing the buildings as they go. As the column moves under covering fire from the APCs, each team makes sure there are no enemy in the buildings on its side of the street and keeps the upper floors of the buildings across the street under observation.

KILLING TANKS

Enemy tanks, infantry fighting vehicles and other hostile armour represent probably the greatest threat you'll face when defending your position on the European battlefield. This threat more than anything else will dictate how you set out your defences.

A Soviet T-62 emerges from a blazing forest, its stabilised 115-mm gun ready for the next target. As an infantryman, the tank is still your most feared enemy and unless you co-ordinate your anti-tank weapons it can smash your defences in minutes.

But preparing to defeat an armoured attack doesn't mean that you should slip into a defensive state of mind. Your tactics should be aggressive, imaginative and effective. This is when the enemy is at his most stretched and his most vulnerable – and you have a golden opportunity to inflict massive tank casualties on him.

Use your ground

Use natural obstacles to hinder and impede the enemy, and to canalise his approach – that is, make him travel

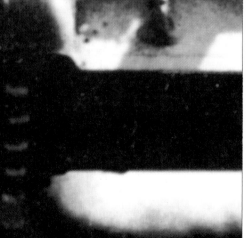

The Dragon system is currently in service with the US Army. The gunner just keeps the crosshairs of the sight on the target, and the tracker automatically guides the missile along the gunner's line of sight.

Milan is a man-portable system (just); the two-man team comprises the gunner, who manhandles the firing post and fires the weapon, and the No. 2, who carries two rockets and loads them on the firing post. Each rocket weighs 11.3 kg and the firing post 16.5 kg.

along the lines you want, to where you can ambush, harass or destroy him at will.

Remember that armoured vehicles are very limited by the ground that they can use. They need bridging or snorkelling equipment to cross anything but the smallest rivers or streams. Marshy or swampy ground is impassable to main battle tanks, and close or wooded country, if not impassable, gives you an opportunity for tank ambush at close range.

Similarly, built-up areas delay and channel the movement of armoured vehicles and make them vulnerable to close-range infantry anti-tank weapons. You can of course thicken up all these natural anti-tank obstacles with minefields and, if you are defending a built-up area, with rub-

ble, overturned buses and any other sort of artificial obstacle.

Use surprise

You can use 'dead' ground to conceal your defending, reserve and counter-attack forces. You can sight your anti-tank weapons in defilade positions (hidden from frontal observation) in order to provide enfilade fire (from a flank). You will then surprise the enemy from a flank and hit him where his armour is thinnest. The tank is also a bigger and easier target in enfilade.

You can also use reverse slopes. In other words, sight your anti-tank weapons several hundred yards back from the crest of a ridge or hill: your positions are then invisible to the enemy until he crosses the crest. You

Fighter ground attack
As well as Lynx anti-tank helicopters, there may be ground attack aircraft such as the A-10 or Harrier GR.Mk 3 available for tank-busting.

Priority target
Warsaw Pact radio procedure is very strictly controlled: only battalion or company commanders are allowed to speak! Everyone else simply maintains a listening watch and passes no information, so if a command tank is knocked out then confusion reigns.

Counter-mobility
The engineers can create anti-tank obstacles or improve existing natural obstacles to further channel the enemy into the killing zone.

Wombat is a 120-mm recoilless rifle still in use by the British Army's Berlin garrison and some Territorial Army units. Although it cannot match the Milan's excellent tank-killing capability, it remains a very worthwhile tool for fighting in built-up areas.

Reverse slope positions
Always consider a reverse slope position first. Not only does it provide a degree of protection from direct and indirect fire, but it also gives a better chance of preserving surprise. But you will need OPs forward to provide adequate warning of enemy approach.

84-mm MAW
An old but extremely solid piece of kit, there are moves to retain it with an improved ammunition while the new 80-mm LAW is perfected. The 84 has a massive blast signature and is almost as impressive at the firing end as it is on the receiving end. If there is time, it is well worth digging secondary, alternative positions and perhaps dummy positions. The essential thing is, you can't afford to miss very often!

66-mm LAW
Great for short-range work on BMPs, BTR-60s etc, LAW could be used against tanks in a desperate situation. If you are taking on a tank with this weapon, fire volleys rather than one shot after another; you are bound to get at least one round on target.

Mines
There are four types of minefield: the tactical large-area minefield, usually laid by the engineers, for tactical use on the battlefield (i.e. to canalise the enemy into killing areas); the protective minefield, the sort that you will plant in front of your position for defensive purposes; the nuisance minefield, designed to hamper and disrupt enemy movement; and the dummy minefield – a wired-off area suitably marked can be as effective as the real thing.

will have been safe from his long-range tank fire but, as he shows his belly when he crosses the ridgeline, you can engage him with maximum effect. Clever use of ground is probably the most effective counter to the tank threat.

Second, you must exploit to the full any conditions that favour you. Despite the most modern night-vision equipment, tanks are more vulnerable at night. Despite the most up-to-date thermal-imaging equipment, tanks are more vulnerable in poor visibility. Finally, tanks do not like either close country or built-up areas. Use these conditions when you can.

The weapon for the job

Well-planned and coordinated use of your anti-tank weapons will enable you to defeat enemy armour. In every battle group there is a combination of weapons systems for anti armour operations.

In the first category are hand-held infantry weapons: the 66-mm LAW, the 84-mm MAW and Milan anti-tank guided missile (ATGW) system.

The second category are the vehicle-mounted infantry anti-armour systems, the 30-mm Rarden Cannon mounted on the new Warrior APC or the Scimitar recce vehicle, and Milan mounted in the Milan Compact Turret (MCT) fitted to the Spartan APC.

In the third category are Royal Armoured Corps (RAC) anti-armour systems: these are the Swingfire ATGW mounted on Striker, the Rarden cannon mounted on Scimitar, the 76-mm gun mounted on Scorpion and, most important, the 120-mm main armament of Chieftain or Challenger – the most potent tank killer of all.

The fourth category consists of anti-tank mines laid by the Engineers: these are mostly designed to make a tank immobile, usually by blowing a track off.

The fifth category, and one that is showing enormous potential, is the anti-tank helicopter: in the British Army this is the versatile TOW/Lynx system, which is capable of firing eight TOW missiles out to 3,750 metres without reloading.

Big guns

The sixth category is artillery: large-calibre guns (155 mm and upwards) can be most effective against a massed

FIGHTING THE ANTI-ARMOUR BATTLE

Tanks combine firepower, mobility and armoured protection to produce what is known as 'shock action'. The quality and quantity of Warsaw Pact armour, combined with their massive indirect firepower capability, forms a serious threat, and with this in mind all defence on the NATO central front is designed around the anti-armour plan.

Chieftain
In positional defence, it is normal to fight in mixed teams of tanks and infantry with dedicated artillery support, as well as some signals and engineers. If you have tanks with you, then make sure the anti-tank plan is co-ordinated to include them. Each tank will have a number of fire positions pre-prepared, the idea being to fire two or three shots and move; this will give the tank a better chance of survival.

Small-arms fire
7.62-mm rifle and GPMG fire will force tanks to close down, making target acquisition more difficult. 0.50 calibre rounds will damage the BTR-60 and similar vehicles.

Weapons siting
In anti-tank warfare your siting of weapons is all-important to minimise your vulnerability to the enemy's direct and indirect fire.

Milan
Quick to deploy and devastating in positional defence, Milan would normally be fully dug in. The long flight time of the missile means you must be able to see the target for a full 12.5 seconds at maximum range, and the missile can be decoyed by other infra-red sources on the battlefield, like burning tank hulks. Milan must be deployed with short-range anti-tank protection (84-mm) and with infantry in a position to defend it.

Above: The 84-mm Carl Gustav anti-tank weapon is recoilless, operated by two men and fires an 84-mm HEAT round. It has a considerable backblast signature and there is some doubt whether it can defeat Soviet main battle tank frontal armour.

Right: The Milan system replaces the ageing 120-mm Wombat; it will defeat all known Soviet armour out to a range of 1950 metres. Again, it has a vicious backblast firing signature which affects survivability of the system.

Striker is a Spartan-armoured personnel carrier fitted with the Swingfire guided missile system. It will defeat any known armour combination from 150 to 4000 metres and is immune to electronic countermeasures.

tank attack. A concentrated artillery bombardment can ruin optics, destroy radio antennas, dislodge and set fire to external fuel tanks and disorient and disconcert tank crews. Multi-barrelled rocket systems such as MLRS can fire rockets that scatter bomblets designed to penetrate the weaker top armour of tanks. Ground attack aircraft such as the Harrier and A-10 are most effective tank destroyers: they are capable of either rocket or bomb attack against tank targets.

You will see from this brief gallop through the systems available to you, or in direct support of your battalion, that there is a vast array of weapon systems capable of defeating a tank attack. It is precisely because there are so many systems that they must be carefully coordinated in order to avoid duplication and waste.

Hands-on

Closest to you will be the hand-held weapons. They are designed for use under 1950 metres. Milan reaches out to this range, and the 84-mm MAW and 66-mm LAW reach to 600 and 350 metres respectively. Each system is designed to be used progressively as the enemy gets closer.

Milan is fitted with a Thermal Imaging system, so that you can use it 24 hours a day and in bad weather. Milan and the 84 mm/66 mm systems are complementary. You can use them to fill in gaps in the Milan defence, or you can use them to provide close anti-tank protection for isolated Milan crews or at distances below Milan's minimum range.

Weapons on wheels

In a mechanised battalion you will have your vehicles near you in your defensive position. Site them so that you can use their weapon systems to best advantage. Use the 30-mm Rarden cannon on Warrior and Scimitar to engage enemy APCs and other lightly armoured vehicles, and concentrate the firepower of tanks and long-range ATGWs on enemy tanks. Rarden is effective out to about 1500 metres. You may also have some Spartan vehicles fitted with the MCR in your vicinity. This system has exactly the same capability as ground-fired Milan but provides a measure of protection for the crew.

Tank support

When you operate in a mechanised battlegroup you will be supported by tanks. The tank is the most effective tank-killer of all. It can fire its armour-piercing discarding sabot (APDS) round out to 2000 metres with great

BRITISH ARMY INFANTRY ANTI-TANK WEAPONS RANGES

This is the coverage of weapons you will use in an infantry battalion. The 66-mm LAW and 84-mm MAW are needed to cover the area between the firing line and Milan's minimum engagement.

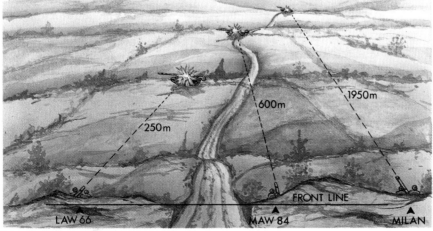

1. LAW can shoot out to 250 m.
2. MAW sight range is 600 m, but effective range is 500 m for static and 400 m for moving targets.
3. Milan can shoot out to 1950 m. Missile flight time is 12.5 seconds; you must be able to track the target for the whole time.

Above: The 66-mm LAW (Light Anti-tank Weapon) is a one-shot, recoilless, throwaway weapon, not particularly accurate and not capable of defeating modern MBT armour, though it has its uses for APCs and bunkers.

Below: Indirect artillery fire will not generally knock out Main Battle Tanks; however, it will cause them to 'close down', restricting their field of view, and fragments will smash optics and radio aerials and damage tracks and running gear.

Above: A light tank like the Scimitar is not designed to fight but to recce; the 30-mm Rarden cannon could damage a T-72 but certainly not knock it out. However, it would be very useful on BMPs and other APCs and thin-skinned vehicles.

accuracy, and at a rate of up to eight rounds a minute.

However, tanks are best used to achieve surprise. You will find that the Royal Armoured Corps no longer use tanks as static gun platforms. That would be a waste of their mobility. Keep them in reserve, ready to cut off and destroy any enemy tank penetration. You are equipped with Milan and perfectly capable of defending your position against tank attack without wasting your own tanks in static defence.

Armoured Reconnaissance Regiments are equipped with the Scorpion recce vehicle and with Striker. The highly accurate Swingfire ATGW is mounted on Striker and gives the Armoured Reconnaissance Regiment the ability to engage tanks out to a range of 4000 metres. This allows reconnaissance troops to cause early attrition.

Mines and choppers

The next component of your anti-tank plan is the minefield. This is a subject in itself; at this stage all you need to know is that the anti-tank mine plays an important part in the overall plan to defeat an enemy armoured attack.

There are several categories of anti-tank mine: the most common are the conventional cylindrical pressure mine (such as the British Mk 7), the bar mine, the off-route mine (designed to attack the side of a tank) and the scatterable mine which can be fired from a gun or launched from a system

mounted on an APC. Well-planned minefields covered by fire from your defensive positions can cause havoc among an enemy armoured formation.

Anti-tank helicopters are also a subject in themselves. TOW missiles fired from Lynx have a range out to 3750 metres. They are likely to engage massed enemy tank attacks of over 60 armoured vehicles well out to the front of you. Your role will be to mop up what is left.

A fighting chance

Add to this array of weapon systems the anti-tank capabilities of both artillery and offensive air support, and you will see that you stand a very good chance of blunting, stopping and destroying even the most concerted armoured threat. The tank is still a potent weapon system but it is no longer queen of the battlefield: the armoured helicopter is emerging as a contender for that title.

US ARMY INFANTRY ANTI-TANK WEAPONS RANGES

This shows the corresponding coverage for the US Army. TOW gives an extra kilometre over Milan, but there are not that many positions that will allow a clear shoot out to that range. Dragon again has better maximum range than MAW, but cannot be fired as rapidly.

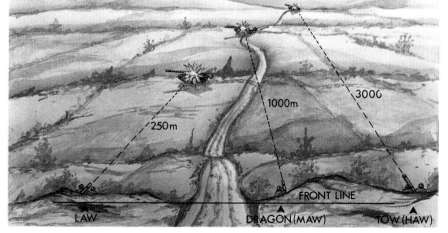

1. LAW: a more realistic range for engaging a tank would be 150 m or less, and volley fire is recommended.
2. Dragon can shoot out to 1000 m, and has a minimum range of 65 m. This gap is covered by LAW.
3. TOW can shoot out to 3000 m and must be carefully sighted to take advantage of this.

TANK HUNTING

Snarling, heavily-armoured, and bristling with devastating armament, the main battle tank can seem unstoppable to the infantryman — but there are occasions when determined and properly armed foot-soldiers can wreak havoc among even a sizeable detachment of enemy armour.

You'll usually carry out such operations at night, as part of a fighting patrol whose mission is to destroy enemy tanks at close range.

Known as tank hunting, this is a task for the ordinary infantryman, as distinct from the expert and highly specialised techniques of anti-tank warfare.

Here, we describe the weapons and techniques of tank hunting and tell you the vulnerable parts of an armoured vehicle that you should aim to hit.

Know the weak spots

The first thing you need to remember is that a tank is not by any means a flexible weapon. Closed down for combat, a tank crew has very limited vision. Close to, a tank is surrounded by blind spots.

TANK VULNERABILITY

1. Tanks have restricted vision when all their hatches are closed.
2. Soviet tanks in particular cannot depress their main armament very far, and are especially vulnerable when crossing a ridge.
3. The sides, rear and belly of a tank have much thinner armour than the front, which is usually proof against infantry anti-tank weapons.
4. Tanks are particularly vulnerable when re-fuelling and re-arming: they are stationary and bunched up.
5. Despite developments in thermal imagers, it is still difficult for a tank crew to spot infantry at night, especially if they use correct camouflage and concealment.
5. Tanks without infantry support are particularly vulnerable to infantry anti-tank weapons, especially in woods or built-up areas.

A Soviet BMP Infantry Fighting Vehicle leads a mixed column of tanks and infantry. Successful tank hunting demands a thorough knowledge of the strengths and weaknesses of enemy armoured vehicles.

The tank's armament is virtually useless against a moving, close-range target, for the simple reason that it can't lower its gun sufficiently to engage a nearby target. As a result, a tank is at its most vulnerable when crossing a ridge — doubly so, in fact, because its tracks and lightly-armoured belly, rear and sides are also exposed then.

Tanks have to refuel and rearm, usually at night. They'll do this either in a 'leaguer' (an administrative compound) or with a 'running replenishment' in the field. In either case enemy tanks will be bunched together, with little room to manoeuvre, and probably surrounded by cover that may screen them but also offers a perfect hiding-place for

infantry. If you can find the enemy's tanks at such a time, they make excellent targets.

Attack by patrol

Imagine that you have been given the task of mounting a tank-hunting patrol. Your mission is to destroy as many tanks as possible as they undergo running replenishment in a

Taking aim with a Carl Gustav 84-mm recoilless rifle: this bulky but accurate weapon will penetrate the side and rear armour of modern Soviet tanks as long as they do not carry reactive armour panels.

village street just behind enemy lines. You know that the enemy has been using that location for two nights and that his tanks will be there again tonight. Recce patrols have already found a route for you between two forward enemy companies. You're to take a 12-man patrol.

As with any patrol, your first job is to make sure you know as much as possible about the killing ground and your route to it. Use maps, aerial photographs, and if possible survey the ground itself from an observation post.

Next, learn everything you can about the type of tank you are going to attack: where its most vulnerable points are, its hatches, radio antennae, and sights. And make yourself familiar with enemy operating procedures.

Finally, rehearse your action on the objective and make sure that you and everyone going with you knows exactly what they have to do.

The weapons to take

Since your best chance of success lies in reaching your objective, making a quick attack and then withdrawing behind your own lines as fast and as unobtrusively as possible, you would ideally use timed charges. However, they are likely to be reserved for Special Forces.

A reasonable armoury of immediate-effect weapons for your 12-man patrol would include two 84-mm medium anti-tank weapons (MAWs), two 66-mm light anti-tank weapons

TANK HUNTING

Tank hunting is carried out by a fighting patrol which can vary in size from a section to several companies. The fighting patrol must have sufficient strength to carry out the mission and defend itself on route out and route back. The basic aim is to attack enemy tanks when they are harboured up, in a defensive position or in a tank leaguer.

Control, concealment and protection
As soon as you start firing your anti-tank weapons your position will be revealed to the enemy, so make sure you deploy these weapons at reasonable intervals, not all together.

Co-ordinate your fire
Make sure you can cover targets with both small-arms and anti-tank fire. A good co-ordinated fire plan will isolate individual tanks from their infantry support, restrict tank crews vision by forcing them to close down, and cut off the unit you are attacking from enemy reinforcements.

Withdrawal route
Make sure you have secure withdrawal ro and leave a protectic back at the final RV. Everyone must knov signal for 'Break Cor and what he must de Withdrawal must be staggered, so that th enemy will not be ke follow you up. Leapf back by half sections the enemy is always fire while you withd

Surprise
Your chances of success depend on catching the enemy unawares: your presence should be announced by a sudden hail of anti-tank and small arms fire. Your patrolling skills and fieldcraft will have to be excellent.

Information

Tank hunting relies on good intelligence information received in time to allow for careful planning and detailed preparation. Every eventuality must be covered.

Other weapons

Don't forget white phosphorus grenades: these are particularly effective against dismounted tank crew and add to the confusion. These grenades are also useful to cover your withdrawal, since they produce instant smoke and discourage the enemy from putting his head up.

Mines

Don't just use the 66-mm and 84-mm anti-tank weapons; plant anti-tank mines on likely enemy routes and approaches. Always mix some anti-personnel mines with the anti-tank mines to discourage the enemy engineers from digging them up.

ZSU 23-4

Remember, these self-propelled anti-aircraft guns can be used against ground targets with devastating effect. Get rid of them first! Even small-arms fire will wreck their optics and radar control system.

The 84-mm is a sizeable beast, but it needs to be in order to fire a large enough round to threaten a Main Battle Tank. In recent years tanks have received new types of armour designed to defeat infantry anti-tank weapons.

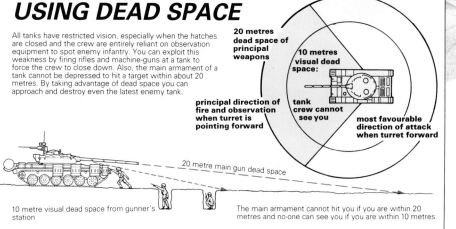

Timed charges and Molotov cocktails

Make sure these have been properly prepared before the patrol. Satchel charges should be double-fused to ensure that they detonate.

Know your enemy

You must be completely familiar with enemy AFVs and their tactics. You have to know what you are firing at.

(LAWs), both firing specialised high-explosive anti-tank (HEAT) missiles. The LAW is effective up to 200 metres, the MAW out to twice that distance. Both will penetrate the sides and rear of any Soviet main battle tank.

In addition you'll be carrying phosphorus grenades, anti-tank mines and personal weapons.

You can attach image intensification (II) equipment or an individual weapon sight (IWS) to the MAW. This will give you an impressive picture of any nocturnal enemy activity at up to 150 yards' range even on the darkest night. Without an IWS, you will need white light – flares – to score a kill at anything but point-blank range.

USING DEAD SPACE

All tanks have restricted vision, especially when the hatches are closed and the crew are entirely reliant on observation equipment to spot enemy infantry. You can exploit this weakness by firing rifles and machine-guns at a tank to force the crew to close down. Also, the main armament of a tank cannot be depressed to hit a target within about 20 metres. By taking advantage of dead space you can approach and destroy even the latest enemy tank.

20 metres dead space of principal weapons

10 metres visual dead space:

tank crew cannot see you

principal direction of fire and observation when turret is pointing forward

most favourable direction of attack when turret forward

20 metre main gun dead space

10 metre visual dead space from gunner's station

The main armament cannot hit you if you are within 20 metres and no-one can see you if you are within 10 metres.

ARMOUR THICKNESS

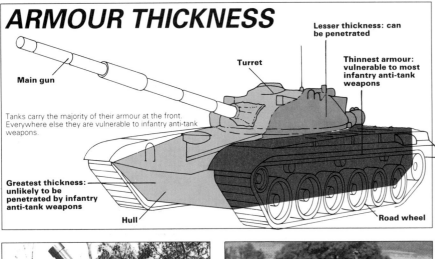

Main gun

Tanks carry the majority of their armour at the front. Everywhere else they are vulnerable to infantry anti-tank weapons.

Turret

Lesser thickness: can be penetrated

Thinnest armour: vulnerable to most infantry anti-tank weapons

Greatest thickness: unlikely to be penetrated by infantry anti-tank weapons

Hull

Road wheel

LAW should have entered service with the British Army in 1987, and will substantially improve the infantry's anti-tank capability. It is a one-shot, throwaway weapon like the 66-mm, but with a much more effective warhead.

You cock the 66-mm by pulling the top handle forward. There is a cartoon 'idiot's guide' printed on the side, but it is not recommended that you read through this in sight of a hostile tank!

Into the attack

You should open fire with both MAWs and LAWs simultaneously. This creates the maximum immediate damage to the target and creates an invaluable psychological advantage.

Imagine the effect on the enemy: he thinks he is in a safe administrative area, behind his own lines, peaceably servicing his tanks. Then, several HEAT missiles slam into the vehicles.

Flames and panic break out everywhere. The tanks are waiting in column to be refuelled. Some reverse, others accelerate, some swerve to avoid other crippled and burning vehicles. At this point you should drop anti-tank mines at each end of the column, causing further damage and chaos. Meanwhile, rake any visible enemy personnel with automatic fire.

About now some enemy crews will decide to abandon their ruined vehicles. At this stage, throw as many phosphorus grenades as you can into the midst of the tanks. This will disrupt any night vision equipment the enemy is trying to bring to bear on your position, and injure dismounting

AIMING POINTS AGAINST WARSAW PACT AFVs

These diagrams show the points of maximum vulnerability on the major types of Armoured Fighting Vehicles used by the Soviet Union and its allies. The tanks have internal fuel tanks and ammunition on the right-hand side, level with the driver.

Key:

✚ **Point of maximum vulnerability**

▨ **Engine compartment**

BMD Airportable APC

ZSU 23-4 self-propelled anti-aircraft gun

BMP Mechanized Infantry Combat Vehicle

BTR-50 Armoured Personnel Carrier

BRDM-1 Armoured Car

BTR-60 Armoured Personnel Carrier

BRDM-2 Armoured Car

In the prone position an 84-mm team is very difficult to spot from a closed-down tank. A reverse slope is a doubly good position, because the tank presents its vulnerable belly.

enemy troops. Having done your job, withdraw as discreetly as you can.

The ambush option

You can bring off an attack as successful as that only against an extremely inefficient enemy. But that is the ideal to aim for. In practice, most of your tank hunting will more nearly resemble an ambush.

If, for instance, you were withdrawing under the pressure of an enemy attack, one way of blunting his advance would be to set up tank ambushes and hit the enemy as he advanced. You'll be able to mount these attacks most easily in close country or in built-up areas. If you can mount a series of ambushes, so much the better.

Choose your ambush site carefully. From it you should be able to get as close as between 100 and 200 yards to the enemy. Spring your ambush, withdraw along a pre-planned route,

reorganise and repeat the process.

Any decently-trained tank crew will, if they can, avoid areas where they're vulnerable to ambush. And if they're forced to advance through close or built-up areas, they'll call on infantry to clear the woods or buildings first. However, in reality, tanks often outrun their infantry support – if

they can get it at all. You will usually find rich pickings in a tank-hunting party working from a well-chosen ambush site.

Where to aim

The largest 'soft' area of a tank you're likely to see is its side. So wait until your target tank turns away from you before opening fire.

Tank tracks are particularly vulnerable. If you can blow off a track, the tank is as good as dead. It's immediately exposed as an easy kill for longer-range anti-tank missiles, and is costly for the enemy to recover.

The turret or the glacis plate at the front of the tank is where a tank's armour is hardest. Don't fire at the front of a tank, therefore, even if it's coming straight at you. Just take cover.

An infantryman hidden behind a building, an earth bank or in his trench is surprisingly safe from a tank. If one motors over your trench, just keep your head down. Then pop up behind it and send a LAW or MAW up its rear end.

Revenge is sweet

Tank hunting is a useful way for the infantryman to get back at the tank. It's not a practical way to destroy enemy armour in large numbers: this is a job for other tanks, long-range anti-tank missiles and anti-tank guided missiles (ATGW) on the open battle-field.

But tank-hunting saps the enemy's morale and raises that of the foot-soldier no end – as well as reducing the threat to you from enemy armour. Tank hunting is the infantry's special contribution to the anti-tank battle.

When it's successful, tank hunting is truly an example of David slaying Goliath.

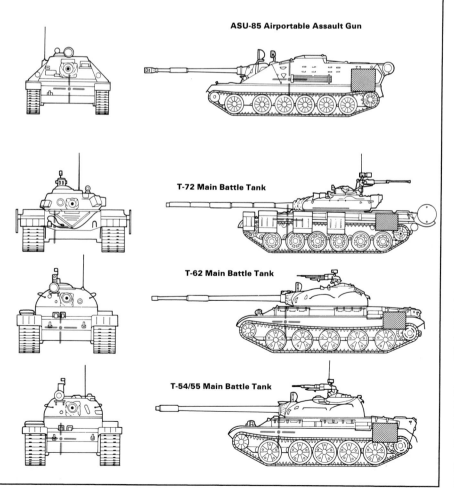

ASU-85 Airportable Assault Gun

T-72 Main Battle Tank

T-62 Main Battle Tank

T-54/55 Main Battle Tank

CHAPTER THREE

INTERNAL SECURITY

The more the military planners know about the enemy the better prepared they are to make constructive and successful moves against him. Much of the very necessary detailed information will come from the activities of the Intelligence Corps, whose covert operations, their means of gathering information about troop movements, numbers, defences, weapons, radio wavelengths, and so on, and the ultra-sophisticated devices they have at their command, are not things which can be discussed here and so must remain secret. Even before hostilities break out it is extremely important that as much fine detail as possible be obtained about any prospective enemy, the weaponry at his disposal, his numerical strength and, hopefully, his plans of campaign.

At the same time there is the need for careful counter-intelligence work to be directed at the enemy's agents who will be doing their best to build up an overall picture of the home side's military strength.

This chapter is concerned with obtaining the kind of information that can be gained about the enemy by observation posts (OPs). First we show how the two kinds of OP are constructed, the covert one and the open one, visible to the enemy but well-guarded and with strong defences. The construction of an OP is not a simple matter, for the enemy should not be aware of it until it is occupied. Its troops must have good contact with HQ, be able to occupy it and retire safely should the enemy make a strong offensive.

The second article describes the duties of a soldier doing his 'stag' in an OP. It will soon be very obvious that only a highly trained and resourceful fighting man can cope with the sophisticated equipment at his disposal and use it to the best advantage in spite of the proximity of enemy units. OPs keep a low profile but at the same time are aware of all movements of people and vehicles, noting index numbers, recording patterns of activity.

Through television, radio and the daily newspapers everybody is aware of the troubles in the Middle East. Prominent in those stories and reports are incidents at road blocks and we have all seen vehicles being waved down and their occupants questioned. But the strongest road block is not effective against terrorists on foot, who can move about over rough ground and where cars and other vehicles cannot go. The value of a road block is that it has the effect of making difficult the transportation of quantities of weapons, explosives and bombs.

There are other advantages too. A road block dominates the immediate area and also provides a show of strength to comfort – or dismay – the local population. At the same time, if there is a disturbance on the 'home side' an effective road block prevents large numbers of terrorists coming to their aid.

With a reliable, up-to-date and accurate list of wanted vehicles and people the soldiers controlling a well-placed road block will be able to spot any likely source of interest before it has the chance to turn off. Then comes the search and questioning, both activities requiring a lot of experience and skill and a constant radio link with back-up forces so that assistance can be called upon in emergency. The subject is covered in the fourth article in this chapter.

Internal security can be a difficult and dangerous business. But today's soldier is not just trained for traditional warfare, the places where troops find themselves today are not always set battlefields.

OBSERVING THE ENEMY

In battle it's vital that you know as much as possible about the strength, movement, positions and intentions of the enemy. Modern warfare is highly mobile and technologically sophisticated, but commanders still acquire some of their best information from static observation posts (OPs) in carefully chosen sites, concealed from the enemy and manned by a few sharp-eyed infantrymen.

This feature gives you information on how to set up an OP, how to survive in its cramped conditions, and what to look out for when on watch.

In conventional warfare mobile OPs are provided either by the Scorpions and Scimitars of reconnaissance regiments and static OPs by infantry patrols. In counter-insurgency or internal security (IS) situations covert OPs are provided almost exclusively by the infantry.

1 Choosing the site

Obviously your OP must provide a good view over the ground that you want to watch. Therefore it should have as wide a field of view and as little dead ground as possible. This is as much for security as for observation – a small infantry OP does not want to be surprised by a larger enemy patrol. It should have a covered and safe approach and exit, and it should provide good cover from view and from fire. In order to achieve the latter, you will probably have to dig in, which should in any case help conceal you. The position should not, however, be an obvious choice for an OP site. The enemy is not a fool.

An OP party is not normally strong enough to take offensive action itself. However, in a conventional war situation it can bring down artillery or mortar fire, and in an IS situation it can direct a quick reaction force to the scene of the incident. Last, an OP site must permit excellent radio communications. It is no good an OP spotting some crucial enemy activity and being able to do nothing about it.

Selecting an OP site

1. **You must be able to see all the ground given in your orders.**
2. **Your field of view should be as wide as possible and include little dead ground.**
3. **You must have a covered approach and exit.**
4. **Your position must offer cover from fire and view.**
5. **Check that you can contact your HQ by radio from the OP site.**
6. **Select some alternative positions in case you encounter unforeseen problems with your first choice of site.**

2 Occupying the OP

Once you have chosen your site (you may have to do this from a map or from air photographs), you will have to set about occupying it. First, the ground must be cleared to make sure there are no enemy in the vicinity and to make sure there are no booby traps around. Next, you must ensure that your communications are not affected by the location. You can only do this by calling your HQ from the OP itself. You may then need to dig trenches, which could take up to 24 hours, depending on the ground. It may not

This Observation Post in South Armagh overlooks the border with the Irish Republic. This is a permanent OP, and is 'overt', i.e. not intended to be hidden, and is heavily fortified.

be possible to move, let alone dig, during daylight hours so you could take two nights to complete your position.

Finally, you must prepare range cards. Look at your map and relate certain prominent objects to your own position in terms of range. This will prove an easy way of determining the range of another location quickly, by using the nearest reference point.

Post routine

The most obvious factor that will affect the routine in the OP is the number of men you are able to take. While it is seldom necessary to have more than two men actually on duty in the OP at any one time, there is a limit to the length of time that a man can closely and continuously observe the same piece of ground. Most people's concentration fades after about 30 minutes. If you put two men on duty for two hours, they should alternate every 15 minutes.

To make life even more complicated everyone in the OP must be ready to move instantly. If there is a real danger of a very small OP party being discovered by a much larger group of enemy, discretion may be the better part of valour and a rapid withdrawal is advisable.

OP work, although it can pay enormous dividends, is usually boring. The only way you can guarantee that the job is done properly is to follow certain procedures. The man who is not observing should act as a sentry and observe the area around the OP. This can also be done by those in an administrative area if your OP is large enough to have one.

You must keep in touch by radio with your HQ, and you should do this at pre-arranged times – if only to

Individual Weapon Sight (IWS)
This is a first-generation image intensifier which amplifies the amount of light available. Because it simply makes better use of the available light it does not work well on a moonless night or in smoky conditions.

IWS sight picture
This is the sort of image you get from the IWS. It is very tiring on the eyes to peer through it, and ideally you should observe for no longer than 30 minutes before handing over to someone else in the OP. Here an arms cache is being unloaded at a deserted farmhouse. The magnification provided by IWS allows you to identify what sort of weapons the enemy are carrying.

Ready to move
All kit should be ready to move at a moment's notice in case a quick bug-out is called for.

Close recce
When it's very dark or there is a heavy morning mist or fog, you might have to carry out a close target recce. Choose a close recce position which you can cover by fire from the OP itself.

Covert Observation Post

Selection of the site for your observation post is absolutely critical. In wartime, the only aids available to you are a map and air photograph, but in counter-revolutionary warfare you may be able to visit and recce possible sites. However, do not rely on this: good appreciation of ground and being able to look at a map and 'see' the ground in your mind's eye is vital. You need to place your OP as far away from the target as is allowed by the nature of the target and your surveillance devices. On some occasions you may be over a kilometre away, while on others you may be right on the enemy's doorstep.

Sketch map
You need a detailed sketch map of the area and an OP log kept of all significant events.

Surveillance devices
As well as binoculars and image intensifiers, thermal imaging, ground radar, intruder systems and seismic sensors are employed on OPs.

M79 grenade launcher
This single-shot, break-action 40-mm grenade launcher is accurate enough to get a grenade through a window at 150 metres. It can give you a valuable edge.

report that nothing has happened. In this way HQ will know your position has not been compromised and that you are safe. Obviously you should send back important information as soon as you can.

What to look for

You should split the area that you are observing into foreground, middle distance and background. In that way you can scan each part methodically and carefully with binoculars from one side to another. Rest your eyes at frequent intervals.

While you are searching the ground, you should look very carefully for anything that does not fit easily with its surroundings. Don't look for a tank, or a trench system. Look instead for an indication that might let you pinpoint a tank or a trench system. In other words, look for mistakes in enemy camouflage.

Look for foliage that is out of place or foliage which is withering for no particular reason. Look for track marks or areas of ground that have been disturbed. Be suspicious if birds or animals are disturbed. Look for something glinting in the sun, look for a vehicle exhaust or a camp fire. You

Changing stag (sentry duty) on a permanent OP on the Irish border. The OP commander briefs the man relieving him on his arcs of observation and responsibility.

Minimum strength
Four people is the minimum required for an OP; this sort of work is probably the most demanding infantry skill. It is physically cramped and exhausting, but you must remain alert all the time you are on duty. If your attention wanders for even a moment you may miss something vital and all your effort will have been for nothing.

Light machine-gun
Automatic weapons are not essential on an OP, but they are a source of comfort. The LMG is more accurate and lighter than the GPMG and ideal for this sort of job.

Summer Time factor
Be aware that short summer nights combined with a long patrol route in will not leave you long to build your OP. It may be necessary to construct your OP over two nights, camouflaging your work in the meantime.

Shotgun
There is nothing like a 12-gauge pump-action shotgun for point-blank range firepower.

Weapons
Weapons should be cocked and ready to hand at all times. Never clean more than one at once. A four-man OP is not intended to fight; it relies for defence on not being seen. You'll need a weapons mix to cover short and long range options.

Stags
Usually two people will be on duty at once: the observer and the sentry. The observer scans the target and notes down any activity while the sentry covers all approaches to the OP in case the position is compromised. The two men swap over functions when using surveillance devices, which are tiring on the eyes.

SITING YOUR OP

1 An OP is essentially a type of patrol: here the four-man OP team, in diamond formation for crossing open ground at night, moves towards an OP site selected from maps, photos, and previous patrol reports.

4 The patrol commander uses the linked legs to pass information. He sends the message on the left and receives it on the right, thus knowing that each member of the patrol has understood.

7 As soon as the recce team moves off, the two men left at the FRV move round to cover 180° each. They recognise the patrol commander by pre-arranged signal when he returns from the OP site. Remember that this is all happening at night, in enemy territory.

2 The patrol commander, having used his IWS to select a good FRV position, passes the message to the rest of the patrol.

5 The OP recce: the OP commander and his radio operator move forward stealthily as a two-man team, covering each other. If compromised at this stage you have to use an alternative site.

8 Another listening stop follows in the FRV before the whole team move out to occupy the OP position.

3 The patrol occupies the FRV (Final Rendez Vous). This should be some distance from the actual OP position and should be easily recognisable at night. Note that in the FRV the patrol covers 360° and has a listening stop to make sure they are not followed.

6 Next you recce the exact spot where you will site the OP. The patrol commander checks that he can actually see the target and that the OP has good all-round observation. The radio operator checks he is 'in comms' with HQ.

9 The OP position: all four members take up their allotted places, cover their arcs and listen for the enemy. When the OP commander is satisfied that the enemy has not seen them move in, he gives the signal for 'packs off' and the team moves into the set-up phase.

---

should search dark areas with particular care. Above all, you should look for movement. It is movement more than anything else that will draw your attention towards an enemy vehicle, patrol or position.

In counter-insurgency operations you must have done your homework regarding terrorist recognition. There will be a 'rogue's gallery' that you will have studied in great depth so that you can instantly recognise a wanted man. You may also have to memorise car registration numbers. In a conventional operation you must be able to

identify enemy armoured fighting vehicles (AFVs). The type of vehicle will often identify the type of enemy formation you are facing. This sort of information is invaluable for your HQ to build up an accurate intelligence picture. In the confusion of battle you must be sure that you do not wrongly identify and engage one of your own AFVs.

Urban OPs

On internal security operations, you may need to set up your OP in an urban environment. Derelict or unoc-

cupied houses or the roofs of apartment blocks can all be used. If you want to use a window for observation, net curtains are useful, but you must stand back from the window. If you are in an attic it is possible to move a tile a few inches so that you can look through. Unless you are situated on a high building most urban OPs will only provide a view down one or two streets but that is probably all that is necessary as it is usually a house or street that you wish to watch. Clearly the injection and extraction of this sort of OP will be much more difficult.

THE SET-UP PHASE

*While the **OP** is being constructed, a sentry is placed on a flank at the limit of noise or vision, whichever is the further. He looks and listens for the enemy, who are hopefully blissfully unaware of the team's presence. Depending on the situation you may need to dig in, either to protect yourself from fire or to conceal yourself if your **OP** site is on open ground.*

1 Armed with a Light Support Weapon, the sentry covers the OP team as they work. In a dug-in OP the work phase could be as long as six or seven hours, in which case sentry duty must be rotated.

2 The OP commander and observer first put up a black hessian screen to work behind. This is secured to the cover with bungees. Remember this is at night, so you must practise beforehand.

3 Meanwhile, the third man pulls the poncho and cam net out of his Bergen. The cam net has already been cut to size and is attached to the poncho. Remember to observe even while you are working, and do not sit or stand up above the level of the black screen.

4 Next you put up the overhead cover, which keeps the rain off and camouflages the position. It must be camouflaged from the air as well as the ground.

5 The poncho is now in place. You must attach the bungees before you start as you'll never find them at night otherwise. Commercially purchased DPM ponchos are best because they are bigger. Do not cut off any branches or disturb the undergrowth.

6 The OP seen from the front without camouflage. At night it is movement which attracts the eye; you will only move behind your black screen.

7 The rear of the OP, fully camouflaged. The cam net which is attached to the poncho should be large enough to fold down over all sides. The overall effect can be improved by the use of local camouflage, but don't cut it from right by the OP position. As it wilts it must be replaced.

8 The front of the OP. Ideally if your position is correctly camouflaged, the only way the enemy should be able to find it is to tread on it.

9 When observing, the observer pushes his head or his surveillance device underneath the black screen. Use of active surveillance devices must be kept to a minimum since they can easily be detected.

PREPARED FOR A LONG VIGIL

Before you move out on the patrol that will put you into position in your OP, you must check your equipment and weapons. Re-supply could compromise your position – a helicopter carrying spare batteries or even a patrol carrying ammunition or stores will attract attention if they are moving in a sensitive area.

Folding digging tools are essential to prepare the position, and a wire saw and secateurs will allow you to cut vegetation to clear viewing points through cover or to garnish the position. An axe or parang is less suitable, since chopping is a noisy business.

A small camouflage net to hang in the observation port, or light chicken wire to attach camouflage garnish are also useful: remember, the hole you look through at the enemy will look like a black hole in green vegetation unless you camouflage it.

Stags of duty

Once you are in position you will need to work out the stags of duty. Two men on and two men off, staggered so that one man is fresh on as the other is half way through his stag, helps ensure that no-one falls asleep or loses concentration. Basic equipment that you need includes the prismatic compass for bearings on contacts and binoculars for detailed

On stag, in an overt OP, training for Counter Revolutionary Warfare (CRW). As a rule, two people will be on duty at any one time. A high degree of concentration is required to remain alert for long periods: OP duty is the most demanding of all infantry skills.

Internal security OP in Ulster is shown here during the early days of the current troubles. Overt OPs are a constant terrorist target: note the wire mesh screen protecting against mortar, grenade and rocket attack, and the filled oildrums designed to prevent car bombs being driven into the position.

An urban OP like this must be adequately defended, and mutually supported by other posts. Note the sandbagging and the GPMG. The hessian screen allows movement and observation without giving a sniper a clear target. Overt OPs limit terrorist activity by their presence.

observation. A radio with either burst transmission facilities, like the Racal Merod system, or frequency agility, which hops through a range of frequencies, will prevent the enemy getting a fix on your OP when you transmit information.

Frequency-hopping

The advantage of frequency agility is that you can transmit as events are happening and so correct artillery fire. If you use burst transmission you will have to format the message on the display and then send it. When you are using SOP (Standard Operating Procedure) formatted messages, burst transmission is the ideal system.

Types of OP
In conventional war, the work is divided between the infantry, who would set up this sort of OP, and armoured reconnaissance regiments of the Royal Armoured Corps, whose Scorpions and Scimitars would provide mobile OPs.

Construction
This type of OP may take several days to construct and uses large quantities of sandbags, angle-iron pickets, wire and wriggly tin (corrugated iron). You may be able to find old doors, or lengths of felled timber (common in German woods) to help with the job. Excavated soil must be disposed of thoughtfully, either spread on tracks or dumped in streams or manpacked some distance away.

The observer
His job is to observe his arc and report any enemy activity. In Germany, OPs would be used to discover the direction of the main thrust of the Soviet Operational Manoeuvre Group seeking to penetrate NATO's defences.

NBC protection
In a future war, OP members will almost certainly need to wear NBC suits, so the use of surveillance equipment must be practised in full NBC kit. If the OP is to be maintained for a number of days, spare suits and gloves will have to be manpacked in.

Protection
This four-man OP relies upon concealment for its protection. It is completely dug in, and revetted like a main battle trench, with at least 45cm of overhead cover for protection against shell splinters.

Kipmat
This makes life easier as it provides insulation from the cold ground.

Rest bay
In a four-man OP party, only two sleeping bags are required as two people are always on duty. They should not be zipped when in use to allow for rapid evacuation. Kit not in use must be packed away at all times. It is unlikely that the tactical situation will allow you to cook, and even if you can you must remember that hexamine smells, and also gives off poisonous fumes which can accumulate dangerously in an enclosed space.

Immersion suits
Aircrew immersion suits are very useful in OPs. Alternatively, wear your waterproofs underneath your combat jacket.

Kit layout
Four Bergens never seem to be enough to carry the required kit. Bergen weights of more than 40kg are not uncommon. One of the four packs contains communications equipment; a second carries the food and uncontaminated water. The other two are for surveillance devices, special equipment, spare clothes and sleeping bags. All members of the OP party must be familiar with the contents of all the Bergens in case of emergency or the absence of a patrol member.

Other electronic aids include the simple dictaphone hand-held tape recorder. Instead of writing notes, sometimes in the dark or in bad weather, you can record the events that you are observing. Again remember spare tapes and spare batteries. If you can work with light, make sure that flashlights are as small as possible and have red filters to save your night vision and reduce the danger of enemy observation – again, make sure the batteries are fresh. The Betalight is useful: it has a long life and compact configuration.

Cameras come into their own when you are in a CRW (Counter Revolutionary Warfare) environment.

A COVERT OBSERVATION POST ON THE CENTRAL FRONT

In order to make informed decisions, commanders need the maximum possible battlefield intelligence about the enemy's strengths, movements, positions, habits, dress, and possible intentions. In any future European conflict, a very effective way of getting that intelligence is by the use of observation posts.

Sentry
He shares with the observer the task of using the wide variety of surveillance equipment. He also operates the radio, and is responsible for the protection of the OP. He may also help with the preparation of a detailed sketch map/range card and assist in keeping the OP log.

Radio
Use of radio must be kept to a minimum to forestall enemy eavesdropping and direction-finding.

Wanted men, suspect vehicles and illegal gatherings can be photographed and checked with intelligence records after the OP is completed and debriefed. Cameras are also useful when you are tasked with enemy vehicle identification.

High-tech aids

Though a laser rangefinder is useful, it is an active source and may alert the enemy to your location. Laser beams can be detected by sensors on enemy AFVs. Passive night vision equipment, either long-range tripod mounted systems or simply the IWS from a rifle, will give you good short-range observation. If you are an artillery observer the longer range systems

Clothing
On the patrol into the OP, you will sweat excessively. Wear a T-shirt under your combat gear to prevent suffering from chilling when you stop moving. The same goes for the work phase when you are setting up the OP: as soon as you stop work and occupy the OP, you must put on several layers of warm, dry clothing. Once inside the confined space, physical movement will be kept to a minimum and you will become much colder than normal; hypothermia may be a problem.

ROUTINE IN A SIMPLE O.P.

In a basic OP, there are four positions. The observer and the radio operator/observer maintain the watch, swapping roles every 20 minutes or so to prevent tiredness. The third man sleeps or attends to personal tasks while the fourth, armed with an LSW, acts as rear sentry. The members of the party rotate anti-clockwise through the positions at hourly intervals.

On a given signal, the observer wakes the sleeper and takes the sleeping bag. The sleeper moves onto sentry duty, while the sentry takes over the radio operator/observer's position. The radio operator passes across the headset and moves onto observation. No equipment or weapons are moved in the changeover of personnel.

THE EYES OF THE ARMY
Equipped for OP Duty

1 Gillie suit
Personal camouflage and concealment must be excellent.

2 Thermos flask

3 Poncho

4 Entrenching tool

5 Sleeping bag
Protect it with a Gore-Tex waterproof bivi-bag, because once wet army issue bags are useless.

6 Bergen
This needs to be comfortable and of large capacity.

7 Kipmat

8 Claymore mine
Good for providing close-in protection should your OP be compromised.

9 M79 grenade launcher
If you are attacked the grenade launcher may help you turn the tables and win the fire-fight.

10 M16 (Armalite) assault rifle
A lightweight weapon ideal for OP work.

11 Camera equipment and lenses

12 Passive night vision goggles
For use on the route in as well as on the OP.

13 Scrim net

14 Hand-held thermal imager

This Royal Marine on a rooftop OP is carrying an Individual Weapon Sight fitted to an SLR. Urban covert OPs are a good deal easier to set up as there is no shortage of suitable derelict housing. Be careful with the IWS; it emits a low whine when switched on which can be heard at 15 metres.

are clearly necessary, but passive systems with a range of 150 metres will allow you to stake out a position by night.

At the other end of the technology scale are the basic bodily functions: eating and defecating. Food cannot normally be cooked as smells carry long distances, but insulated containers may allow you to take hot food into the field. There are some chemical-based systems such as the US Zesto-Therm, which consists of a small chemical sachet, and insulated bag or pouch. By putting one in the pouch, adding water and placing in a food sachet, you can have warm food. The only drawback there is a slight chemical smell which may compromise the position or may simply be unpleasant to live with.

Waste disposal

Food and water will have to be carried in, and all waste carried out. Use plastic bin liners for all rubbish: double ones are best, and do not overload them. Remember, you will have to take them out in your Bergens! If you take an anti-diarrhoea tablet when you are in the OP this will induce constipation and get you through the OP patrol, but may be

Electronics have transformed the art of night surveillance. The hand-held thermal imager seen here is in use with a scan converter, allowing the image to be viewed (and recorded) on a TV monitor. Better still, the observer can view the display at any convenient secure location some distance from the imager.

Unlike the IWS, the Thermal Imager (TI) is not obscured by battlefield smoke or fog, and remains effective even on the darkest night.

rather disruptive to your bowels.

Communications in the OP may be by speech, but it may also be necessary to use cards, carrying messages such as 'Your Stag Now'.

Last resort

Hopefully you will not have to fight in your OP; if you do, something's gone very wrong. Weapons need to be compact, but capable of a high rate of fire. The Colt 733 Commando assault rifle, with a 30-round magazine, is ideal. Pistols with a silencer will allow you to kill an enemy who may have blundered into the position.

Area mines like the British PAD mine or the US Claymore will give good overall cover against infantry, but may compromise the position when they are emplaced: like unattended ground sensors (UGS), which have to be pre-positioned in a perimeter around the OP, they may be detected by the enemy. UGS, however will give you advanced warning of enemy movement, whether wheeled, tracked or even men on foot. UGS can even be configured to detect speech, seismic tremors and metallic masses such as AFVs.

Finally, good-quality clothing and a first-aid kit and medically-trained team member are essential. The kit should not only contain morphine and first field dressings and pads, but also plasters for minor cuts that might become septic in the OP, and simple pain killers for headaches and stomach troubles.

Warm clothing

Personal protection will include sleeping bags with a Velcro and zip opening to allow quick exits in the event of an emergency. Quilted clothing and even quilted foot wear may be necessary, since OP work can be cold and there is absolutely no opportunity to move about to improve circulation. Thermal underclothes and thermal boots may also be required, plus gloves as both camouflage and for protection.

Perhaps the most important thing about OP work is being able to get on with your mates. You may have to sleep, eat and defecate in their company, so make friends fast.

A successful OP requires a high standard of camouflage and concealment, effective patrolling techniques, highly efficient administration and preparation, good terrorist or AFV recognition, effective survival techniques – and the patience of Job. If you can master all this you are a professional.

Above and right: British troops at an observation post in Belize may be experiencing a climate very different from that of South Armagh, but the watch on the Guatemalan border requires patience and concentration just as much as in an OP in Ulster's bandit country. Inside the post, the spotting scopes are prominent. Note the large photograph with the OP's arcs of observation and ranges marked on.

ALTERNATIVE OP LAYOUTS

Star formation

Layout depends on the size, location and the nature of the cover in which the OP is located. When digging the OP, be careful not to spill loose earth around the position, and keep the turves used on the overhead cover in good condition: you may even need to water them. The star formation is generally considered the best.

1 Sentry
2 Observation position
3 Rest bay
4 Rest bay (personal admin)
5 Central well holding spare kit

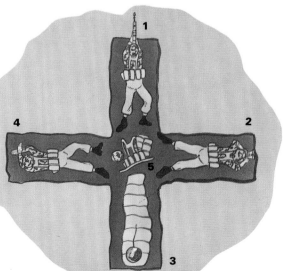

Pairs

The pairs layout is good for putting into linear features such as fencelines and boundaries. Observation ports should be kept small, with a face veil or camouflage net draped over the opening. The observation bay is screened from any light source within the OP by a black hessian screen

1 Rest bay and personal admin
2 Kit well
3 Observer and sentry

Top to tail

This layout is largely intended for use underneath or within bushes. Again, it is good for use along linear features and it is suitable for all-round observation.

1 Sentry
2 Rest bay (personal admin)
3 Rest bay
4 Observer

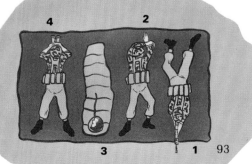

A Beirut roadblock capable of withstanding a lot of punishment.

SETTING UP ROADBLOCKS

Roadblocks are usually mounted in an internal security (IS) or counter-insurgency situation. You can use either snap or permanent roadblocks; the purpose of both is to check traffic going through a particular point or to completely block a road to prevent its further use. The siting of the roadblock is important. Preferably, it should be around a corner or beyond the crest of a hill so as to take the driver by surprise, and should be flanked by hedgerows or ditches so that it is difficult or impossible for a car to turn round.

Terrorists have to use wheeled transport to move weapons, explosives, supplies and other equipment to safe hiding-places, from which they will have to move them again when they intend to use them. The best way to counter this threat is to create a permanent infrastructure of roadblocks, or vehicle checkpoints (VCPs) as they are called in Northern Ireland, upon which you can superimpose as many extra snap or temporary roadblocks or VCPs as the operational situation demands.

Permanent roadblocks

The basic, permanent VCP will impose restrictions on the terrorist. Even though he knows it is there and the surprise element is lacking, it forces him to use other routes, thereby reducing his options; it also reduces the number of routes upon which you need mount snap or temporary VCPs. Snap VCPs can be set up by foot patrols, by vehicle patrols or by patrols dropped from a helicopter. This latter technique is known by the British Army in Northern Ireland as an Eagle Patrol (see Chapter Five).

Freedom fighters or terrorists use similar tacts to the security forces. Here an El Salvadorean guerrilla demonstrates his control of this section of the coastal highway only 50km from the capital. Burning trucks provide an adequate road block.

THE AIMS OF ROADBLOCKS AND VCPs

They should:

1. **Dominate the area, deterring terrorist activity and movement.**
2. **Prevent reinforcements of enemy or terrorists reaching sensitive areas or riotous gatherings.**
3. **Deny contact between terrorists and local inhabitants.**
4. **Prevent supply of arms, ammo, food and medical supplies to the enemy.**
5. **Win public confidence and impress the local inhabitants.**
6. **Facilitate other operations against the enemy or terrorists.**
7. **Gain information and intelligence.**

LAYOUT OF A VCP

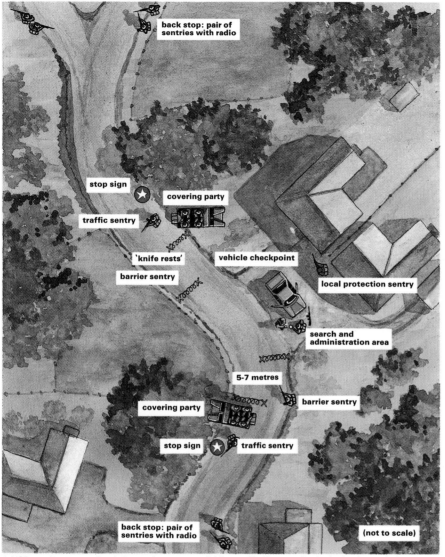

A VCP can be set up simply by putting two parallel lines of knife rests (barbed wire frames) about 50 metres apart on the road; you can do the same with vehicles. The enclosure formed can be used as a search area. The number of troops you'll need for the job depends on how many roads you are covering and how busy they are. If possible, all road blocks should be co-ordinated and manned by civilian police along with the military personnel.

Labels in the illustration:
- back stop: pair of sentries with radio
- stop sign
- covering party
- traffic sentry
- 'knife rests'
- vehicle checkpoint
- barrier sentry
- local protection sentry
- search and administration area
- 5-7 metres
- covering party
- barrier sentry
- stop sign
- traffic sentry
- back stop: pair of sentries with radio
- (not to scale)

Above: A Royal Marine Commando lifts an anti-tank mine laid by Argentine forces on the verge of one of the roads approaching Port Stanley. Permanent roadblocks can remain effective long after the end of the battle.

Permanent roadblocks or VCPs must be well defended, permanently manned and well equipped. The smallest practical unit that can look after itself is a section: this is just big enough to run a shift system 24 hours a day. The position should provide safe accommodation for those not on duty and reliable communications to your HQ. Your perimeter should be well defended with wire to prevent attack or fire, and with concrete bollards to prevent terrorists leaving a car bomb alongside your position.

Surveillance aids such as remotely-controlled CCTV cameras can monitor approaches that you may not be able to see all the time. Your road-block will probably be sited on a busy road or border crossing, and your job will be to check the identity of all those passing through your position and also to search them. Your aim is to limit the movement of both terrorists and their weapons and explosives.

Proper planning

Clearly, if the road is very busy you will not have sufficient men to search all vehicles without causing a major traffic jam. Either you will have to select vehicles at random for checking, or you will need additional police or military manpower. If you intend to bodysearch females you will need female soldiers or policewomen. If your roadblock is to be effective at night, floodlights will be necessary.

A permanent roadblock is vulnerable to attack and therefore it must take on all the characteristics of a military base. It will tend to suck up more and more manpower, and you must use all your ingenuity to use as few men as possible by employing mechanical items such as 'sleeping policemen', chicanes, surveillance devices, secure and strong defences, good communications and so on.

Snap roadblocks

When you mount a snap roadblock you are under fewer constraints: because you will be in position only for a short period, the enemy is unlikely to have the time to organise and mount an attack upon you, unless you compromise him in a roadblock and he tries to evade it or crash through it.

Snap roadblocks can be mounted by section-strength foot or vehicle patrols whenever and wherever the moment is right. The technique is to half-block the road with your vehicle and, if you have two vehicles, to create a chicane effect by blocking alternate sides of the road at an interval of per-

In conventional warfare, roadblocks are designed to slow down or channel an enemy's advance. Mining adds to the effectiveness, as shown by this Israeli soldier prodding gently for mines.

haps 25 metres. This will force traffic to slow down to be checked.

If you are on foot or have been dropped from a helicopter, you won't have any vehicles to help you. You may have a portable Caltrop (an extendable arm with upward-pointing spikes designed to cause punctures to car tyres), but this is normally used in an emergency to stop an escaping vehicle. Often you will have to rely on vehicles heeding your signal to stop. Law-abiding citizens will of course do this.

Stopping and checking

At least two members of your patrol will need to carry out the job of stopping and checking passing vehicles, and at least another two men should be employed to cover the checkers. These men should be far enough back so as not to get in the searchers' way, but close enough to be able to see what is going on.

A BAD NIGHT IN BELFAST

A car that had burst through an army/ RUC vehicle checkpoint was pursued by a chase vehicle to this rather unfortunate end; it crashed during the high-speed chase. The Army's job in the province is complicated by drunken joyriders and car thieves, who could just as easily be heavily-armed terrorists. You cannot open fire just because a vehicle fails to stop.

crashed the roadblock, short of opening fire, which will not usually be possible unless the occupants of the car have opened fire at you.

Escaping cars

There are not too many options open to you for halting a car that is quite determined not to stop. Caltrop can be very effective if you can deploy it in time, and armoured vehicles are even more effective if you are part of a vehicle patrol. However, if you are unable to stop an escaping car you should either have a pursuit vehicle ready to give chase or be in radio contact with a police or military vehicle that can give chase. At the very least

Precise orders for opening fire will have been given. In an IS situation, this usually means that you can only open fire if your own or one of your comrades' lives, or that of another innocent person, is threatened. You must be absolutely sure that you understand your orders: a car simply failing to stop at a roadblock is not normally sufficient reason to open fire.

Argyll and Sutherland Highlanders search a suspect's car at a roadblock in Aden. Note that the searcher is covered at all times by his number two.

As well as the men employed in stopping and checking the traffic and those covering them, you will need to position 'long stops' in both directions down the road. Their task is to cut off anyone who approaches the roadblock, sees it, thinks better of going through it and turns round to go back the other way. Alternatively, they can attempt to stop someone who has

Traffic control
If traffic volume is heavy, members of the checkpoint must bear in mind basic road safety and prevention of accidents.

Layout
Stop groups should be on each side and well clear of the search area so that they can watch approaching traffic, prevent vehicles or people evading the VCP and watch out for snipers or other enemy forces moving into position. It should not be possible to drive round the VCP, so it must be sited with ditches or obstacles on each side of the road. Vehicles placed in an arrowhead formation will make it impossible to drive through at speed, while permitting a slow through-flow of traffic.

Communications
A VCP must have excellent communications so that information about suspect vehicles or individuals such as number plate or identity checks can be rapidly obtained. Revised instructions or orders must be passed swiftly from HQ, as well as immediate reaction from stop groups or hot pursuit vehicles.

you will have a description of the car and a registration number, which should make its subsequent apprehension quite easy.

Roadblocks are relatively simple to mount. Remember these basic rules, and you can successfully apprehend wanted men or uncover a haul of illegal arms or explosives.

Early warning devices
Unmanned ground sensors such as Classic can be set to detect vehicles or personnel approaching the VCP from up to several kilometres away. Ground radar and infra-red devices can also be used.

Security
A VCP must have enough men to defend itself from enemy ambush, especially when moving in and setting up. It should be treated just like a patrol. Remember, a security force VCP is a high-value terrorist target.

Concealment
A good VCP should be sited where it is difficult for a terrorist to turn his vehicle round or reverse out without being noticed by the VCP. Sharp bends or dips in the road are the places to go for.

A VEHICLE CHECKPOINT

Vehicle Checkpoints (VCPs) are set up during emergencies both to apprehend wanted persons and to prevent the smuggling of arms and equipment. Checkpoints also enhance the visibility of the forces of law and order, acting as a deterrent.

Below: The ultimate roadblock. There is no squeezing your car-bomb past this in a hurry! A T-54 of the Shi'ite Amal militia guards the approaches to the Beirut residence of the Amal leader, Nabit Berri. Tanks are effective, moveable roadblocks with massive firepower: even when knocked out by terrorists, they are still 40 or 50 tonnes of metal blocking the middle of the road.

Automatic fire
Machine-gun fire can be called for by the commander on the spot in the same way that he requests single shots, if in his judgement it is the minimum force required and that no other weapon can be used effectively. Short bursts minimise risks to bystanders.

Stop groups
These are more effective if they are concealed. If you have time, dig in. Make sure communications between the stop groups and the search area are duplicated (e.g. both radio and field telephone). The stop groups should have weapons capable of stopping a car, and pre-designated arcs of fire and killing zones. A quick and effective way of blocking the road should be available, such as vehicles or Caltrops, shown here.

Moving out
Before leaving the position, make a detailed search along the sides of the road in both directions to the limit of visibility. You may find some things that people with guilty consciences dumped out of car windows while approaching the VCP.

SEARCHING VEHICLES

When the security situation deteriorates, the armed forces are called in to provide assistance to the civil power. Current policy in Northern Ireland is for the RUC to be backed up by the Army in high-threat areas. Here an RUC officer armed with a Sterling SMG mans a control point in Belfast city centre.

It doesn't take much explosive to kill someone. Just imagine how easy it is to hide a matchbox in a vehicle and you have some idea of how difficult a thorough vehicle search can be — it's like looking for a needle in a haystack. Highly specialised training is needed to search a car properly, and one place you are likely to have to do so is in Northern Ireland, having stopped a vehicle at a roadblock.

These are the general points and principles of car searching; you need a lot of practice and experience before you can regard yourself as competent not only in knowing what to look for, but also how and where to find it.

There are three types of vehicle search:

1 Quick search
2 Thorough search
3 Workshop search

Normally, you will carry out quick or thorough searches. Workshop searches involve stripping down a vehicle completely, which is a specialist job requiring specialist equipment.

As always, what you will do depends on circumstances. A quick search might well progress into a thorough search at the OC's discretion, either because of information received or just the intuition of the searchers that something is not right with the vehicle.

The threat: a car bomb explodes outside the Crumlin Road Courthouse. It was intended to kill Jane Watt, the barrister daughter of a judge. However, the deviced was noticed in time and she scrambled to safety. Large car bombs have the capacity to level whole blocks of buildings and one of the main functions of a VCP is to make it more risky for the terrorists to plant them.

TIPS FOR SEARCHING SOME MAKES OF CAR

1 VW Beetle
The dashboard is accessible from under the front bonnet and provides a good 'hidden' space.

2 Renault 4
The rear wheel arches extend high into the bodywork, enabling small arms to be safely stashed.

3 Hillman Avenger
The rear panel above the bumper is double-skinned; a hole can be cut from the boot to gain access.

4 Maxi
Large voids in the air hoses under the front wings deserve extra examination.

5 Mini
Some models have a boot floor instead of a mat to cover the spare wheel — where weapons could be stored.

Never let the driver rush you in your examination. Invariably, people will be in a hurry to 'meet a relative' or 'pick the kids up from school'. The inconvenience of a checkpoint search can make even the mildest drivers angry. Act calmly and formally – never put yourself into the position of having to answer back.

The deterrent effect

Searches are carried out for two reasons; the first is as a deterrent. The purpose here is to put the terrorist off carrying out his clandestine activities. If, for instance, you habitually search all cars leaving and entering a military base, it is unlikely that terrorists will attempt to conceal weapons in a vehicle as they are likely to be caught.

Even random searches of vehicles at road checkpoints help to prevent the regular smuggling of arms or drugs, as long as the searchers are efficient at their job.

The specific search

The second type of search is more direct: it is one where Intelligence suggests that a particular car is likely to contain items of interest to the Security Services. The advantage here is that the search party know what to look for, and can thus be especially vigilant.

Left: A 'Brick' commander radios in the registration number of a suspect vehicle to 'Vengeful', the Northern Ireland computer system which provides up-to-date information not just on stolen cars but also on the driver.

EIGHT TRICKS TO MAKE SEARCHING SIMPLER

1 Look for evidence of recent activity.
2 Ask yourself where *you* would hide something.
3 Look above and below as well as at eye level.
4 Keep thinking where the spaces are and how to reach them.
5 Have a change of kit handy; you might get messed up.
6 Strong smells of talc or perfume may be hiding the powerful smell of explosives.
7 Get the driver to open the bonnet and the boot; don't do it yourself.
8 Look carefully at the driver – is he or she nervous?

Planning a search

An experienced searcher will also ask himself six questions to ensure that he has prepared thoroughly.
1 Who is being searched?
Will the owner of the vehicle be there? Will he mind? Perhaps he may need to be calmed down – especially if the search reveals nothing and you have ripped up his vehicle! Note his appearance and attitude – are they suspicious?
2 Why is the search taking place?
Has the car been deliberately identified as suspect, or is it just a deterrent search?
3 What am I looking for?
Are you trying to discover explosives, incriminating letters, arms, ammunition, maps, money, drugs, detonators, radio equipment? Or are you just looking for anything of interest? This will dictate how thoroughly you search.

SOME TYPES OF EXPLOSIVE DEVICE

1 Time delay
This is attached to a simple timing mechanism such as an alarm clock; it could be concealed in the glove compartment.
2 Pressure switch
This activates an explosive device when touched, for example when the accelerator pedal is pushed down.
3 Release switch
This pulls a trip wire when a door is opened or a chair lifted, and can be made using an ordinary clothes peg.
4 Tilt switch
This is set off by a tilting movement and so is quite suitable for attaching around axles. It can be detonated by jacking the car up to look underneath.
5 Heat switch
This could be located in the engine compartment or on the exhaust pipe, where the device explodes upon reaching a certain temperature.
6 Remote-controlled device
This could be quite sophisticated; radio control allows the operator to detonate the charge from a safe distance, at the time when it will cause the most damage.

Left: A hastily installed tilt switch device which takes seconds to clip to a car and contains enough PE 4 explosive to kill you easily. The bomb would normally be placed well underneath the car.

Right: A section of steel pipe packed with explosive with a simple circuit and battery and clothes peg circuit breaker with an insulated switch in place, which pulls out when the car drives away.

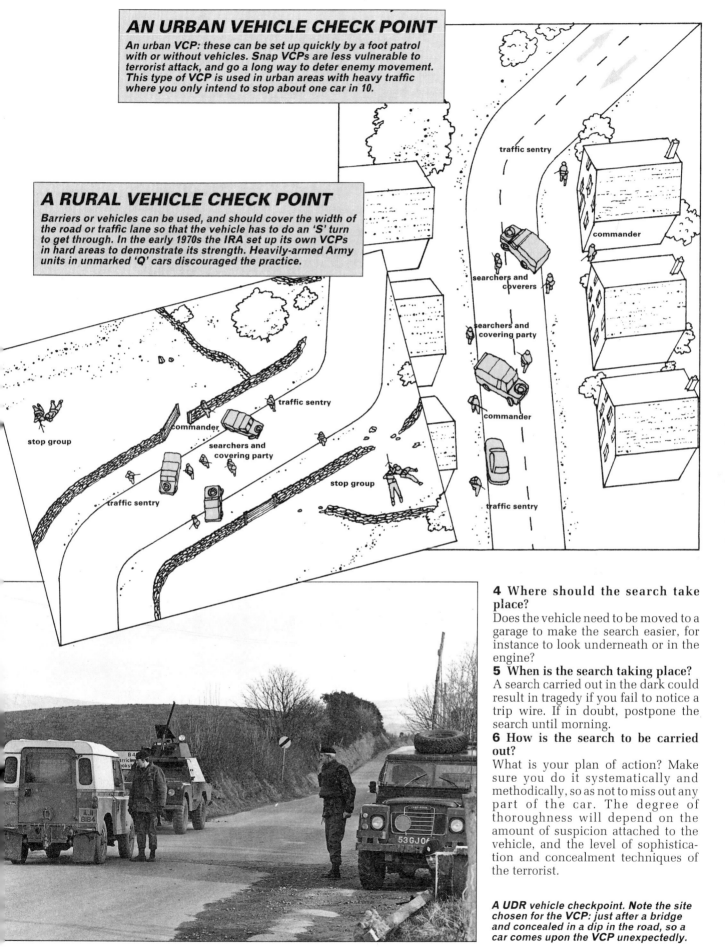

AN URBAN VEHICLE CHECK POINT

An urban VCP: these can be set up quickly by a foot patrol with or without vehicles. Snap VCPs are less vulnerable to terrorist attack, and go a long way to deter enemy movement. This type of VCP is used in urban areas with heavy traffic where you only intend to stop about one car in 10.

traffic sentry

commander

searchers and coverers

searchers and covering party

commander

traffic sentry

A RURAL VEHICLE CHECK POINT

Barriers or vehicles can be used, and should cover the width of the road or traffic lane so that the vehicle has to do an 'S' turn to get through. In the early 1970s the IRA set up its own VCPs in hard areas to demonstrate its strength. Heavily-armed Army units in unmarked 'Q' cars discouraged the practice.

stop group

traffic sentry

commander

searchers and covering party

traffic sentry

stop group

4 Where should the search take place?
Does the vehicle need to be moved to a garage to make the search easier, for instance to look underneath or in the engine?

5 When is the search taking place?
A search carried out in the dark could result in tragedy if you fail to notice a trip wire. If in doubt, postpone the search until morning.

6 How is the search to be carried out?
What is your plan of action? Make sure you do it systematically and methodically, so as not to miss out any part of the car. The degree of thoroughness will depend on the amount of suspicion attached to the vehicle, and the level of sophistication and concealment techniques of the terrorist.

A UDR vehicle checkpoint. Note the site chosen for the VCP: just after a bridge and concealed in a dip in the road, so a car comes upon the VCP unexpectedly.

103

HOW TO CONDUCT A THOROUGH CAR SEARCH

Car searches are nearly always carried out by more than one person; in this case one person should direct the search so that it is carried out methodically and systematically. He should also note down all the items found and where they were located, and should check off each area of the vehicle as it is completed.

The simplest way to carry out a search is to break down the areas of examination into five stages:

1 Exterior bodywork
2 Underneath
3 Interior
4 Boot
5 Engine

It is vital that you proceed logically so that no part of the vehicle is left out.

1 The layout: one sentry forward, one rear, one man standing in the road to stop traffic, and the fourth covering him.

2 Stop the vehicle and check its registration against the wanted car list. Check the driver's licence.

3 Ask the driver for his registration number and where the spare wheel is: if he has to look before answering he may be driving a stolen vehicle.

4 You notice something suspicious: in this case the petrol cap has been ripped off the car. You decide to conduct a thorough search.

5 Start with the outside of the vehicle and keep the owner with you to watch the search.

6 While one soldier searches the car in company with the owner, another soldier covers him at all times.

7 After doing the outside, search the underneath of the car: look for fresh paint, disturbed underseal and unconvincing 'exhaust systems'.

8 Next search the boot: get the owner to open the boot and any luggage inside. Take out the carpet and spare wheel.

10 Next you search the engine, again getting the driver to open the hood and in this case the filter.

11 Searching the passenger seat area: make sure you reach into all the cavities.

12 When you have finished the owner is to sign an indemnity certificate stating he has suffered no damage or loss during the search.

What to look for

There is a wide range of specialist terrorist devices, but you are looking for one of three elements.

1 The absence of the normal/presence of the abnormal

Ask yourself, "Does the car look right?" Do the carpets fit properly, or have they been lifted recently? Why?

2 The sophisticated booby trap

A trigger switch, for example, could have been placed under the hollow of the front seat, and will be activated the moment the seat is lifted.

SEARCHING MOTOR BIKES AND BICYCLES

Their small size makes them fairly easy to search, but look out for the following surprises:

1 False partitions in petrol tanks.
2 Weapons concealed in the hollow of rubber handlegrips.
3 Anything concealed in tubular framing, especially under the saddle.
4 Saddle and tool bags concealing explosive.
5 Electrical devices connected to lamps and bells or horns.
6 Wires taped to underside of mudguard and crank case.

9 Grenades can be easily concealed in the space between the boot carpet and the floor or sides.

3 The hastily-laid booby trap

A heat-activated device can easily be tied to an exhaust, and the effect of the engine heat will be fatal if the bomb remains undetected. A device like this could be planted in seconds.

If you find something

If your search reveals an explosive device or something that looks like one, clear the area immediately. Then hand over to civilian or military bomb disposal units, who will attempt to render the device harmless.

AREAS TO SEARCH

This cutaway shows the main areas to search on a typical saloon car. Check any large box sections or double-skin areas to which access can be obtained with the minimum amount of alterations. It is essential to be systematic when searching, or you may well miss something.

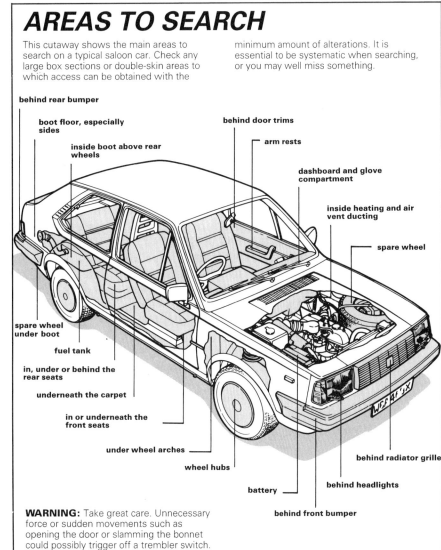

- behind rear bumper
- boot floor, especially sides
- inside boot above rear wheels
- behind door trims
- arm rests
- dashboard and glove compartment
- inside heating and air vent ducting
- spare wheel
- spare wheel under boot
- fuel tank
- in, under or behind the rear seats
- underneath the carpet
- in or underneath the front seats
- under wheel arches
- wheel hubs
- battery
- behind radiator grille
- behind headlights
- behind front bumper

WARNING: Take great care. Unnecessary force or sudden movements such as opening the door or slamming the bonnet could possibly trigger off a trembler switch.

13 If you find anything suspicious, leave it where it is and arrest the driver. Alert EOD (Explosive Ordnance Disposal).

14 Once you have found something, search the suspect. Here a soldier checks the driver's hair.

15 The terrorist suspect is restrained and should be handed over to the police as soon as possible.

CHAPTER FOUR

URBAN COMBAT

Of all the various kinds of ground over which battles can be fought – plains, jungles, mountains, deserts, ice and snow – should any trained soldier be asked where he liked fighting the least he would almost certainly say 'Streets' for urban combat is the most hazardous and dangerous time for troops on the ground. Everywhere in a built-up area there are places for well-concealed snipers and machine-gun posts and even AFVs, some of whose large calibre guns can be well concealed in a ruined building and will totally destroy nearby structures. Also, of course, in enemy territory there is the possibility of offensive action by the population, who will at any rate have agents among them, indistinguished from the ordinary civilians, but who will be engaged in gathering intelligence.

In this chapter, which concentrates on the difficulties of urban combat, you will read about the seven life-saving rules a rifle quad must remember when the time comes to assault a building known to be occupied by the enemy. One lapse of memory, even thoughtlessly entering a room the wrong way, or turning a doorhandle without considering that it might be boobytrapped, can bring that explosion which will take one or more of the squad out of the engagement. Those seven ways of staying alive are listed and detailed here. From the rooftops and attics down to below street-level and including the sewers and tunnels defenders can harry the troops who have taken the area and whose job it is to make it safe for follow-up units and non-combatant personnel.

A street in the hands of the enemy is a dangerous place even to approach. The experienced assault team does not push forward and storm the houses one by one, they will fail if it is occupied by the enemy and probably die in the attempt. The walls of houses, so comforting to those who live there in normal times, are often the best 'doors' through which to gain access. The damage to what after all might be someone's home is disastrous but it must be remembered that the inhabitants will be long gone or at the least sheltering in the cellar should there be one.

In battle, a soldier stays alive by keeping constantly alert and in urban combat the need for awareness is doubly so. No building can be considered safe and empty unless entered and thoroughly searched. But it may not remain in an empty state if the enemy is still in the area and has the means of moving about, so sensors or some other device have to be planted inside.

Entering premises, whether or not they are damaged, is fraught with danger. There may be enemy concealed there, or boobytraps, tripwires, or the building might be in the sights of a large-calibre weapon down the street. All these hazards have to be contended with and it is usually nothing but bitter experience that makes a trained soldier into an effective urban fighting man.

There are special drills for crossing alleys and intersections, moving up or down stairways and all need well-trained teamwork; and once inside a building there is a right and wrong way of moving about. One unhinking error and you may not live to regret it.

Getting out fast from a threatened building might be necessary and one of the most likely ways of doing so is rappelling, or abseiling as it is otherwise called. Troops who some day might be engaged in urban combat will need to know how this is done.

INFANTRY TACTICS IN BUILT-UP AREAS

Street fighting, especially the difficult and dangerous job of house-clearing, is some of the most nerve-racking work you will ever do as a soldier. City streets are deadly places for the attacking soldier. Every doorway and window, every pile of rubble and seemingly abandoned vehicle, every rooftop and underground passage, could contain a fatal hazard for the unwary.

On a city street you can make no assumptions until you've seen, checked and double-checked for yourself; and even then you must expect the unexpected at any moment, day or night.

Your life depends on your alertness, and you must rely on your basic training to see you safely through.

This article is based on the US Infantry Fighting Manual. It is the first in this Chapter and looks at all the skills a soldier needs to survive in an urban battle.

The tricks of the trade

The rifle squad is the basic unit for street fighting. Every member of the squad must know all the tricks of his trade: how to move through the streets, how to enter and clear build-

Seven life-saving rules of movement

There are seven basic rules of movement.
1   Never allow yourself to be seen in silhouette, and keep low at all times.
2   Avoid open spaces.
3   Select your next position in cover before you make your move.
4   Hide your movements any way you can.
5   Move fast.
6   Stay clear of covering fire.
7   Be alert and ready for anything.

Look first, move later. This simple formula has saved the life of many a patrolling foot-soldier.

Before going into the building, the experienced infantryman sends a grenade in ahead to kill, stun or drive out anyone who may be inside.

These two infantrymen are working as a team to minimise the danger from enemy forces inside the house, during the American invasion of Grenada in 1983.

ings, how to use grenades, how to choose firing positions, what camouflage techniques and special weapons (flame-throwers and smoke bombs, for example) to use to best effect.

Movement

The moment you stop moving, your attack stops too. Then you are at the mercy of the enemy forces who possess the advantage of a secure defensive position. The attacking force must dictate the pace of the battle or lose the initiative.

The important rule is to move as fast as possible to present the smallest target.

Moving in the open

You should try to move down a street through the buildings on either side by making holes in their internal walls. If you must move in the open, use smoke screens and covering fire at all times. Stay close to the walls, and in the shadows. Keep low, don't present your silhouette and, above all, move fast. This way, it will be very difficult for an enemy gunner inside the building to get a clear shot at you without exposing himself to covering fire from your teammates. Always remember: work as a team. Everyone then stands a better chance of surviving unhurt.

These US Marines are using what available cover they can in an attempt to take out an enemy sniper during the battle for Hue, South Vietnam, in 1968.

Urban movement techniques

Moving from place to place under fire is always a dangerous business. Movement in towns and cities calls for a different set of skills from those used out in the country, but you must still be alert to every possibility of danger.

Mind your head
Be careful when you pass by ground floor windows. Always be sure to keep your head well down below the level of the sill.

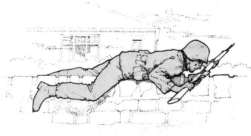

The lie of the land
Looking around corners carelessly is a quick way to get killed. Do it at ground level. Always remember to keep your weapon well back out of sight and wear your Kevlar helmet.

Over the wall
When crossing a wall you must keep as low a profile as possible. Roll over it, with your body flat. If you don't know what is on the other side, throw a grenade over first – but be sure that shrapnel splinters can't reach you through the wall.

Firing positions

The infantryman looks for two things in a firing position – concealment for himself and his weapon, and a wide field of fire. His assessment of any situation must be second nature.

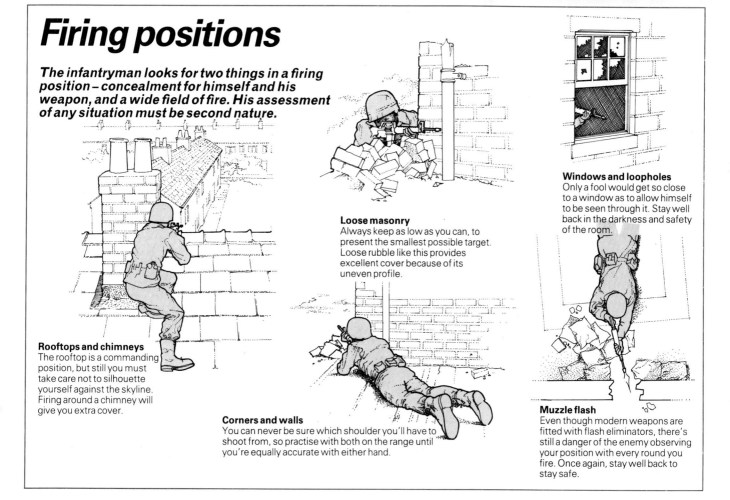

Rooftops and chimneys
The rooftop is a commanding position, but still you must take care not to silhouette yourself against the skyline. Firing around a chimney will give you extra cover.

Loose masonry
Always keep as low as you can, to present the smallest possible target. Loose rubble like this provides excellent cover because of its uneven profile.

Corners and walls
You can never be sure which shoulder you'll have to shoot from, so practise with both on the range until you're equally accurate with either hand.

Windows and loopholes
Only a fool would get so close to a window as to allow himself to be seen through it. Stay well back in the darkness and safety of the room.

Muzzle flash
Even though modern weapons are fitted with flash eliminators, there's still a danger of the enemy observing your position with every round you fire. Once again, stay well back to stay safe.

Never cross an open space directly. Always take the long way round if that lets you stay in cover. If you must be out in the open at all, make it as short a time as possible.

If the whole of your fire team is on the move, don't cross open spaces one at a time: the first man may get through, but it will give any enemy a good opportunity for an aimed shot at anyone following on. Move as a group, and use smokescreens and covering fire. It does make for a bigger target, but this technique still reduces the risk to a minimum.

When you have to cross alleyways and narrow streets, spread out into a line, with three to five metres between one another. On the squad leader's signal, all cross together – fast!

As soon as you have taken up your new position you must be ready to give covering fire to the other members of your squad, and that means you have

Watch your feet
Basement windows can be a source of danger, too. Keep a careful lookout for them, and always be sure that you don't expose your legs to view. Make sure to jump well clear of the window, or use whatever is available to step above it. Even if you get past unhurt, the next man may not.

Stand clear of the doors
Don't use doorways if you can avoid it – they are just too obvious as targets. If there really is no alternative, be sure to pick out your next position before you set out.

Keep covered
Don't ever do anything as obvious as leaving a house by way of the door without covering fire from at least one of your team. And be sure that the position you move to will allow you to cover him, when it comes to his turn to move.

Moving as a fire team

Covering fire
You can't get too much supporting fire. Properly placed, it will keep the enemies' heads down and allow you to move in comparative safety.

The squad rush
Move as a spread-out group, not as one individual after another, so that the enemy has no warning of your movements.

to be ready to use your weapon from either shoulder. Never, ever fire over the top of your cover. You will be silhouetted against the building or sky behind. Always fire around your cover and don't take any chances by exposing yourself to enemy fire. Take every chance you can to practise firing your weapon from the shoulder that you don't normally use – you never know when you'll need to be able to do this.

Firing positions

The individual rifleman succeeds or fails in his job through how he chooses and uses firing positions. There are two things to keep in mind: how to put fast, accurate fire down on to the enemy position, and how to avoid exposing yourself to return fire.

In attack you will almost certainly have to use improvised methods called 'hasty firing positions'. These may be from round the corners of buildings, from behind low walls, through windows, from behind roof ridges and beside chimneys, and through holes blown in walls by heavier weapons.

Don't stand up

When firing from round the corner of a building, don't use the standing position. This will place too much of your body in view and your head will be precisely at the height the enemy expects it to be. Kneeling is good, but lying down is better.

Fire around walls, from as low a position as possible, and try to use any rubble or fallen stones and bricks to give extra cover.

The most common mistake made when firing from a window is to get too close to it, in order to widen your field of fire. You won't be able to give your full attention to a field of fire that

When the time comes to move, do it quickly, with no hesitation. These US Marines of Company H, 2nd Battalion are seen closing in on a group of VC during the battle for Hue.

Fighting through the streets and alleys of a city is some of the toughest work an infantryman will ever be called upon to do. It's dangerous, dirty and very, very demanding in terms of strength and physical fitness. Team work, too, is all-important, with each member of the squad acutely aware of what everyone else is doing.

Careful observation
One member of the squad should scout out the ground carefully, looking for snipers, difficult obstacles to cross and signs of particularly strong enemy activity.

wide, so don't expose yourself to un-expected fire. Stay well back in the room – the end of your rifle muzzle should be at least one yard inside the room, and preferably two. The muzzle flash will then be hard to see, and so will you. Just because you can see out of a window, even from the other side of the room, doesn't mean that an observer on the outside can see that far in. It is almost impossible to see more than a metre inside, unless a room is lit from another direction as well as through the window you are using.

Loopholes

The same rules apply to firing from 'accidental' loopholes – holes that have been blown in walls by fire from heavy weapons. Stay well back inside the room to hide both yourself and the muzzle flash, even though this will reduce your field of fire. Fire from a lying or kneeling position wherever you can.

Roof-top positions are useful. They give you an excellent field of fire, and put the enemy at the disadvantage of having to fire up into the air. Use the side of a chimney or any other side wall or structure to give yourself extra

cover, and try not to expose your silhouette straight over the top of the roof-ridge. Remember, when no cover is available, reduce the size of the target you give to the enemy by all or any of these means:
1 Fire from the lying position.

2 Fire from the shadows.
3 Don't present a silhouette.
4 Use tall grass, weeds and bushes, rubble and ruins to hide in – they won't stop an enemy bullet but they will stop him from seeing you.

Alley-crossing as a team

Open spaces, streets and even narrow alleyways present a greater obstacle to the infantryman than walls or piles of rubble ever can. The procedure is to cross as a group, spread out with to five metres between one man and the next. Once every member of the squad is in position, the leader gives the order and everyone goes at the same time. That way, the enemy forces aren't given any warning of your intentions.

TAKING OUT ENEMY POSITIONS

At first sight, urban combat is a one-sided business: whichever side holds the 'high ground' — the buildings — has a natural advantage. But, sooner or later during an assault on a built-up area, you'll be called on to leave the streets and flush out the enemy from the buildings. There are in fact a host of techniques and tricks that you can use to put the occupiers not only on the defensive but positively on the losing side. This second article on urban combat skills tells you how to go in after the enemy and take out his positions.

Entering a house

Just because you haven't come under fire from a particular building, that doesn't mean it isn't occupied by the enemy, or – possibly worse still – that he didn't booby-trap it before he left.

Cities play an increasingly important role in military operations. Here an Israeli soldier cautiously advances up an alleyway in Beirut.

Seven life-saving rules of entry

1 Select your entry point long before you get to the building.
2 Stay away from windows and doors.
3 Use smoke whenever possible.
4 Make new entrances with explosives, tank rounds or rocket-propelled grenades (RPGs).
5 Send a grenade into a building or room before you go in yourself.
6 Go in immediately after the grenade has exploded.
7 Go in under covering fire.

Movement in buildings

Entering a room
It takes three men to enter a room safely – one to provide security and two actually to go in. The first man throws in a grenade, and goes in after it has gone off. He flattens himself against the wall while his partner searches the room.

Mouseholes
A 'mousehole' is a hole about 60 cm wide, blown or cut through a wall as an alternative entrance to a room. Doors are easy to booby-trap so you should try to assault through a mousehole, throwing a grenade in first as usual.

Moving past windows
In the stress of clearing a house of enemy troops, it's all too easy to forget that you can be seen from outside if you walk past a window. Don't expose yourself to danger in this way. Always stay below the level of the sill.

Hallways and corridors
Don't use hallways and corridors unless you must. If you can't make your way from room to room directly, make sure you present as small a target as possible by keeping in tight to the walls.

Until you know for sure that a building has been cleared, always assume the worst. Don't go in through the doors or the ground floor windows if you can possibly avoid it. Treat as suspect any hole you haven't blown in a wall yourself.

Clearing from the top

Although nothing to do with house-clearing can be said to be safe, the best way to do it is from the top. It's a lot easier to fight your way down than up, and it also gives the enemy somewhere to go! If you corner enemy forces on the top floor of a building, they have no alternative but to try and fight their way out. If you drive them down to the ground floor, there's a good chance they'll try to make a run for it — straight into covering fire from the rest of your squad.

Although entering at the top floor of a building does present some problems, they're not as bad as you may think. Once one house is cleared, you have access to the roof of the next. It's only the first house that presents a problem, and that can be solved easily enough if helicopter support is available. Otherwise you can use ladders, drainpipes or, at worse, ropes.

The easiest way to get a rope up to the top floor or roof of a building is with a grappling iron — three or four large metal hooks welded together and attached to the end of a rope. Don't use too thin a rope; although it will weigh less, it is much more difficult to climb than a thick one. You can knot the rope every 30 cm or so to improvise steps but, if you do, it will not pay out so easily when you throw the hook.

Watch out for snipers

Remember that you will be extremely exposed to sniper fire while you're climbing the wall. Take as few chances as possible, and spend some

Throwing a grappling hook

Stand as close to the building as possible to reduce your vulnerability to enemy fire. In your throwing hand you have the hook and a few coils of rope; the rest of the rope is in loose coils in your other hand. The throw itself should be a gentle, upward, lob. Check that the hook has a solid hold before you begin to climb. Knotting the rope beforehand at 30 cm intervals will make it easier to grip.

Incoming fire
You'll never be more vulnerable than when you're roping down the side of a building. Before you set out be sure that there are no enemy forces able to get a clear shot at you.

Rappelling
It's certainly much quicker and much less effort to go down a rope than to climb up one. Where you can move across the roof from one building to another, rappel down to the top floor to start the house-clearing operation.

Weapons security
Roping down the side of a building requires both hands, so you will have to sling your weapon and you won't be able to get at it until both your feet are on solid ground again. You should have plenty of grenades to hand, though, ready to throw into every window you come to.

time before the attempt in checking any possible sniper positions – and have them cleared.

If you do have to go past windows on the way up, give them a grenade when you're still below the level of the window sill, and always put a grenade through the window you're going to enter.

It is much easier to come down a rope than go up one. When you can, go up to the roof level, staying well down from the ridge so you don't present your silhouette, and rope down to the entry window.

Rappelling

The US Army uses the French name for roping down: rappelling. It's also known as abseiling. There are a lot of different ways of doing it, but they all rely on the friction of the rope across your body and through your (gloved) hand. A 'free' rappel, where there is no wall to bounce off to slow your descent, is used to come down from a helicopter that has no room to land.

Rappelling needs practice. When you're on the rope you're on your own. If you make a mistake and fall, no one can save you. Practise in a group with an experienced teacher, and start off low – from a height that won't injure you if you fall. Never try it alone, or without the right equipment.

Making a sling rope seat

Rappelling, also known as abseiling, is used to descend from the roof of a tall building and in through a window. Urban fighters should be familiar with the sling rope seat.

1 Place the centre of the sling rope on the hip opposite your brake hand. If you are right-handed, use your right hand as the brake hand; if you are left-handed, use the left.

2 Wrap the rope around your waist, keeping the centre of the rope on your hip.

3 Tie an overhand knot in front of your body.

4 Bring the ends of the rope between your legs, front to rear, then around your legs and under the waist loop.

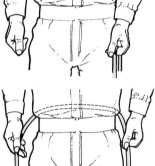

5 Tie the ends with a square knot and two half-hitches on the side opposite the brake hand. Tuck the loose ends into a pocket.

6 Place the snaplink through the single rope around your waist and through the top ropes that form the overhand knot. Insert the snap link with the gate down and the opening towards the body.

7 Rotate the snap link one half-turn so that the gate is up and opens away from the body.

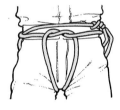

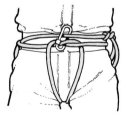

Not all your fire team may be able to see you while you're rappelling down, so you must give them a clear signal, both when you start the descent, and when you finish. Where noise doesn't matter, shout 'On Rappel' and 'Off Rappel'. In a situation requiring a silent approach, work out a system of tugs on the rope, and make sure everyone understands it.

Through the window

When you come to the point of entering the window, you can get in very quickly by positioning yourself just above, throwing in the grenade, and then bounding the last couple of feet. If you have to enter while climbing the rope, go up above the sill so that gravity helps you down through the window and into the .room. Even after you've thrown in a grenade, you have to get through the window as quickly as possible.

In house clearance, it's always a good idea to 'cook-off' the grenade before throwing it in the window. Grenades have timed fuses to prevent them from exploding in your hand as soon as you pull the pin. If you don't want to throw it too far – just drop it into a room, for example – you need to use up a part of this delay before you throw the grenade. Pull the safety pin and let the firing clip go. Then count 'One thousand and one, one thousand and two,' before throwing the grenade. This will use up two seconds of the delay and reduce the chance of someone throwing it back!

You should never throw a grenade without a secure place for you to shelter. Once a grenade has left your hand

In urban combat part of the squad advances; the other men cover possible enemy positions. This picture was taken during house-to-house fighting in Managua, Nicaragua, in 1979.

Ground-level entry

Don't use doors and windows if you can avoid it. Here are three methods of entering a building via windows.

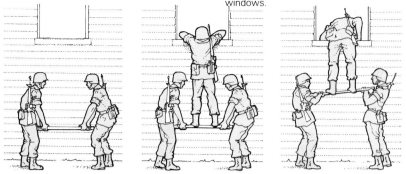

1 Two-man lift
Two men bend down facing each other with cupped hands or holding a plank. They support the climbing man as he reaches for the window sill and lift him upwards so that he can climb in.

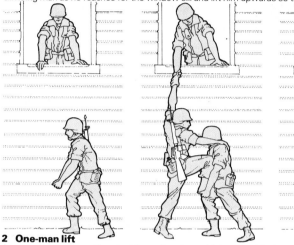
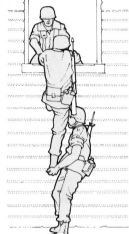

2 One-man lift
One man braces himself against the wall and cups his hands while the man already inside reaches down. Together they help the climbing man through the window.

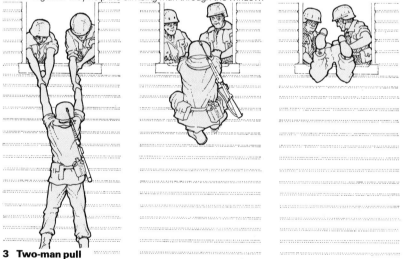

3 Two-man pull
Once the first two men are inside, they can pull the third man up by his hands as he scrambles up the wall.

it is a very unpredictable weapon. It could take a bad bounce or explode prematurely. If you can, use a grenade launcher such as the M203 attached to the M16 rifle, or the bulkier M79 grenade launcher. These two weapons propel a grenade much further and more accurately than you can throw one.

Once again, speed means safety. After you have completed the standard tactic of throwing a grenade in

first, you must be through the window as quickly as possible. If the window is above your head you will need the help of one or two members of your squad to push you into the room. Remember that it is always safer to call up armoured or RPG support if you can. Such heavy weapons can knock a hole in a wall for you to enter the building at a point the enemy could never have considered when he set up his defences.

CLEARING AN ENEMY-HELD BUILDING

When you're inside a house where enemy troops are installed, the grenade takes over from the gun as your first-line weapon. When clearing buildings — perhaps the most dangerous job an infantryman is called on to do — there's no time to wonder how the enemy's going to react. You have to do it to them before they do it to you. And do it quickly, safely and surely, risking your life and those of your team as little as possible.

This section of the urban combat chapter looks at clearing buildings room by room, and setting up defensive positions once that task has been completed.

Watch the outside

There are two problems involved in moving about in buildings occupied by enemy troops — and only one of them comes from inside. The essential point for a soldier to remember in house clearance operations is that enemy forces on the outside are just as dangerous to you as those on the inside. Never stand at windows, in doorways or in holes blown through walls. If you do have to cross in front of windows that could be targeted by the enemy, either keep well back in the room or crawl beneath the level of the window sill.

Inside the house, the danger zones are found in hallways and corridors. The rooms opening on to these are useful hideouts for enemy troops who can then ambush the forces clearing the building. If you are forced to use an entrance hallway or upstairs corridor, always present yourself as the smallest target possible by flattening yourself against the wall. If you come to a turning, treat it as you would a

REORGANISING YOUR FORCES

When you have completely cleared the building, you should:

1. **Resupply and redistribute your ammunition.**
2. **Mark the building so that friendly forces will know it is safe.**
3. **Provide covering fire for assaults on other buildings.**
4. **Treat and evacuate any wounded.**
5. **If the building is to remain occupied, organise a defensive position.**

SECURING UPPER FLOORS

As the rest of the team storm into the enemy-held building, a security detachment is left on the roof to guard against enemy counter-attack. The assault team blows a hole in the roof or adjoining wall using a demolition charge, and begins to clear the building from the top downwards. Further demolition charges can be used to blow holes in floors so that the stairs, which may be booby-trapped, need not be used.

Covering entrances
Once the building has been captured, all entrances and covered approaches to it must be guarded by a security detail. Pay particular attention to rooftops and underground routes into the basement.

Security detail
Always leave a security detail behind to block possible enemy action and to communicate with friendly forces following on behind. A building must be secured from top to bottom: and don't forget to check for cellars or a basement.

Entry through roof
Roofs and upper walls are much thinner than the lower walls of a building, and much less explosive is needed to blow an entry hole.

Room clearance
The roof area of the target house can be effectively cleared by an M60 machine-gun. Inside a building with lightly-constructed interior walls, the same technique can be used for room clearing by shooting through walls and ceilings.

Fire-escapes are useful avenues of approach from top or bottom and they are usually situated at the back of a building where there is more cover for the assault team.

room. Never make any assumptions until you have seen for yourself.

When you are approaching a room always keep a sharp eye out for booby-traps. These aptly named devices are hidden bombs with disguised trigger mechanisms. Although they are normally left behind by enemy forces after they have evacuated a position, they have proved useful in the defence of buildings as well.

Constantly bear in mind a few simple rules and you will avoid being a booby. Never touch everyday household objects such as light switches or door handles. Don't be tempted by attractive souvenirs, for their appearance can be deceptive. A handsome gold watch lying on a table could in reality be the trigger to an anti-personnel bomb underneath the furniture. Watch your feet: a favourite location for booby-traps is where you have to walk — the treads of a staircase, for example.

If possible take the most difficult route; it could save your life. Bear in mind that the enemy may have had as long as he wanted to place booby-traps, and don't ever try to render these bombs safe — that is the engineers' job. If you do find a booby-trap, mark its position with tape, chalk or aerosol paint, and give it a wide berth.

Go for the grenade

Infantrymen are taught in basic training that their rifle is their best friend. However, when the soldier is clearing a house the grenade replaces the rifle in his affections. Its explosive strength is increased by the small enclosed spaces, and it provides a quicker source of firepower in a situation where speed is safety.

When you are ready to enter a room, don't use the doorhandle; it could be booby-trapped and its movement warns the enemy who might be inside that you're about to come in. Instead put a short burst of automatic fire through the door and kick it open. If it is a stout door, get a shot-gun and load it with solid charges. Blast the hinges and then kick the door.

The first thing through the door is not your foot but a grenade. Let it 'cook off' first: pull its pin, wait two

3. STOCK

Fighting from room to room

Clearing an enemy-occupied building demands split-second timing and practised team work. Make full use of grenades and demolition charges, and remember that you can fire straight through thin walls and ceilings – but remember too that the enemy can do the same.

seconds, and then throw it in. Be very careful of thin walls, however — grenade fragments can penetrate them and injure you or one of your comrades.

Bursts of fire

Rush in fast, as soon as the grenade has gone off in the room, firing a short burst from your weapon. The first man in must get his back to the wall, in a position where he can engage any target in the room. Don't try to get off single, aimed shots. Two- or three-shot bursts are more effective. The second man into the room searches it carefully. He is protected not only by his teammate inside the room with him, but also by a support party outside the door.

Always shout messages to your support party. Keep them informed. When you're sure that the room is clear, say so in a loud voice; when you're coming out, once again yell a warning. The same applies to movement up and down staircases.

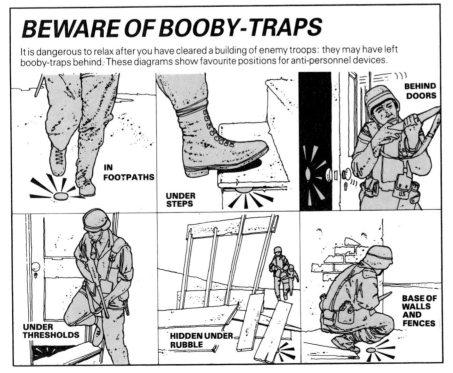

BEWARE OF BOOBY-TRAPS

It is dangerous to relax after you have cleared a building of enemy troops: they may have left booby-traps behind. These diagrams show favourite positions for anti-personnel devices.

IN FOOTPATHS

UNDER STEPS

BEHIND DOORS

UNDER THRESHOLDS

HIDDEN UNDER RUBBLE

BASE OF WALLS AND FENCES

Before entering a room, 'cook off' a grenade by pulling the pin out and waiting 2 seconds, and throw it inside as hard as you can – if you lob it in gently you might give the enemy the split second he needs to catch it and send it back.

As soon as the grenade has gone off, one man rushes into the room and moves to one side of the doorway while firing on full auto. He occupies a position where he can see the whole room.

No-one must stand directly outside the closed door to a room: doors can be fired through or booby-trapped.

Don't make the mistake of setting up a pattern as you move from room to room. A clever enemy, lying in wait for you, would be able to work out exactly what you are going to do and when. Instead, vary the way you tackle each room. Use demolition charges or light anti-tank weapons to blow holes in sections of walls so that you can enter from an unexpected direction: but always lead off with a grenade. When a room has been cleared, mark it with tape, spray paint or chalk.

Keep what you've won

Once a building has been secured, it may be necessary to prepare its defence. Barricaded windows, fortified loopholes, sniper positions, anti-tank positions and machine gun posts are all examples of the sort of hardened firing positions you will need. Each one has different needs and they will be examined in turn.

When barricading a window, leave just a small port through which to put fire on to the enemy. You can use

Once you are inside, the priority targets are the staircase and rooms that overlook approaches to the building. It is important to isolate the enemy troops inside the building and to make it impossible for them to be reinforced.

A sniper takes aim from a position concealed by shadow. If you are going to prepare a building for defence, knock out the glass from the windows and put a wire mesh anti-grenade screen over the gap.

material taken from the internal walls of the building you've occupied, or – better by far – already prepared bags of sand or earth. Don't just barricade the windows that you want to use as firing positions. You will tell the enemy exactly where you are to be found. Don't make the firing ports that you leave in the barricade square or of an even shape. That, too, makes the enemy's job easier. Reinforce the walls below and to each side of the window. A modern high-velocity round will go straight through a brick wall and still have enough energy left to cause casualties.

Watching at the window

Remove any glass left in the windows to avoid injury from splinters, but if there are curtains leave them, so long as they don't restrict your view. If possible, put wire mesh up at the windows to keep out grenades. Arrange it so that you can vary and change your position as much as possible. When firing from an upstairs window, for instance, try to have a table or similar piece of furniture close at hand, so

that you can increase the angle of fire downwards by standing on it.

Loopholes should be protected in much the same way as windows. Because you have the choice of where to make loopholes. They can often give a better field of fire than windows, and are more difficult for the enemy to spot.

Floors and ceilings

As well as protecting the walls to the front and sides of your firing position, you can put a double layer of

Knocking holes in a roof or wall can give you a firing position with a wider field of fire than that provided by existing windows and doors. It is also harder for the enemy to spot where you are shooting from.

sandbags or similar bullet-absorbent material on the floor under your feet. This is most useful if you're above the ground floor. You can also build a protective roof with a table and more sandbags. Think about camouflage as well as out-and-out protection. Make dummy firings positions to fool the enemy into wasting time and ammunition.

Sniping points

These points apply to sniper positions as well as to ordinary fire points, but with extra attention paid to camouflage and concealment. Because the sniper operates at ranges of 500 yards and more, his field of fire is very wide, even if he has a very narrow view. Because of this, he can afford to fire through the smallest hole as long as it still gives him a good view. He must take good care that the muzzle flash from his rifle is not visible to the enemy. In this way he can stay undetected for a long time, and make the very most of his value as a weapon.

FIRING ANTI-TANK WEAPONS FROM INSIDE A BUILDING

Although intended primarily for anti-tank action, the following weapons can be very useful in house-to-house fighting. But backblast is a serious problem, and the following steps must be taken; otherwise you are likely to score an own goal. Remember that the minimum range of the TOW anti-tank missile is 65 metres, which restricts its value in urban combat.

1 Remove all glass from the windows in the room.
2 Wet the floor to reduce the amount of debris thrown up by the backblast.
3 All men in the room must wear earplugs.
4 Everyone must be forward of the rear of the weapon when it is fired.

5 Ensure there is no inflammable debris behind the weapon.
6 There must be an open door or at least two square metres of ventilation behind the weapon to allow the backblast to escape.
7 The ceiling must be at least 2 metres high.

LAW

Must have 1.2 metres clear behind weapon.

Dragon

Minimum room size: 4.5 × 3.6 metres.
Minimum muzzle clearance: 16 cm

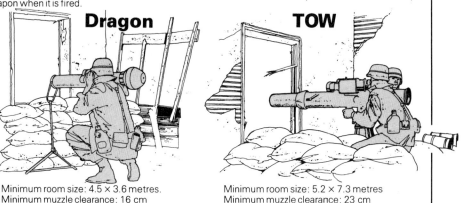

TOW

Minimum room size: 5.2 × 7.3 metres
Minimum muzzle clearance: 23 cm

DUMMY SNIPER POSITION

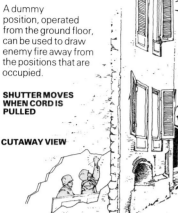

A dummy position, operated from the ground floor, can be used to draw enemy fire away from the positions that are occupied.

SHUTTER MOVES WHEN CORD IS PULLED

CUTAWAY VIEW

Right: How not to do it – US Marines in house-to-house fighting in Vietnam lean out of the window to shoot at a building occupied by North Vietnamese troops. By pushing his rifle out of the window this Marine is letting everyone know where he is firing from: if at all possible, you should fire from the interior of the room.

An infantry fire team will often be reinforced by an anti-tank squad in urban fighting. The team leader must be aware of the extra needs of the anti-tank gunners, and the partiular difficulties they face when they fire from hiding.

Modern anti-tank weapons are rocket propelled. This means that the round goes in one direction, and a huge blast of flame goes in the other. So it's extremely important to site them in such a way that the back-blast will not injure the crew or other friendly forces. This may often mean the demolition of walls facing away from the direction of the enemy. It will certainly mean that the supporting infantrymen must pay very close attention to where they put themselves when a rocket-propelled weapon is in operation.

Machine-gun team

Machine guns are the other type of crew-served weapon likely to be attached to fireteams in urban combat. They too deliver heavy firepower and must be protected by the supporting infantrymen, but they are easier to site because there are no problems with back-blast. A machine-gun can utilise a wider field of fire so may need a larger aperture to shoot from. Otherwise, the things to be remembered when choosing a site for it are identical: good concealment, good protection and a good resupply route.

Both anti-tank weapons and machine guns are crew-served: it takes more than one man to operate them. Because of their valuable high firepower, and because their crew members cannot move as quickly under the weight of their weapons should they come under attack, the supporting infantry has to give a high priority to ensuring their safety. They must always be able to give covering fire to their heavier weapons, as well as receiving it.

IDEAL ANTI-TANK FIRING POSITIONS

In urban combat, anti-tank weapons are used against enemy-held buildings as well as against tanks.

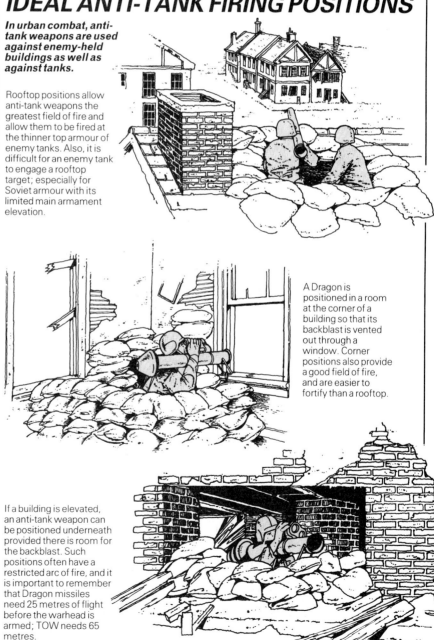

Rooftop positions allow anti-tank weapons the greatest field of fire and allow them to be fired at the thinner top armour of enemy tanks. Also, it is difficult for an enemy tank to engage a rooftop target; especially for Soviet armour with its limited main armament elevation.

A Dragon is positioned in a room at the corner of a building so that its backblast is vented out through a window. Corner positions also provide a good field of fire, and are easier to fortify than a rooftop.

If a building is elevated, an anti-tank weapon can be positioned underneath provided there is room for the backblast. Such positions often have a restricted arc of fire, and it is important to remember that Dragon missiles need 25 metres of flight before the warhead is armed; TOW needs 65 metres.

CHAPTER FIVE

HELIOPS

As soon as the helicopter became reliable it was very quickly recognised as being of immense value to the world's armed forces. We now are all familiar with the sight and sound of the 'chopper' clattering about at no great height above our heads, 'chopper' coming from the chopping sound the machine makes in flight. In the days before the helicopter was established, aircraft had to take-off by having sufficient room to gain flying speed and of course landings could be hazardous if the same amount of room, or a little less, was not available. The helicopter's greatest asset to the armed forces is that it can be flown off and landed in a space not much larger than the area swept by its rotor blades.

Each branch of the services has its own special use to which helicopters are put. In Vietnam their use as mobile, flying artillery led to the introduction of gunships with considerable firepower. But their uses are too many to be described in this chapter, which is confined to but a few of the ways the chopper is used by the Forces.

It is as a vehicle for inserting patrols that we begin this chapter. In places such as Northern Ireland a sudden local disturbance or terrorist activity might call for the fast installation of road-blocks in areas where people wanted in connection with the trouble might be driving. A helicopter can take a patrol out and put them down in time to intercept suspects before they get away across the border. These operations are known as Eagle Patrols and at times they have been very successful.

There will be areas in wartime that have few if any roads, places where it is difficult to get troops to in a hurry. Such an area is typical in parts of South Africa. In this chapter we deal with heliops in activities against terrorists in the bush regions. Here is where the helicopter again proves extremely useful, but the soldiers must be well-drilled and disciplined in operations of this kind.

On arrival, deplaning has to be done fast and in a pre-arranged and well-practiced order, with the troops forming a pre-set defensive position as soon as their feet are on the ground. This is just in case their arrival has been anticipated, the landing zone is targetted and there is a well-armed 'welcoming' party.

Military helicopters can assume an offensive role too. Armed with anti-tank missiles, rockets and heavy-calibre MGs they can hit a ground target very hard and keep the defenders' heads down while the assaulting infantry do their job. The US Army uses the Hughes Apache and the Bell Cobra for this role and their armament is detailed as well as the tactics their crews employ to knock-out pre-selected targets. This chapter also talks about how such an operation is planned to take into account hazards such as AA installations.

Joint operations, action between different sections of the forces or cooperative work while acting as spotters for artillery or knocking out AFVs holding up an advance, are ideal jobs for the choppers. A feature covers this kind of military support, and the chapter closes on yet another prime role for the helicopter – combat rescue. Once the exact site is identified, the machine can hedge-hop and hug the ground on its way to pick up a pilot or wounded soldier and get them back to base, while fighter cover hovers above.

The military para-rescueman has an important part to play. Not only is he well qualified in advanced first-aid, he is a trained fighting soldier as well.

In the campaigns of not too long ago, often desperately wounded soldiers had to lie out on the shattered battlefield and had nothing to sustain them but the hope that some kind of help would eventually arrive. Today things are very different, first aid treatment is carried out very soon after an engagement and any serious cases are soon back in a base hospital getting the full benefit of the sophisticated level of modern medicine.

FLYING THE EAGLE PATROL

An RAF Puma swoops low over the countryside, keeping within 15 metres of the ground to avoid shoulder-launched anti-aircraft missiles. The Eagle Patrol will be landed to set up a surprise road block on an isolated road, which will catch the terrorists unawares.

Eagle Patrols are the name given by the British Army to the technique used in an IS situation in which patrols are inserted by helicopter to mount a snap road block or ambush. They are usually in reaction to something the patrol commander has seen from the air himself or something that has happened within flying distance since the patrol has been airborne. In this sort of situation the helicopter gives the patrol the advantages of surprise, flexibility and speed of reaction.

Versatile deployment

Modern helicopters have a good radius of action and effective communications. Only very bad weather or exceptionally high terrain are likely to impede your movement in a heli-copter. You can strike in any direction, you can deploy reserves quickly, you can cut the enemy off during a pursuit and you can carry out detailed air reconnaissance and observation.

Night flying

What is more, you can operate efficiently in a modern helicopter at night as well. You will need to fly at higher altitudes than by day to avoid obstructions, and usually some sort of landing aid is required though this need only be in the form of a basic layout of lights.

Eagle Patrols at night are difficult because of the random nature of landing sites, but they may be possible in good weather conditions using helicopter searchlights as a landing aid.

Below: A section in Northern Ireland with a Wessex helicopter in the background. By inserting heli-borne troops into rural areas the Army makes it more difficult for terrorists to transport arms and ammunition.

For all their advantages, helicopters are intricate pieces of machinery. They are vulnerable to SAMs (Surface-to-Air Missiles), small arms fire and artillery fire, especially when on the ground. The pilot himself is very vulnerable and in operational areas he wears a nylon armoured vest and sits in an armoured seat.

Low and fast

The best way for a helicopter to avoid either small arms fire or SAMs is to fly low and fast. In Northern Ireland helicopters have remained remark-

Above: Many rural roads in Northern Ireland are so easily mined that road travel is prohibitively dangerous. Here, Army transport lies wrecked after command-detonated bombs caught several vehicles.

Above: Permanent Observation Posts near the border with the Irish Republic are usually supplied by air because of the danger of road travel.

Find Report
This should include:
1. The date and time of the find.
2. Location of find.
3. A detailed description of the hiding place.
4. A detailed description of what you have found.
5. Why you conducted the search.
6. Details of any arrests.
7. Any follow-up actions you have initiated.

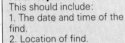

Deployment
Time on the ground or in the hover must be kept to a minimum. Speed is essential; the patrol should be off the chopper and down in all-round defence in less than the time it takes a terrorist to get to a weapon, acquire a target and fire an aimed shot.

Vulnerability
Movement by air is a good deal safer than by road in the real bandit country of South Armagh, where PIRA have had considerable success with massive command-detonated land mines etc. Helicopters are themselves very vulnerable to ground fire; Wessex, Puma, and Lynx are not armoured and rely on the tactical flying skill of their pilots to avoid small arms fire.

Weapons
Be careful: they may be booby trapped. Do not clear them; contact an RUC or RMP Finds Team.

Action on a find
If you find anything suspicious, do not touch it. Think about the possibility of a covert operation (this may not be practicable), make sure the area is clear and secure it, keep everyone away from the scene, and, finally, tell your HQ.

EAGLE PATROL

Eagle patrols can react quickly to short-term intelligence and are ideal for snap vehicle check points, cordon and search operations and inserting the QRF (Quick Reaction Force). Helicopters provide commanders with immense flexibility and speed of reaction.

The border
South Armagh is a largely rural area with many isolated farms, derelict buildings, and a population indifferent if not actively hostile to the Security Forces. This, coupled with the proximity of the border, provides an excellent environment for terrorist activity.

Assessing the situation
Once the area is secure you have to think about what help you need: If you have found an IED (Improvised Explosive Device) you will need an ATO (Ammunition Technical Officer) or a Royal Engineer search adviser. You may need dogs, engineer digging equipment, a photographer, RE diving team, or even a community relations officer.

Searching
Farms provide many hiding places for weapons and explosives and are notoriously difficult to search – especially dairy farms, which have underground storage for manure.

Suspects
These should be searched, restrained, segregated and handed over to the RUC as soon as possible. Prisoners must be signed for when they are handed over to the police.

ably immune – their tolerance to several hits is considerable.

Although some have been forced to land by damage caused by small arms fire, few have been 'shot down'. Where, however, terrorists or guerrillas have managed to obtain hand-held surface-to-air missile systems, such as the Soviet designed SA-7 'Grail', helicopters have been brought down: there is photographic evidence of successful engagements of Soviet helicopters in Afghanistan by the Mujahideen.

The counter to the SA-7 is to fly at 15 metres or less, so that the operator

does not have sufficient time to acquire his target, fire the missile and achieve lock-on with the infra-red heat-seeking system during the brief exposure time of the target.

Army Air Corps

If you are going to operate with helicopters you must be familiar with the different types in use with the Army Air Corps and the RAF and you must understand their requirements. The Puma and the Wessex are the two helicopter types in the RAF that are most suitable for 'Eagle Patrols': they are twin-engined transport helicopters

An Eagle Patrol airborne in a Wessex helicopter in Northern Ireland. Women are included to search any female drivers stopped by the patrol.

A GPMG gunner gets into position to cover the rest of the patrol while they organise the 'snap' vehicle checkpoint. You must never forget all-round defence when on Internal Security operations.

The Wessex climbs back into the sky after dropping off the patrol: helicopters are at their most vulnerable when on the ground, so it is essential that you disembark swiftly.

that are capable of carrying 12-16 fully armed and equipped troops. The Army Air Corps Lynx, though it only carries eight men, can also be used in this role. If you are operating with any of these types, you may be responsible for choosing a suitable landing site or LS for your helicopter. The ground should be reasonably even and solid if the helicopter is going to land rather than hover. All solid obstacles, loose items and inflammable material must be cleared from the site: the term 'cleared to ground level' is used to indicate the requirement.

If ground obstructions cannot be cleared, you can embark and disembark your patrol without the helicopter actually landing. However, your chosen LS should still offer as good an approach as possible and suf-

ficient room for the pilot to manoeuvre on and around the LS. But because of the relatively high engine power required during hovering, loading and unloading is best carried out with the helicopter actually on the ground.

Pilot's decision

Obviously in an emergency situation, such as an urgent casualty evacuation, pilots are prepared to land or hover in far from ideal circumstances. The pilot will decide himself whether a landing is feasible.

Once you have met up with your helicopter you will then need to get your patrol on board. As patrol leader you should kneel by the door of the helicopter and count your patrol into the helicopter. Get in last and sit by the open door. That way you can see out and you will know where you are and what is going on.

Beware the blades

Remember to brief everybody to crouch as they run in towards the helicopter, nor should anybody move towards the helicopter until the pilot gives the 'thumbs up'. Windy conditions can make the rotors dip low and there have been terrible accidents with rotating helicopter blades decapitating unwary passengers.

Once the helicopter is airborne you will fly to your planned area of operations. It is then up to you and the heli-

The marshaller should stay in cover until he hears the helicopter approaching. He should wear the fluorescent panel under his combat jacket and flash it at the helicopter as it appears. Stick commanders must have prepared plates to give to the crewman, containing radio frequency, callsign and grid references of the LS and dummy LS (landing sites).

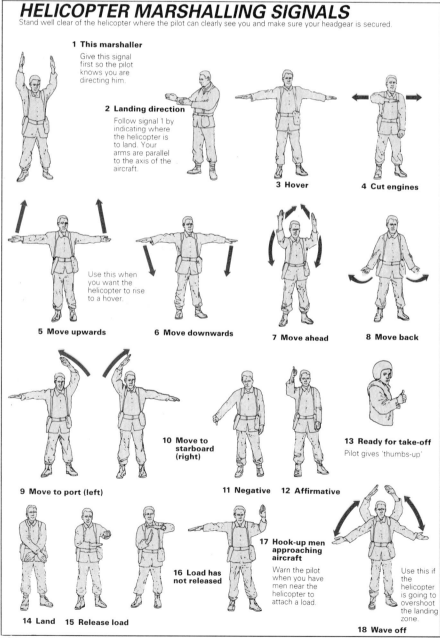

HELICOPTER MARSHALLING SIGNALS
Stand well clear of the helicopter where the pilot can clearly see you and make sure your headgear is secured.

1 This marshaller
Give this signal first so the pilot knows you are directing him.

2 Landing direction
Follow signal 1 by indicating where the helicopter is to land. Your arms are parallel to the axis of the aircraft.

3 Hover

4 Cut engines

5 Move upwards
Use this when you want the helicopter to rise to a hover.

6 Move downwards

7 Move ahead

8 Move back

9 Move to port (left)

10 Move to starboard (right)

11 Negative

12 Affirmative

13 Ready for take-off
Pilot gives 'thumbs-up'

14 Land

15 Release load

16 Load has not released

17 Hook-up men approaching aircraft
Warn the pilot when you have men near the helicopter to attach a load.

18 Wave off
Use this if the helicopter is going to overshoot the landing zone.

copter pilot who will be talking to you over the intercom to select a likely target – probably a suspicious looking car on a lonely stretch of country road – and to swoop down ahead of it and mount an instant vehicle check.

Surprise landing

The trick is to use the contours so that your suspect does not see you landing ahead of him; in that way he will suddenly round a bend and find a snap roadblock where he least expects it. Your helicopter will drop you and then immediately take off and loiter somewhere safe rather than present a static target on the ground. As soon as you have carried out your check you can recall the helicopter on the radio, resume your patrol and repeat the process somewhere else.

Your tasks on the ground need not be confined to mounting snap vehicle check points. You may be dropped in a particular location to mount an ambush or act as a cut-off party in a larger operation. Once you are on the ground the same rules apply for your road block as if you were operating in a vehicle or foot patrol.

Instant tracking

The great advantage of mounting a road block from a helicopter is, if someone does evade or crash through your roadblock the helicopter will be instantly available to track the car.

Once you have carried out your vehicle check you can call in your helicopter and move on to the next task. If sufficient helicopters are available Eagle Patrols are a cost-effective

If you are commanding an Eagle Patrol your place is in the doorway with the helicopter crewman. Count your men into the helicopter and enter last. Observe the ground below as you fly to the operational area.

and efficient method of dominating a large rural area with limited resources. If you carry out an Eagle Patrol in bandit country, remember the rules associated with working with helicopters: keep your wits about you, and remember that the car you decide to stop and check from the air may be carrying terrorists.

Eagle Patrols work in close association with troops already on the ground, and can be used to insert a roadblock ahead of a civilian vehicle that has avoided existing checkpoints.

HELICOPTER ASSAULT TACTICS

The cabin of a troop-carrying helicopter going into battle is a confusing place. The noise is truly ear-shattering, and every available space is cluttered with essential equipment and a jostling crowd of excited men keyed up to fever pitch. Time after time heliborne operations ('heliops') have proved their worth in anti-terrorist and counter-insurgency campaigns.

This article on helicopter operations shows how the South African Defence Force uses helicopters as combat and support craft in anti-terrorist operations.

The helicopter's main strength in combat is its ability to get troops into areas that they could otherwise reach only on foot, perhaps after days of cross-country marching. It gets them there so quickly that a successful operation can be mounted before the enemy has any idea that they're aware of his presence.

Because airborne operations take place at such high speed, it's extra-important that each member of the air-crew and the airborne troop knows exactly what he has to do at all times. Helicopters are expensive to operate –

every hour of flight costs many hundreds of pounds – and have only a short radius of action.

Know your job

Helicopter drill has two purposes: to cut down time wasted through mistakes; and to make sure that both aircraft and personnel stay as safe as

possible. There are no short cuts. Everyone concerned has to do things

Fire Force in action: South African soldiers fly into action aboard an Aérospatiale Puma helicopter. They are kept on standby to launch instant attacks on terrorist gangs the moment they are discovered by patrols, hidden observers or aerial reconnaissance.

STICK LEADER'S PRE-FLIGHT DUTIES

As the leader of the stick, you must make a series of checks before the helicopter is airborne. Once in the air you use the spare headset to communicate with the pilots and keep an eye on the ground over which you will be operating.

1. Brief the men on the signals that will be used during emplaning and deplaning.
2. Ensure that everyone has taken off their caps or jungle hats.
3. Check that no one is loosely carrying equipment such as water bottles, machetes, ammunition pouches etc.
4. Make sure that all straps on packs and equipment are tucked away.
5. Remove the aerials from the radios and stow them away.
6. Check that weapon slings are tight, carrying handles folded down and that bayonets are not fixed.
7. Check that all weapons safety precautions have been observed.

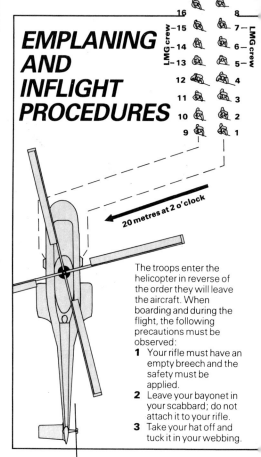

20 metres at 2 o'clock

The troops enter the helicopter in reverse of the order they will leave the aircraft. When boarding and during the flight, the following precautions must be observed:

1 Your rifle must have an empty breech and the safety must be applied.
2 Leave your bayonet in your scabbard; do not attach it to your rifle.
3 Take your hat off and tuck it in your webbing.

exactly by the book. When the order comes to start a heliborne operation, the stick leader must make sure that each member of the team knows his place and what to do immediately after leaving the aircraft. He should form his squad up in the reverse of the order they will leave the aircraft. Then he waits for the pilot's signal to emplane – a clear nod of the head and a thumbs-up sign, for example. When in the helicopter it is vital that no infantryman interferes with the crew, and that no one touches any of the controls.

Overwhelming noise

The noise in a helicopter is quite deafening. The stick leader should always put on the spare headset so that he can communicate with the pilot and any other crew members.

Weapons safety, at all times, is vitally important. A round fired off by accident could hit a vital piece of machinery and cost the life of everyone aboard. For this reason weapons must be carried with the breech cleared. On those rare occasions when the stick has to come out of the aircraft fighting, then the weapon can be charged and cocked, but the safety must be on, to make it impossible to loose off a round by accident. Because of the cramped conditions, bayonets should never in any circumstances be fixed on board.

The man in charge

The pilot is in command of the aircraft at all times. He is responsible for it, and for every person on board. His commands must be obeyed immediately. He alone decides how many men can be carried, and when and how they will enter and leave the aircraft. For operational reasons, he transmits his orders through the stick commander.

The stick commander also has his

Troops relax en route to the landing zone in the operational area up-country in southern Africa. The mood will soon change once they've landed in a hostile area.

own responsibilities. These are mainly to do with the safety of his men and how they behave in the aircraft, but he must also pay attention to the ground they are above, looking for possible future landing sites, useful terrain features such as sources of fresh water and potential defensive positions, and, of course, signs of the enemy.

Contact!

The real strength of heliborne counter-insurgency operations is the speed with which they can be mounted. Experience of actual operations has

shown SADF that concealed static observation posts are much more effective in gathering intelligence about enemy movements than mobile patrols. A patrol moving cross-country gives itself away very easily, especially by being seen and reported to guerrillas by civilian sympathisers. These static OPs must be in constant

LANDING ZONE PROCEDURES

Just as counter-insurgency troops rely on the helicopter crew to get them safely in and out of the battle, the pilot and crew depend on the men on the ground to carry out certain tasks.

Clearing and marking the LZ is the most important job. A heavily-laden helicopter can't land or take off straight up and down. When it's full of cargo or passengers, it behaves more like

an ordinary aircraft, and must land and take off at a shallow angle. A track must be cleared so that the pilot can bring the aircraft safely into and out of the LZ.

Another advantage the helicopter does have over fixed-wing aircraft, however, is that it is much less influenced by the wind direction when landing and at take-off. Instead of having to head into the wind at take-off, the

helicopter pilot has a wider choice: he only has to pay attention to wind direction when it's really strong. This in turn makes the ground crew's job a lot easier – the same LZ can be used in all sorts of conditions.

At night the LZ must be marked with lights. Five is the best number, arranged in the shape of a T, with the top bar into the wind if this is important. Otherwise the bar will be opposite the shallowest possible approach path.

Battery torches are a good source of light. They should be placed 10 metres apart, with the beams shining up at an angle of

Puma landing zone

To land safely, a Puma helicopter needs a landing zone at least 50 metres in diameter, with a central area 35 metres in diameter cleared to ground level. At the centre of the LZ there must be a hard surface 15 metres in diameter.

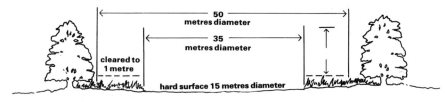

HAND SIGNALS

The noise inside a helicopter makes voice communications practically impossible so hand signals are used:

Emplaning signal (day): Pilot or crew member gives the thumbs up or vigorously nods his head. It is now safe to approach the helicopter (in a stooped attitude, to avoid the rotors).

Emplaning signal (night): Intermittent flashing of the helicopter navigation lights.

Do not emplane yet: Pilot or crew member raises open right hand with the palm outwards.

Some members of the stick to emplane: Pilot or crew member extends a number of fingers indicating how many men are to board the helicopter.

Prepare to deplane: Pilot or crew member motions with his left hand.

Target direction: This is indicated by the pilot or crew member pointing.

Deplane: Pilot or crew member nods his head vigorously. You must now exit the plane in the pre-arranged order as fast as you can.

SEATING PLAN

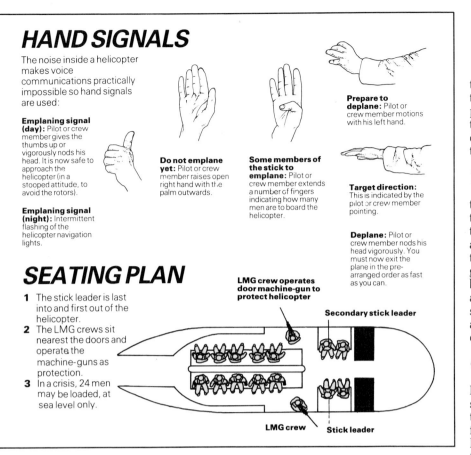

1. The stick leader is last into and first out of the helicopter.
2. The LMG crews sit nearest the doors and operate the machine-guns as protection.
3. In a crisis, 24 men may be loaded, at sea level only.

LMG crew operates door machine-gun to protect helicopter

Secondary stick leader

LMG crew

Stick leader

radio contact with the operational base.

When a report of terrorist activity comes in, it should be only a matter of moments before assault troops are called together for a briefing. This will include all the essential information about the contact: map reference, a short report of the circumstances, the number of assault troops required, whether they are to be supported by helicopter gunships or other air strikes, how they are to approach the target, rendezvous (RV) position with troops already on the ground, and the radio frequencies, call signs and passwords that are to be used for the operation.

All this can be accomplished in the time it takes the aircrews to warm up the helicopters and carry out their pre-launch checks. Within minutes, the assault sticks can be out on the dispersal point, waiting for the signal to emplane.

Troop commander

The troop commander always travels in the helicopter gunship. If there is no gunship support, he has to travel in the lead troop carrier. Where a gunship is involved in the operation, it must be possible for friendly ground forces to identify it easily. The best way to achieve this is by means of a series of smoke grenades, tied to the step or undercarriage of the gunship, and triggered by the troop commander.

Going in to land

When the assault force arrives at the RV, contact with the forces who have spotted the enemy will make sure that the commander has up-to-date information about the guerrillas' behaviour. While the troop carriers orbit the RV on a high and wide course, the ship carrying the troop commander goes in low, so that he can see the enemy disposition for himself. The observers in the static OP should have reported the presence of any anti-aircraft weaponry with the guerrilla band, and the troop commander must bear this in mind when deciding how close to the enemy he can get. Where

---

between 30 and 40 degrees. Because the helicopter's main rotor generates a very powerful down-draught, the torches must be partly buried in the ground, to prevent them being blown over.

If there are more than five torches to hand, the number of individual lights is not increased. Instead, two torches are used at each location, one angled as before, the other pointing straight up into the sky.

Other light sources can be used instead of torches. Hurricane lamps or pressure lamps are both good enough and, as a last resort, sand in an open-ended tin can be soaked with a gallon of petrol and set alight. The helicopter pilot will bring his craft to land slightly to the left of the three lights that form the vertical line of the T, so the lights are best placed slightly to the right of centre of the LZ.

In an emergency, vehicle headlamps can be used to mark the LZ. Parked at the edge of the cleared area, the vehicles should be between 20 and 25 metres apart, and angled at 45 degrees so that their headlights meet in the centre of the landing zone. The aircraft will approach them from behind, and come in between the vehicles, so they must not have radio aerials sticking up.

Night landing

To guide a helicopter onto the landing zone at night, lay out five lights in a 'T' shape pointing into the wind. Lights can be either lamps dug into the ground or torches pointing towards the direction the helicopter will be coming from. Put each light 10 paces apart.

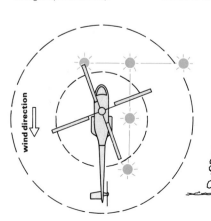

wind direction

approach path

Vehicle-lit emergency night landing zone

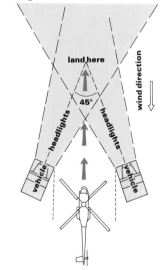

land here

45°

wind direction

headlights

headlights

vehicle

vehicle

Position two vehicles 25 metres apart and facing into the wind. Turn them slightly towards each other so that the intersection of their headlights forms an angle of 45°. This will be the helicopter's landing point.

Troops must exit or enter the helicopter at incredible speed: in one operation in Angola, paratroopers had to clamber on board while under fire from a Cuban tank!

DEPLANING PROCEDURE

The troops must exit the helicopter as fast as possible, throwing packs out of the door and assuming an all-round defensive position. The two machine-gun (LMG) crews must exit first to provide covering fire for the rest of the stick. Normally the helicopter will land to emplane or deplane personnel but over long grass, bushes or uneven terrain, men and equipment are dropped while the helicopter hovers at between 1.2 and 1.8 m. In order to prevent the aircraft from rocking too much when the troops depart from a hovering helicopter they must not leap out sideways, but drop straight to the ground from the steps provided.

5,6,7 LMG Crew

12

16

8

Secondary Stick leader 9

1 Stick leader

10

2

11

3

LMG Crew 13,14,15

DANGER ZONE 60°

4

possible, the gunship should go in close to soften up the enemy with strafing fire before troops go in on the ground.

On the troop commander's signal, the transports will come down to prearranged positions in the LZ (landing zone). Where possible, they will touch down, but over rougher terrain such as long grass or badly broken

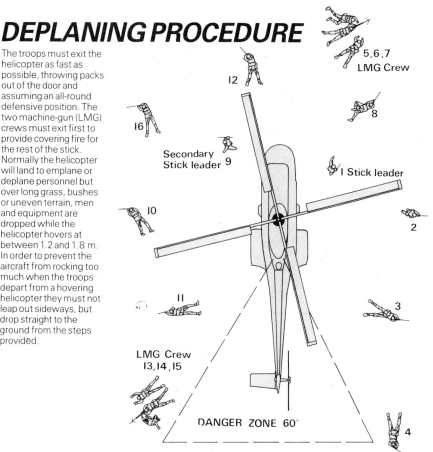

Aérospatiale Puma
The Puma is one of the main helicopters used by the South African Defence Force. It flies at treetop height to avoid anti-aircraft fire, which now includes heat seeking SA-7 missiles supplied by the Soviet Union.

Troopers and their kit
Each stick (helicopter-load of troops) must be prepared for an extended period of operations on the ground, pursuing and fighting the terrorists. In the dense bush it is easy for a stick to become isolated, so it must be able to communicate, navigate and defend itself against superior enemy forces. The stick leader should have a ground/air radio, a map, compass and protractor plus mini-flare and heliograph. The men must have rations and bedding for prolonged operations but should otherwise be lightly equipped. Everyone should carry a torch, as patrolling often involves searching native huts. In case the stick bumps into a large concentration of terrorists it must include at least one gun group with a light machine-gun.

ground they will stay in a low hover, one or two metres above the ground. Troops must be prepared to jump out, making sure they have all their equipment with them, and being careful not to upset the aircraft in the process – something that happens all too easily to a hovering helicopter. Unless they are in hot pursuit, with the enemy in sight, troops will make a defensive ring around the aircraft. Each trooper knows his position in the defensive structure, and goes to it without being told.

Trying to hide

Rather than try to run for it, insurgents may choose instead to go to ground, hoping to escape by hiding. This is especially true in open country. This means that pursuing forces have to be prepared to mount lengthy search operations whenever they are sent in to eliminate a guerrilla group. This causes a number of problems: it becomes necessary to re-supply with rations, to carry bedding and survival equipment and to have enough weaponry and ammunition for every conceivable circumstance.

In search and tracking operations, the fighting forces also need the help and support of specialists – especially intelligence officers and dogs and men trained in search and tracking techniques. The helicopter is the usual means of transport for these, to get the right people into the right place in the shortest possible time.

As soon as the ground forces have been deployed from the aircraft, most of the helicopters will return to the nearest defended supply base, where

The Rhodesians pioneered the Fire Force System, although their resources were very limited. This is an Alouette III spotting for a mortar shoot against an enemy position.

they can be immediately refuelled and made ready to return to the combat zone. One or two craft will remain within a very short flight-time of the ground forces, to be available to move troops from place to place within the combat zone if this becomes necessary.

Fire Force

The Fire Force technique uses helicopter-borne troops to launch surprise attacks on terrorist groups. The troops are kept at instant readiness so that the moment a terrorist group is detected in the operational zone, troops can be airborne and on their way. Aircraft and helicopter gunships are used to soften up landing zones before the vulnerable troop-carrying helicopters come in to land.

Stick leader
During flight, the stick leader's job is to communicate with the aircrew, look out for enemy movement on the ground and to build up a mental picture of possible landing zones, dropping zones and watering holes that might be of use on this or future missions.

ATTACK!
ATTACK!
ATTACK!

When the first attack helicopters poked their ugly, gun-loaded noses over the Vietnamese horizon in the early days of the war in South East Asia, the Viet Cong and NVA units they decimated could not have known that they were experiencing the first taste of a weapon that would change the face of battle.

Now one of the US Army's primary anti-tank weapon systems, the AH-64 Apache is the most powerful helicopter gunship in NATO. Swooping low across the battlefield, flying and fighting with an attack helicopter demands the skills of a tank crew and the quick reactions of a flier.

The gunner sits in front of the pilot and operates the gunship's weapons using a helmet-mounted sight. The crew compartment is armoured and will protect you even if the helicopter is shot down.

Carrying anti-tank missiles (ATMs), line-of-sight rockets and heavy rapid-firing machine-guns, and capable of a speed of almost 200 mph yet able to turn in not much more than its own length, the modern attack helicopter not only reaches the targets that other gear cannot reach – it destroys them, too.

Gunships

The early attack helicopters were known as helicopter gunships, which reflected the way in which they were armed and operated. Using modified infantry machine-guns mounted in the nose, in belly pods and in the open doorways, they went looking for detachments of enemy infantry in much the same way as a fast patrol boat would scout around for suitable targets.

All this changed with the development of light, accurate guided missiles capable of destroying Main Battle

ANATOMY OF A GUNSHIP

The US Army uses two types of helicopter gunship, the Hughes AH-64 Apache and the older Bell AH-1 Cobra

APACHE
Armoured against weapons up to 23mm cannon, the Apache is designed for battlefield survivability as well as great offensive power.

COBRA
Armed with TOW missiles the Cobra was the first purpose built gunship and performed very well in Vietnam.

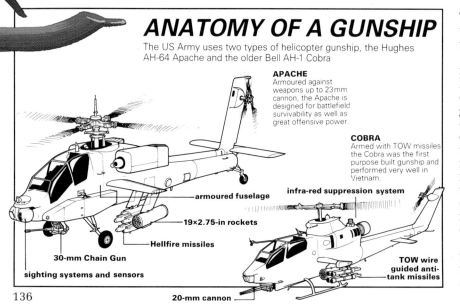

armoured fuselage

infra-red suppression system

19×2.75-in rockets

Hellfire missiles

30-mm Chain Gun

sighting systems and sensors

TOW wire guided anti-tank missiles

20-mm cannon

Tanks and other heavily-armoured vehicles and fortified ground positions at ranges of a mile or more.

With the change of the helicopter's role from infantry hunter to tank killer, there came a profound change of tactics. Gone were the days of lone gunships going out on search-and-destroy missions. Instead, the helicopter pilot's job came more and more to resemble that of the tank commander – operating in teams, giving mutual support from covered positions, overwatching advances, hull-down concealment, and movement from place to place using every scrap of natural cover and protection.

All the operational manuals – and this section is taken from the US FM 17-50, Attack Helicopter Operations – stress the need for the aircraft to be

HELICOPTER ATTACK

In combat you have little time to plan your attack and the distribution of your fire. This is the sort of engagement order you can expect: "Attack enemy forces in Engagement Area Bravo from Battle Positions Two, Three and Four."

Front and rear
When you attack an enemy column from both sides, the attack from the right goes against the rear of the enemy and shifts its fire towards the middle while the left flanking element starts from the front.

Target allocation
The attack element leader decides the weapons mix and the allocation of individual targets to individual helicopters, following your SOPs.

Long-range attack
Attack helicopters keep spread out but pointed towards the enemy forces. You attack from the longest range possible, making maximum use of cover and concealment.

Beyond enemy range
Long-range engagement may allow you to attack enemy tanks beyond the effective range of the ZSU 23-4 self-propelled anti-aircraft guns which accompany them.

KW

Moving fire inwards
Modern anti-tank guided weapons whether laser- or wire-guided, cannot criss-cross the battlefield without getting their guidance systems hopelessly tangled. Outside elements of the attack force should engage outside elements of the enemy and move their fire inwards towards the enemy centre.

Right and left
When the attack is to come from one flank, the element on the left of your force attacks targets to its front and works towards the left of the enemy column. The right-hand element attacks the enemy to its front and then works to the right of the enemy column.

Target indication
Target indication is similar to that used by infantrymen: you use obvious terrain features as reference points and identify enemy units by their position relative to them. However, you must give a compass bearing from the reference point since helicopters could be approaching the target from any direction.

ATTACK PRIORITIES

Standard operational procedure (SOP) lays down two ways of deciding in which order targets are to be attacked: **Target Priority** and **Engagement Priority.**

Target Priority is the order in which different types of target are to be engaged:
1 Air defence artillery
2 Attack helicopters (if they are a direct threat)
3 Command tanks
4 Other tanks
5 Command and control vehicles
6 Anti-tank vehicles
7 Direct artillery fire
8 Mechanized troop carriers
9 Troop concentrations

The second method, **Engagement Priority**, is a sort of sub-group of the first set, depending on:
1 Immediate threat to yourself
2 Immediate threat to other platoon members
3 Immediate threat to other friendly forces
4 Other targets of opportunity

Widespread use of armed helicopters dates from the Vietnam War, when utility helicopters like this Bell UH-1 were fitted with a variety of improvised weapon fits: in this case a pair of Browning .30-cal machine-guns.

used aggressively. 'Seize, retain and exploit the initiative', they tell you, time and time again until it's second nature.

These new tactics mean that you have to learn a new repertoire of low-level flying techniques. Contour following is the less terrifying of the two methods. Plotting a course in something like a straight line, you adjust your altitude to keep a constant height above ground.

Ground level
Hedge-hopping, it used to be called; but the fixed-wing pilots who coined that phrase in World War II would have a collective heart attack if they saw the lengths that modern attack helicopter pilots go to. You really do hop hedges — and trees, garden sheds and even low walls, so close to the ground do you fly.

Even closer to the ragged edge is a technique called Nap-of-the-Earth

(NOE). To fly NOE, you use the same ground-hugging manoeuvres as in straightforward contour-following flying, but you fly a meandering course that makes use of every scrap of cover – a country lane, for example, where there are hedges to hide the main body

of the aircraft, the rotor blades skimming their tops. Or down the bed of a river wide enough for the tips of the blades to clear the trees on each side.

Helicopters such as the AH-1 Cobra and AH-64 Apache, along with the fixed-wing A-10 Thunderbolt II tank-buster, are the mainstay of US ground support operations. Masterpieces of technological sophistication, their computer-controlled Target Acquisition and Designation System/Pilot Night Vision Sensor (TADS/PNVS) allows the crew of pilot and gunner to find and lock onto targets in unbelievably bad visibility.

Computer control

The weapons system, fully integrated into the TADS computer and capable of being operated by voice alone, is just as advanced. Fire-and-forget missiles, rockets, and the 30 mm quick-firing cannon combine to give just one relatively small helicopter the sort of fire power that could previously only be amassed by a squadron of tanks.

And compared with other military aircraft of similar performance, the US attack helicopters *are* small – the overall length of the AH-1 is 13 metres, only two-thirds that of the Mi-24 'Hind', the Soviet Bloc's nearest equivalent. It's narrow, too – because the pilot and gunner sit in tandem, the overall width can be kept down to just one metre across the cockpit: a very hard target to hit under battlefield conditions.

Even if you do receive incoming fire

from ground forces, there's a good chance not only that you will survive, but that you'll be able to continue with your mission. All the vulnerable parts of attack helicopters are fitted with

Because you sit in tandem in the AH-64 Apache the helicopter presents a very narrow target to the enemy, and by hugging the ground as you fly across the battlefield you further reduce the enemy's chances of bringing you down.

titanium armour. Light in weight but very strong, this recently-introduced material is capable of stopping small-arms fire of all types, including that from the 12.7 mm heavy machine-gun.

Finding the target

Scouting and reconnaissance are not carried out by the attack helicopter; it's not equipped for that purpose. This job is the province of small, fast, scout craft, fitted out to spot and mark targets for the attacking aircraft. When the scouting detachment has identified a target and made its report to the area commander, it performs a local holding action, co-ordinating whatever force is available in the area.

It also gathers local intelligence, ready to pass an accurate situation report to the attack helicopters when they arrive at the pre-designated holding area. This holding area will be just minutes' flying time away from the target, but in a secure location that

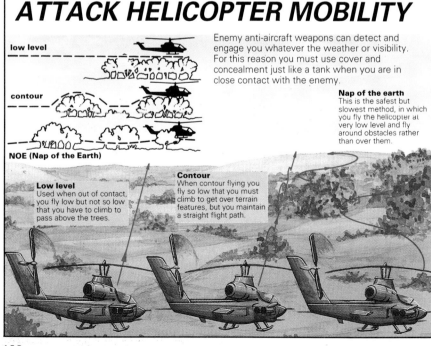

ATTACK HELICOPTER MOBILITY

low level

contour

NOE (Nap of the Earth)

Enemy anti-aircraft weapons can detect and engage you whatever the weather or visibility. For this reason you must use cover and concealment just like a tank when you are in close contact with the enemy.

Nap of the earth
This is the safest but slowest method, in which you fly the helicopter at very low level and fly around obstacles rather than over them.

Low level
Used when out of contact, you fly low but not so low that you have to climb to pass above the trees.

Contour
When contour flying you fly so low that you must climb to get over terrain features, but you maintain a straight flight path.

offers cover and concealment.

The attack and scout force commanders will use this information, constantly updated, to prepare a plan of action. To achieve surprise, the attack helicopter pilot uses all his skill and the flying aids at his command to get into an attack position unseen. By this stage the attack force will have split into two elements, in order to provide mutual 'fire and movement' protection.

Target position

As soon as you reach the attack position, you'll be notified of 'target handover' by the scout force commander, who has been responsible for the action until this point. Now you take your first quick look at the target, a procedure called 'partial unmasking'. This usually requires you to gain height until you can see over the tree-tops, record the scene in front of you with the TADS built-in video-recorder, and then return to concealment.

The sophisticated computer software then allows you to choose a target, unmask completely, acquire the chosen target, designate a weapons sub-system, and fire the weapon – all in less time than it takes for enemy anti-aircraft defences to line you up.

The first element of the attack force will fire two or three missiles in this way. The second element observes, looking especially carefully for anti-aircraft fire, which it will immediately suppress. Then the second element uses its main armament on any target

still in action while the first element is changing position.

The massive firepower and short time-on-target capabilities of the attack helicopter platoon give the ground forces commander a better chance of securing local superiority quickly than he's ever had before. So it would be very tempting to call down an attack helicopter strike at every opportunity, but, sure enough, sod's law will ensure that there is never enough of anything to go round, and so the doctrine of economy of force has evolved.

Economy of Force

Attack helicopter and air cavalry (heliborne infantry) are among the most effective 'economy of force' units

The Apache's arsenal: Hellfire missiles, pods containing 19 2.75-in unguided rockets, and a 30-mm Chain Gun with 1,200 rounds. An AH-64 is more expensive than a Soviet tank and must be able to destroy large numbers of hostile AFVs.

available – a little goes a long way! The ground commander must learn never to use the air strike capability where conventional ground forces can do the job, and, where he does use it, to use it decisively. Ground forces must always be in a position to use the advantages handed to them as a result of the attack helicopters' efforts. At the same time, the ground force commander must do everything in his power to guarantee the helicopter force's security.

FIRING THE HELLFIRE

The Hellfire missile homes in on a tank 'illuminated' by a laser beam from another helicopter or a soldier on the ground. This enables you to strike at the enemy without them seeing you and taking defensive action.

3 The missile will home in on the target being illuminated by the laser beam, and you can pop back into cover.

2 You pop up from behind a clump of trees and fire a Hellfire missile.

4 So long as the scout helicopter can continue to point the laser at the tank, the missile will hit and blow it to pieces. The scout has not fired any weapons, so its position is not betrayed by any telltale flash.

1 A scout helicopter aims a laser beam at an enemy tank.

ON THE OFFENSIVE

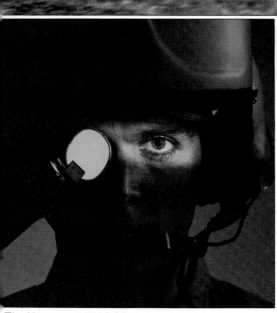

The Honeywell **IHADSS** (Integrated Helmet and Display Sight System) has an electro-optical system which provides flight information and data on targets in the glass over your right eye.

You have to move fast in attack, especially when you're at the controls of an attack helicopter. You've got the firepower, you've got the range, the endurance, the speed and manoeuvrability. Top that off with your own hunting instincts, and the whole package adds up to one of the most formidable weapons on the modern field of battle.

Attacking a defended position when the enemy knows you're coming is an expensive and dangerous business. The defender has great advantages: the main one is that he has chosen the place.

Pick your moment

But he has a big disadvantage, too – he doesn't choose the time. You do. And you make sure that you use that edge to the best possible effect by concentrating your combat power at the points where the defence is weakest.

By using surprise, concentration of forces and out-and-out aggression, an attack can succeed even though the odds may be against it. Attack helicopters are the best possible vehicle for this sort of offensive.

Tailor your movement to the terrain, using concealment techniques like contour following and Nap-of-the-Earth (NOE) flying. Use supporting fire and suppression techniques, but above all, know your enemy. How is he equipped? What is his main threat? How well does he use the kit he's got?

These things add up to the effective range of his anti-aircraft fire. If the

Suppressing the enemy with a hail of 70-mm rockets, an AH-64 Apache swoops in to the attack. In offensive operations one of the main missions of the attack helicopter is to gain or re-establish contact with fast-moving enemy forces. This demands rapid movement, decentralised control and the ability to organise hasty attacks against opportunity targets.

effective range of your offensive weapons is greater than that, then you've got him – but only if you do everything just right.

You may be involved in five main types of offensive operations:

1 Movement to contact
2 Hasty attack
3 Deliberate attack
4 Exploitation
5 Pursuit

These operations tend to follow on, one from another, but you have to keep flexible. At any stage you must be ready to back up and consolidate in the face of effective opposition, or skip a stage or two and turn a static situation into a running chase.

Movement to contact

Often, you may not know exactly where the enemy forces are situated. You can find them by sending out reconnaissance patrols, but often it's more effective to move a considerable force forward until contact is made – it's quicker, and you gain ground as you go.

But because it involves rapid movement and decentralisation of command and control, it can lead to disorganisation and reduce the attack force's ability to fight effectively unless communications function really well.

One thing you can be sure of in a multi-million-pound attack helicopter is top quality communications hardware, and that's just one of the reasons why a helicopter force is often at the forefront of a movement-to-contact operation.

The attack helicopter company commander must establish FARPs (Forward Arming and Refuelling Points) able to resupply five attack and three scout helicopters simultaneously.

Find the enemy's weak spots. Use the best combination of friendly forces to mount the attack. Maintain security. Strike a balance between control and aggression. Now move! Seizing the initiative early will give you the best chance of catching the enemy off balance.

ASSEMBLY AREAS AND HOLDING AREAS

In the rear of the fighting front, far enough back to be out of range of enemy medium artillery, the attack helicopter units will establish an assembly area where they can rest and resupply.

The closer to the fighting front the assembly area has to be established, the sparser will be the range of combat support services available, until we reach the point where only the attack helicopters and their crews are present. By that time the assembly area has turned into a holding area.

You choose an assembly area according to these considerations:

1 Entry and exit routes
2 Cover and concealment
3 Space
4 Proximity to friendly units
5 Proximity to main supply routes
6 Security

Helicopters flying in and out of the same place day after day are bound to attract attention, and the attention is likely to be closely followed by artillery fire or air raids. As well as offering physical cover, assembly areas should be either out of radar range, or masked by the terrain, and the entry and exit routes likewise.

The chosen assembly area must provide good cover and concealment not only for aircraft, but for the vehicles and equipment of the maintenance and re-supply crews.

Built-up areas are generally preferable to sites out in the countryside. Supermarkets, warehouses and factory sites all provide good hardstanding for the helicopters and metalled roads for the vehicles, as well as the sort of buildings that can be adapted for aircraft maintenance. The buildings can be blacked out at night so that maintenance work can continue round the clock.

The whole assembly area should be spread over as wide an area as possible – a company will need two or three square kilometres – to minimise the risk from artillery or air strikes.

An attack helicopter unit has a very small complement of men, and all of them have specific mission responsibilities. Wherever possible, local ground forces should provide security, and in any event the helicopter unit commander should be in very close touch with his counterpart on the ground.

On the ground, just as in the air, the attack helicopter unit is organised into teams along with the air scouts who fly with them. Ideally, the fighting units should be grouped around the perimeter of the assembly area with the operational command post at the centre.

Individual team members stay with their aircraft at all times with the exception of the unit leaders, who stay at the operations centre where they are immediately available.

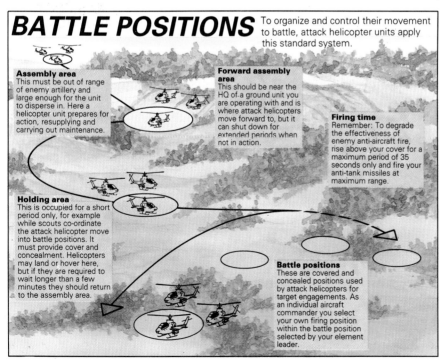

BATTLE POSITIONS

To organize and control their movement to battle, attack helicopter units apply this standard system.

Assembly area
This must be out of range of enemy artillery and large enough for the unit to disperse in. Here a helicopter unit prepares for action, resupplying and carrying out maintenance.

Forward assembly area
This should be near the HQ of a ground unit you are operating with and is where attack helicopters move forward to, but it can shut down for extended periods when not in action.

Firing time
Remember: To degrade the effectiveness of enemy anti-aircraft fire, rise above your cover for a maximum period of 35 seconds only and fire your anti-tank missiles at maximum range.

Holding area
This is occupied for a short period only, for example while scouts co-ordinate the attack helicopter move into battle positions. It must provide cover and concealment. Helicopters may land or hover here, but if they are required to wait longer than a few minutes they should return to the assembly area.

Battle positions
These are covered and concealed positions used by attack helicopters for target engagements. As an individual attack commander you select your own firing position within the battle position selected by your element leader.

When you do make contact with the enemy, the speed of the attack helicopter gives you the option of launching a hasty attack or reporting the position and bypassing, leaving it to be assaulted by other arms.

The decision will be based on the strategic value of the enemy detachment and on your own actual mission. You may find that your massive firepower means that you can take the target out on your way past. But don't get side-tracked into attacking a target of opportunity when your real objective is elsewhere – you always run the risk of upsetting a wider plan.

Hasty attack

A hasty attack is generally planned on the move, and carried out with a maximum of aggression and violence. Unit SOPs (Standard Operating Procedures) are of very high value when it comes to planning an attack – or a defensive action – when time is very short.

Instead of having to describe individual manoeuvres in detail, if they form part of the SOP you can refer to them just by name, and everyone will know what they have to do. The smaller the attack force, the more important it is to be properly drilled in the procedures.

You can often use a hasty attack to gauge the enemy's strength and will to resist, but it needs fine judgement on the part of the attack force commander to decide when to press home an assault that looks as though it might find itself in difficulties, in the hope of winning a quick victory, and when to re-group and plan the operation more carefully.

Deliberate attack

During the deliberate attack, the helicopter force will operate within strictly controlled limits as part of the combined arms team. The long-range anti-armour capability of the ATGMs (Anti-Tank Guided Missiles) is the most important part of your armoury, and so suppression of enemy armour will be your first task.

As soon as enemy tank activity is contained, then the attack helicopters are switched to other targets, to:
1 Attack and contain pockets of resistance by-passed by the main force.
2 Provide a fire-base for advancing ground forces.
3 Dominate key terrain not yet under friendly control, to stop the enemy from mounting an effective counter-attack.
4 Destroy or repel any counter-attack the enemy is able to mount.

5 Attack withdrawing enemy forces or reserves.

Exploitation

Once you've hurt the enemy badly with an assault – or, better still, got him on the move – he must be prevented from re-grouping or conducting an orderly withdrawal.

The attack force will keep on at the

An AH-1 flies over a column of M113 APCs on exercise. When on the offensive, attack helicopters can fix the enemy and allow ground forces to manoeuvre and assault under covering fire.

enemy, advancing towards his rear areas where the command posts and supply stations will be located. Small pockets of resistance will be by-passed, but lightly defended installations should be destroyed in passing.

PICK OFF ENEMY ANTI-AIRCRAFT WEAPONS

Your primary target in an enemy mechanized or tank unit will be the ZSU-23-4 self-propelled radar controlled anti-aircraft guns. If you can eliminate these quickly, the rest of an enemy unit can be destroyed in relative safety. Their maximum range is 3,000 metres and the maximum range of a TOW anti-tank missile is

3,750 metres so make sure you use this vital margin.

Use the 70-mm rockets against enemy armoured forces to compel them to close up. Once their hatches are shut, all tanks except the T-64 are unable to fire their anti-aircraft machine-guns and they will find it very hard to see you.

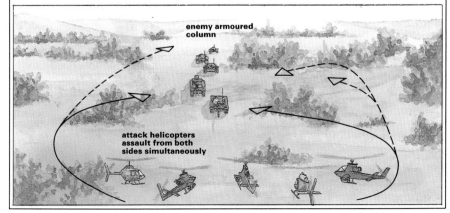

enemy armoured column

attack helicopters assault from both sides simultaneously

Attack helicopter and air cavalry units are really well suited to operations such as this, though support from ground forces is desirable, and may be downright essential if the enemy has ATGM detachments still operating, and the terrain allows him to set up anti-aircraft ambushes with them.

Pursuit

It's one thing to force the enemy to withdraw from territory that he's been holding, and to do so is generally regarded as a victory. But in the long run that gives him battle-hardened troops that he can re-group and re-equip, and then insert back into the war. Better to get him moving – at your pace, so his command structure can't cope – and then take that opportunity to kill or capture the forces concerned.

Once again, it's attack helicopters that are the most efficient means of carrying out this sort of operation, whose prime requirements are speed, arms and armour and good communications.

The Apache is designed to withstand battle damage: each main rotor blade is built from five steel spars separated by glassfibre and covered with a steel skin. Incredibly, they can withstand hits from 23-mm cannon shells.

Operating in company strength, attack helicopter battalions act as an encircling force, getting around the moving columns of enemy troops and attacking them from ambush and from the flanks while they're on the move.

Special operations

As well as operating as part of the main battle force, attack helicopter units will often be called on to form part of a special operations task force. The sort of jobs you may be called upon to do include:

1 Reconnoitre in force
2 Raid
3 Feint
4 Demonstrate fire-power superiority
5 Relieve friendly forces

Reconnaissance in force

Reconnaissance in force can be to obtain information, which may well include taking prisoners for examination and interrogation, or it could be to pinpoint enemy locations and test their strengths and reactions. Attack helicopters can operate alone, or with air cavalry units.

Raiding

A raid is an attack on enemy-held territory for some special purpose, other than to take or hold territory. It may be to destroy a particular unit, installation or stores dump. The one common feature is that the raiding force always withdraws when the operation is over.

Attack helicopter and air cavalry forces, because they are permanently linked to their vehicles, are ideal tools to tackle this sort of job.

Feints

It's sometimes necessary to mount a diversionary supporting attack to draw the enemy's attention, or some of his strength, away from the main effort. Helicopter units – because they can draw enemy troops out and then use their superior speed to leave them

Maximum range
Use your missiles at maximum possible range where you will be safest from enemy anti-aircraft weapons.

Attack priorities
The attack helicopter crew must:

1 Assess the battlefield situation for themselves
2 Acquire the most dangerous target
3 Select the most effective weapon
4 Engage and destroy the enemy

Radar warning receiver
Your radar warning receiver will tell you when you are being tracked by known types of Soviet radar.

Scout helicopters
Their job is to spot the enemy first, co-ordinate with the ground forces commander and select firing positions.

Smoke
Smoke is used to suppress or screen targets which threaten the success of your mission. However, it should be used carefully so it does not hinder other helicopter attacks, close air support or artillery observation.

stranded away from the mainstream of events – are particularly useful in mounting a feinting operation.

Demonstrating firepower

In many ways, setting out to demonstrate your overwhelming superiority of firepower to enemy troops should be considered as tactical deception, but the operational techniques are much the same as for any other type of special operation.

Even though the objective may not even be to cause enemy casualties, you must take the normal precautions when planning and flying a mission such as this – co-ordination with friendly ground forces, SOPs, fallback positions and security procedures.

Mobility
Despite your armour protection, your best defence lies in not being hit. Use frequent changes of position to evade enemy anti-aircraft fire.

First element
You attack in two elements, using fire and movement in a similar way to an infantry section. The first element attacks the enemy, firing two or three missiles, and moves to a new firing position.

TANK BUSTING

Flying an attack helicopter, you follow this sequence when you move into action against enemy armoured forces:

1. **Move forward to the holding area.**
2. **Receive a quick briefing from the scout helicopters who have located the enemy.**
3. **Fly to a battle position which allows you maximum cover and concealment and the longest possible fields of fire.**
4. **Rise slightly above your cover (US pilots call this 'unmasking').**
6. **Unmask far enough to give your weapons clearance above your cover.**
7. **Fire.**
8. **Remask.**
9. **Move to a different firing position to confuse enemy anti-aircraft gunners.**

Artillery
Artillery and close air support from jet aircraft such as A-10 Thunderbolts should be co-ordinated with the attack helicopters' assault. Scout helicopters provide liaison with other friendly forces.

Tank weak spots
Hellfire and TOW missiles will penetrate and destroy any Main Battle Tank that they hit, but do not forget that your 30-mm cannon can penetrate the engine deck of T-54, T-62 and early T-72s. Soviet tanks often carry external fuel tanks, which make good targets.

Teamwork
The key to success is good teamwork between the scouts and the attack helicopters. The scouts must locate and identify targets and hand them over for the attack helicopters to deal with.

Second element
The second element observes the attack of the first, looking out for enemy anti-aircraft weapons. These will be ZSU-23-4 SP anti-aircraft guns and shoulder-fired SA-7 'Grail' surface-to-air missiles.

JOINT OPERATIONS

Attack helicopters, although strong individual weapons, don't operate alone and unsupported. There are times when you can make good use of ground-based combat support, especially air defence artillery, and ground-to-ground fire support such as artillery, mortars and even naval gunfire. On top of that you work closely with the second-echelon support services such as intelligence and engineering units.

Combat support is provided by the ground forces for whom you're working at the time, and it's controlled by the ground force commander. He has the responsibility and the command, and he will co-ordinate the support available, switching from one sector to another depending on need and the resources available.

Combat support can be direct – applying artillery fire on a precise map reference to take out a particular enemy position; general – providing suppressive fire over a wider area; or attached – moving and working

*Helicopters will not fight alone if **NATO** forces find themselves with their backs to the **R**hine and endless columns of Soviet tanks trundling westwards. The attack helicopters will co-operate with **NATO** close air support **(CAS)** aircraft like this **US** Air Force A-10, seen here firing a Maverick missile.*

*The helicopter attack must be co-ordinated with friendly artillery. As the AH-64 engages enemy armour with its Hellfire anti-tank missiles, **US** artillery fires shells fitted with **VT** fuses which burst in the air above the tanks. This forces the tanks to close down, sharply reducing their visibility and preventing all but the T-64s from firing their anti-aircraft machine-gun.*

ARTILLERY AID FOR ATTACK HELICOPTERS

1. **Directed by scout helicopters, artillery can force the tanks to close down before the attack, making it very difficult for them to locate the attack helicopters.**
2. **By keeping enemy armoured vehicles closed down their rate of advance is also slowed, and it is harder for them to co-ordinate their defence.**
3. **The radar system of the dreaded ZSU-23-4 anti-aircraft gun is vulnerable to shell splinters and can be knocked out by an artillery barrage.**
4. **Units adjacent to the ones being attacked by the helicopters can be suppressed by artillery to stop them interfering with the helicopter attack.**

SEQUENTIAL ATTACKS

When a target area is small or the avenues of approach are limited, attack helicopters and A-10 aircraft attack in turns. While the jets are making their attack, the helicopters can manoeuvre to new firing positions so that the enemy vehicles are hit from a different direction after each pass from the aircraft.

An A-10 fires a Maverick missile at an enemy tank, then pulls out to let the helicopters make their attack

The A-10 flies out of the way while the helicopters make their attack in turn

directly with the attack helicopter unit. Engineering and intelligence support fall into this category.

An attack helicopter may seem, to enemy ground forces, to be moving so fast that it doesn't provide a possible target. But to enemy aircraft, with their much wider field of vision and superior speed and weapons systems, they're very vulnerable.

Cover and concealment are your best defence, but there's also general support from Air Defence Artillery (ADA). This support is provided on an area basis, not dedicated to individual aircraft. Most ADA is computer-controlled, picking up and tracking any aircraft that comes into its sector, so it's vital that all friendly aircraft can identify themselves to the gunnery control system automatically – there won't be time to respond manually!

This system is known as IFF (Identification Friend or Foe), and is in the form of a radio beacon that transmits a coded message. Check that it's working – regularly – and make very sure that you know all the appropriate code settings. There are three stages of 'alert status' for ADA systems:

1 Weapons Hold: fire only in self-defence
2 Weapons Tight: fire only at aircraft positively identified as hostile
3 Weapons Free: fire on any aircraft not positively identified as friendly

Enemy armour

One of the most effective uses of direct fire support is to take out enemy ADA to allow you to get on with your main task – destroying enemy armour. The support can be distant: from field artillery units or, if you're within contact range, from a naval task force lying off the coast. Or it can be local, coming from the attacking infantry company's own mortars.

Mortars can also be used against dismounted infantry whose man-portable anti-tank/anti-aircraft systems are proving troublesome, and also to provide illumination. Because of their high trajectory, mortar rounds are particularly effective against units located in dead ground such as the far side of a ridge, where you can't get at them without coming into range of their ADA fire yourself.

Where possible, a member of the artillery unit will fly with the attack helicopters, probably as observer in one of the scouts. He's specially trained to call down supporting fire with the least possible delay. This may not always be possible, however, so you must be able to do the job yourself should it be necessary. The artillery arm provides training officers for attack helicopter units for this purpose.

Suppression

If the target proves particularly difficult, and can't be suppressed even by a combined attack helicopter/artillery support operation, then the next step is to call in the air force.

A close air support mission (CAS) is run by the air force alone; the only thing you might be asked to do is pro-

COMBINED ATTACK

This demands split-second timing. The aircraft and the helicopters do not attack at exactly the same moment; instead, the helicopters begin their attack as the jets approach the target. As the A-10s pull up to launch their missiles, the helicopters pop back into cover and attack again as the aircraft complete their escape manoeuvre and leave the target area.

Helicopters fire just before and just after the A-10s attack

A-10s pull up to fire their missiles then escape under covering fire from the helicopters.

vide transportation for the forward air controller (FAC).

But that's not to say that you'll be loitering in the rear somewhere! The CAS, if properly controlled and co-ordinated, will leave the enemy in a state of chaos – but not for long, if you're facing well-led, battle-hardened troops. You'll have only a few moments in which to exploit the advantage the CAS gives you. Using cover and concealment techniques, you wait in the holding area, taking your attack timing from the forward air controller.

Joint air attack

The most difficult support operation to mount, control and co-ordinate is the joint air attack team (JAAT) operation. In any operation that involves ground forces, supporting artillery, attack helicopters and close air support, all working together, there is bound to be some confusion.

The JAAT operation starts with scout helicopter teams going in to reconnoitre the target area for battle positions, avenues of approach, choke points and engagement areas. It's particularly important that they locate all the enemy's air defence systems, so

SECTOR ATTACK

Sector attacks are the easiest to manage and they reduce the risk of friendly aircraft endangering each other during the attack. The aircraft attack one part of the target while the helicopters deal with another. Both units attack independently and do not have to co-ordinate their firing.

Helicopters engage targets in their designated sector

The road marks the dividing line between the sectors

A-10s attack targets in their designated sector

that they can be suppressed at an early stage, before they can engage the close support aircraft. When these targets have been acquired, the scout helicopters must keep them in sight until they're satisfied that they've been destroyed.

When the targets have been identified, the artillery units can start to lay down indirect fire, guided by the forward artillery aerial observers, who will shift targets and call for changes of ammunition and fuses as necessary. Scout helicopters stay on station right

An A-10 opens fire with its 30-mm GAU-8 cannon, which have a core of depleted uranium to bore through enemy tank armour. For this reason the latest Soviet tanks are being fitted with extra armour on the turret.

Its armoured skin pierced by a hail of 30-mm shells, a tank disintegrates as its fuel and ammunition explodes. NATO ground forces rely heavily on the ability of tactical aircraft and helicopters to destroy enemy armour.

SURVIVING AN ANTI-HELICOPTER AIR ATTACK

To protect their tank forces from attack helicopters, the Soviets intend to use specialist helicopters of their own, purpose-built to take out NATO helicopters like the US Apache and Cobra and the British Lynx. The 'Hokum' and the 'Havoc' will both be equipped with air-to-air missiles, and their introduction into Soviet service will add a new dimension to air combat over the battlefield.

'Hokum'
This new Soviet helicopter carries air-to-air missiles intended specially for you. Unless you spot the missile launch you are probably doomed: the only way to avoid destruction is to fly as low as possible and try to get some terrain feature or obstacle between you and the incoming missile.

Keep your eyes open
Most successful air-to-air engagements occur when one aircraft sees an enemy and attacks it without being seen. The best defence against enemy helicopters is, quite simply, to see them before they see you. Your cannon and even unguided rockets can then be used against him once he is in range.

Sharp turn
When attacked by a jet aircraft, turn sharply towards him. This will make it difficult for him to track you and present a tricky deflection shot for his cannon.

Exploiting weaknesses
If you are attacked by an enemy fighter aircraft, remember that his closing speed is very high and his downward visibility is generally poor.

through the operation, in order to:
1 Locate and identify targets
2 Provide local security for attack helicopters
3 Guide indirect fire
4 Maintain visual contact with both friendly and enemy forces
5 Look for alternative firing positions for their attack helicopters
6 Pass information back to the battle commander

Because the real thrust of a JAAT operation comes from the air, the main threat to it is anti-air weapons. They must be located, identified and destroyed at the very earliest stages of the attack, by any 'asset' that is available and suitable for the purpose.

Briefing a JAAT

Because of the difficulties and complexities in controlling an operation where four different types of offensive troops are deployed, the longer the period involved between thinking up the operation and it taking place, the better – so long as your security is tight – to allow really comprehensive briefing and planning.

Each member of the JAAT task force must supply a minimum of information – the close air support team, for instance, will supply details of the types of weapons they have available and how long they can loiter (stay over the engagement area looking for other targets to hit).

All this 'asset information' is co-ordinated and a plan of attack put together that makes the best use of what's available.

The CAS aircraft – probably A-10s – are built to take anti-aircraft fire. They go in first, flying Nap-of-the-Earth from the holding area, transmitting intelligence back to the battle commander so that he keeps an up-to-date picture of the situation. The strike air-

AH-1 Cobras wait their turn to attack in a Forward Assembly Area. A TACP (Tactical Air Control Party) from the US Air Force is usually attached to the attack helicopter unit when operating in conjunction with close air support aircraft.

craft are followed closely by the attack helicopters flying at even lower level.

When the CAS team is over the target, the level of air defence artillery fire will increase as the enemy opens up with everything he's got; that's just what the attack helicopters are waiting for. With every target identified and acquired by the scout helicopters in their stand-off positions, the enemy ADA can now be taken out by air-to-ground missiles operating from outside the anti-aircraft guns' effective range.

Close air support

With effective training you will be very much more comfortable with JAAT missions. Experience shows that a bare minimum of information – target location, description and attack time – are all that's needed to set up an effective helicopter/CAS operation.

When these two very different types of aircraft operate together in ground strike operations, there are three basic strategies available:

Teamwork
You can expect enemy jets to attack in pairs, and your safety depends on doing likewise. As Soviet helicopters receive air-to-air missiles, so US choppers will probably receive modified Stinger heat seeking missiles. These should be particularly valuable against enemy jets which overshoot you.

Self defence
At present the prime mission of US Army attack helicopters is to provide support for NATO forces on the ground, not to fight it out with enemy helicopters. Do not attack enemy helicopters just for the sake of it.

Blind side
If you have detected the enemy helicopters first, manoeuvre into cover so you can attack them from the side or, better still, the rear. Once on their blind side you can open fire with all available weapons.

Air defence artillery
Co-ordinate your flight with US anti-aircraft weapons on the ground. Concentrations of ADA will provide you with safe zones and even the potential to lure enemy aircraft into an ambush, providing the ground personnel can distinguish you from Soviet helicopters.

Watch your shadow
In strong sunshine you will cast a giveaway shadow on the ground which will betray you to enemy aircraft above you. Do not fly over large stretches of open territory: skirt round them instead, using all available cover.

Ground clutter
This is the term given to the effect that the ground has on radar systems. Enemy aircraft and their radar systems are designed to fight at high altitude and have great difficulty 'locking on' their radar homing missiles on a very low flying target.

1 Sector attack
2 Sequential attack
3 Combined attack

Sector attack is the most straightforward. The two parts of the assault force are each assigned to a sector of the engagement area, and operate separately while still supporting each other.

If the engagement area is small, or the avenues of attack narrow and limited, it may be necessary to mount a sequential attack – helicopters and strike aircraft attacking one after the other to vary the characteristics of the attack and the types of weapons used, to make life more difficult for the defenders on the ground.

In practice, this becomes a sort of three-dimensional fire-and-movement exercise. The CAS aircraft engage the target while the helicopters are taking up their positions. As the A-10s break off, the helicopters unmask, acquire their targets, and fire their weapons. During the time the enemy is occupied with the helicopters' ATGMs, the A-10s have taken a new avenue of attack and resume the

engagement with their Avenger cannon and rockets.

When the target warrants it, the two airborne arms can work even more closely together, in combined attack. Both engaging the targets at the same time, they can be fairly certain that whatever counter-measures the enemy takes, he won't be able to acquire enough of the targets to prevent his destruction.

Remember that flying at low altitude is not just a defence against enemy anti-aircraft weapons but also makes it difficult for hostile jet fighters to get a clear shot at you.

HELICOPTER COMBAT RESCUE

Taking a helicopter to rescue one of your own pilots behind enemy lines is incredibly risky and demanding. All air forces have helicopter rescue crews who receive training for survival in conditions ranging from the leech-infested heat of the tropics to the bitter cold of the arctic, all of this while coping with an enemy's defences to bring off a behind-the-lines rescue. Among the crew's obvious concerns is to make certain that the rescue succeeds and that the crew – and helicopter – do not themselves become casualties!

A typical rescue helicopter crew consists of pilot, co-pilot and two para-rescue specialists, sometimes called Para-Jumpers or PJs. All of these men must be disciplined, alert and resourceful.

A rescue mission is about to begin. One of your pilots has been hit over the enemy's territory. After ejecting and parachuting into a low gully not far from enemy troops, he uses his hand-held beeper (actually, a small voice radio) to report his position to friendly forces.

If any doubt exists that this really is the downed pilot, members of the airborne command post in the region – likely to be a C-130 Hercules transport – will ask the man on the ground questions that have been arranged in advance: 'What is your mother's maiden name?' 'Where did you go to school?' This information on all pilots has already been given to your rescue units. In the immediacy of a battle, there is usually no doubt, but if the enemy is suspected of using an imposter to lure rescue forces, a Q and A session will tell you of the ruse.

An HH-60A helicopter of the US Air Force, modern-day successor to the HH-53s which were used in Vietnam to rescue shot-down aircrew from the North Vietnamese or Viet Cong.

During land hoist training, a para-rescueman or PJ simulates the rescue of a wounded survivor who will be hoisted to the rescue in a litter.

Wearing the maroon beret which distinguishes these elite air crew, a para-rescueman checks the rescue hoist on an HH-53E 'Jolly Green Giant'.

Today, a wounded soldier can swiftly be evacuated by helicopter from the combat zone.

Left: The treeline around the landing zone is blasted with a 7.62-mm Minigun. Electrically powered, this can saturate the target area with up to 100 rounds a second.

JOLLY GREEN GIANT TO THE RESCUE

A downed US Air Force pilot is whisked to safety under fire from the North Vietnamese. Helicopter rescue remains an important task in the 1980s: the elite para-rescuemen are now trained to drop miles away from the downed airman, locate him, provide medical assistance if necessary, and only then call in the helicopter.

Skyraiders

In Vietnam the veteran A-1 Skyraiders played a vital role in the rescue of downed airmen. Their slow speed made accompanying helicopters an easy business and their incredible warload enabled them to suppress the North Vietnamese with rockets, cannon and napalm, giving the helicopters the chance to go in.

The cast of thousands

An airborne rescue mission can involve a large number of personnel and aircraft, from the helicopters at the sharp end to fighter-bombers, aerial command post aircraft, re-fuelling tankers and electronic warfare aircraft monitoring and jamming enemy communications and radar.

Ground fire

In Vietnam the enemy regularly set traps for the rescue units, luring helicopters over concentrations of machine-guns and anti-aircraft missiles. If communication can be established with a downed pilot, a few pre-arranged questions like 'what is your mother's maiden name' can be used to make sure you are flying to the right man.

Vulnerability

The thin metal skin of a helicopter can be pierced by a ball-point pen if it is slammed against the fuselage in a cupped hand. A single accurate burst from an enemy machine-gun can bring down the helicopter and increase the number of aircrew needing to be rescued.

Pilot's choice

At the rescue site, if weather, terrain conditions and the enemy's strength and location make it possible for him to attempt a pick-up, the pilot must make the final decision whether to go in.

Head-on target

Above all, the helicopter crew must avoid presenting their extremely vulnerable frontal arc to the enemy. The glass canopy is the helicopter's weakest spot and the route in and out of the rescue site must be carefully chosen to avoid known or likely enemy concentrations.

Para-rescueman

Although their primary purpose is to save lives, these men may have to fight the enemy in order to bring about a successful rescue. Para-rescuemen have to be able to use anything from a Colt .45 to an M-16 rifle and the 7.62-mm Minigun carried on the rescue helicopter.

Improvised codes

The enemy may be able to listen to radio messages between a downed pilot and the rescue team. One solution is to use double talk: some frame of reference they cannot understand. One rescue team used the layout of a golf course they and the pilot knew to describe where the downed airmen should go next to avoid the encircling Viet Cong.

Second helicopter

Because helicopters are so easily damaged it makes sense to send in rescue helicopters in pairs. The 'Alpha' chopper is the primary helicopter; the 'Bravo' is the back-up.

With a combat rescue mission now about to unfold, the C-130 command post is joined by tankers (to refuel aircraft in the rescue force) and fighters (to cover the rescue helicopter during its mission). Electronic warfare aircraft may also be operating in the vicinity, foiling the enemy's radar while his ground troops beat through the bush searching for the survivor.

Crew responsibility

Hundreds of people, including ground communicators, may be involved in the rescue attempt. But in the end, success or failure will rest in the hands of the helicopter's crew. The noisy, shuddering, very uncomfortable helicopter will be within a short distance of the enemy and it will be important for each man to check and double-check his readiness.

The pilot is always in command and is responsible for the helicopter's role in the mission, including the decision to abort if there is a mechanical problem or if he suffers battle damage. He must not forget one of the fundamentals of aviation, namely a thorough pre-flight check of the helicopter before taking off. This may be performed by someone else, but it is the pilot's reputation on the line.

The co-pilot

The co-pilot provides a second pair of eyes and ears, as well as a hand on the throttle. The pilot may ask him to handle the controls at critical periods during the mission. He should not forget to keep glancing at the pilot, to make certain he is unhurt, in control, and in command. The co-pilot may handle some of the communications with other elements of the rescue force. He will usually have a solid knowledge of the flying characteristics of the helicopter and be pre-

155

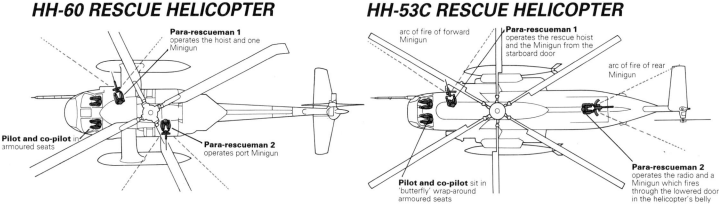

Para-rescueman 1 operates the hoist and one Minigun

Pilot and co-pilot in armoured seats

Para-rescueman 2 operates port Minigun

arc of fire of forward Minigun

Para-rescueman 1 operates the rescue hoist and the Minigun from the starboard door

arc of fire of rear Minigun

Pilot and co-pilot sit in 'butterfly' wrap-around armoured seats

Para-rescueman 2 operates the radio and a Minigun which fires through the lowered door in the helicopter's belly

pared to assume the pilot-in-command job if the pilot is disabled or killed by enemy fire.

An élite breed of para-rescue specialists is essential to any rescue force. They are trained in parachuting, helicopter rescue work, and survival in a variety of conditions. They also receive first-aid training and are expected to keep current on ways to provide medical help to a survivor.

Two rescuemen

The helicopter carries two such rescuemen, usually a senior noncommissioned officer (NCO) and a more junior airman. The two men should remember to carefully inspect each other's gear to make certain that parachutes are properly packed and equipment properly slung, so that they can use their equipment with maximum ease and comfort. A small error in the fit of a strap supporting a bulky item such as a parachute or medical kit could cause serious injury.

If their mission is to rescue a survivor at sea, the men may make use of their training in parachuting into the

sea while equipped with SCUBA (self-contained underwater breathing apparatus). If their rescue will take place under polar or arctic conditions, a scrupulous check must be made of the bulky boots, coveralls, parkas and other gear essential to survival.

Into the mission

On the way towards enemy territory, where the downed pilot is in radio contact and hoping to be picked up before the enemy can take him prisoner, two rescue helicopters in communication with a flying command post approach at low altitude. They are called the 'Alpha bird' (the primary helicopter for the rescue) and the 'Bravo bird' (a back-up).

Experience has shown that sending one helicopter alone, into a region where the enemy may have ground troops, surface-to-air missiles (SAMs) and other defences, is simply not practical. The chances of being shot down with loss of crew are bad enough, but even greater is the prospect of at least minor damage from enemy fire. Having two helicopters provides flexibility.

Talking to the pilot

The survivor now communicates directly with the helicopter pilot as the 'Alpha bird' and 'Bravo bird' approach him. Fighter pilots flying cover, or one of the helicopter pilots, may see a better way to position the survivor for a rescue. If enemy ground troops are approaching through a thick forest to the north, they may direct the survivor to hike towards a riverbank to the south, where a rescue can be attempted with less exposure to enemy fire.

A present-day para-rescueman wears his full kit for a combat rescue with his Sikorsky UH-60A Nighthawk helicopter in the background. The oxygen mask will enable him to leap into the area from over 3,000 metres. He will free-fall until the last possible moment, using his altimeter to judge opening time.

The old HH-53C Jolly Green Giant remains the primary rescue helicopter of the US Air Force. Here a para-rescueman has lowered himself via the rescue hoist and lifted the downed airman to safety. One problem with the HH-53 is that the Minigun is in the same place as the hoist, making it hard to use both at once.

The crew tries to communicate with the survivor using doubletalk, so that he will understand and the enemy, who may be monitoring communications, won't. During the Vietnam war, one downed pilot was given directions to move towards a safer area by using the numbers of his birth date to describe compass headings. The survivor understood, but eavesdropping enemy radiomen did not.

In the Vietnam conflict the PJ was essentially 'married' to the helicopter and would leave it only at the immediate scene of a rescue. In recent times, more flexible tactics have been developed. The helicopter pilot may drop a rescue specialist, by hoist or by parachute, some as distant as 10 miles from the survivor with instructions to trek overland and reach the survivor before the helicopter appears to expose itself at the rescue site.

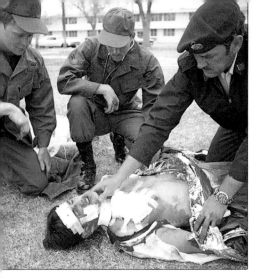

SMSGT Jim Spears, one of the US Air Force's most experienced para-rescuemen, instructs trainees in medical techniques. Unless a casualty is stabilised before evacuation he is likely to die even if successfully rescued.

If the survivor is injured or wounded the rescue expert may be able to administer first aid to render him more mobile, so that he can be moved to a location where terrain or the enemy's position is more favourable for a pick-up.

Moment of decision

When the weather allows the two-ship helicopter force to 'ingress' the area where the survivor is hoping for rescue, when friendly fighters have delayed the enemy's troops and suppressed his ground fire, and when the survivor is finally in a location where a rescue attempt can be made, everything boils down to the judgment and decision making abilities of the four men in the helicopter.

Some actual case histories have been far from total successes. In one well-known rescue operation, the enemy succeeded in hiding several machine-gun positions near the survivor. Enemy troops were close enough to seize the survivor but wanted, instead, to use him as bait for the rescue helicopter. Sadly, the enemy's trick worked. Just as the chopper was hovering overhead and lowering the rescue hoist, the machine-guns opened up. The helicopter was shot down and three of its four crewmen, along with the original survivor, were captured. Only one of the helicopter crew, a para-rescueman, evaded the enemy and was eventually rescued by another helicopter.

In Vietnam, all sorts of tricks were attempted. A Vietnamese communist soldier was dressed in the standard K2B American flight coveralls, positioned high on a ridgetop with a signal mirror, and instructed to act like a downed American pilot. This deception fooled the rescue forces for only a brief time, but this caused one of the helicopters to become bait for a MiG fighter lurking nearby, the only time in the entire war a MiG shot down an HH-53C chopper, with the loss of all on board.

More often, diligence and perseverance by the helicopter crew pay off. Using communications to guide the survivor to a reasonably safe pick-up site, your rescue crew reaches him before the enemy can. The value of the Miniguns aboard the rescue helicopter should not be overlooked, either. While a direct confrontation is best avoided, those guns can lay down a withering stream of fire on a small unit of enemy soldiers. In the case of today's rescue, the guns are not needed: your PJ lowers himself on a sling, clutches the survivor in a bear hug, and lifts him to safety.

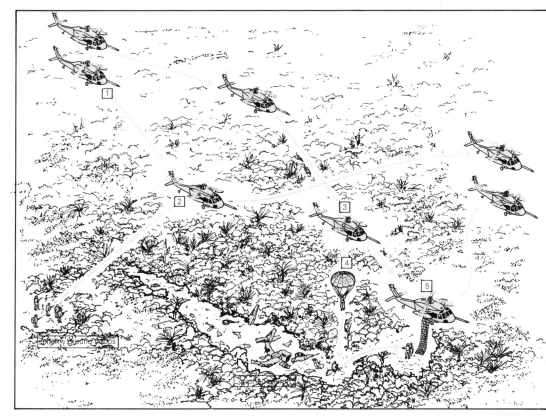

HOW A RESCUE WORKS

The rescue mission uses a pair of helicopters in case one of them is hit by groundfire and has to abort. Accompanying aircraft engage enemy ground troops while the para-rescueman is dropped to reach the survivor and guide him to the nearest usable landing zone that is not under enemy fire.

1 Flight of two rescue helicopters arrives.

2 'Bravo Bird' joins fighter-bombers in suppressing enemy ground troops near the survivor.

3 'Alpha Bird' moves in for the rescue.

4 'Alpha Bird' drops para-rescueman by hoist or parachute.

5 Para-rescueman reaches the survivor and guides him to the chosen landing zone.

CHAPTER SIX

U.S. SPECIAL FORCES

It was the late and much lamented Earl Louis Mountbatten who, during a meeting with General George C. Marshall, then the U.S. Army's General Chief of Staff, towards the end of World War Two, suggested the foundation of the unique Special Forces.

In South Vietnam the Special Forces were closely engaged in many covert operations and since then, when 'military advisers' have been requested in various parts of the world the experts of the Special Forces have comprised a high proportion of the numbers.

This chapter, then, presents an idea of the kinds of activity the Special Forces engage upon and where possible a few details of the way they operate, but of course much of the *modus operandi* must remain secret and in the manner of the British Army's S.A.S. and S.B.S. it is far better kept that way. There are times in war when there is useful intelligence to be gained from getting well-trained units into the enemy's own backyard, and the first of the articles in this chapter outlines the way that this is accomplished.

During World War Two the actions of the various resistance bodies on the Continent and the successes they achieved in blowing up bridges and military installations and troop trains and assassinating brutal individuals shows how effective such groups can be when having the backing and being supplied with weapons and explosives. The Special Forces units act in the same way but on a highly organised basis, and by setting ambushes they can create confusion among the enemy who felt that their ground was secure and under control. The use of friendly locals, often needed where the target is uncertain, can be encouraged but reprisals when the Special Forces pull out must be considered.

When dropping from the air, Special Forces members have to be prepared to go into free-fall for up to three minutes before pulling the rip-cord of their parachutes. The method is fast, accurate and silent if all goes well. A section in this chapter describes how the six-men HALO teams go into action this way and the signals they need from the ground so that a night jump will bring them in a close-knit group right to the DZ. These drop-zones are where such an operation can succeed or fail, for if the wind speed or direction changes during the flight out the team can end up well away from the target area.

The use of the skyhook is a spectacular way of getting into an aircraft without the machine touching the ground. It is dramatic and a test of skill and nerve for the pilot and crew and demands courage and confidence in the system for the soldier about to be whisked off the ground in a harness and hauled up into the aircraft as it climbs away.

Not all Special Forces operations are carried out on land or from the air. When the enemy territory has a coastline there are other means of gaining entry for specialist forces engaged on sabotage or surveillance work. In the manner of Britain's S.B.S. the U.S. Special Forces have groups which concentrate on striking from the sea. This can be accomplished by the use of surface vessels, submarines, submersible dinghies or mini-subs, the latter evading radar searches by keeping below the surface and running silently on electric batteries and carrying the passengers to the shore.

This chapter, the last in this COMBAT title, must of necessity omit many facets of the operations of the Special Forces but what can be said illustrates their high level of many military skills.

US SPECIAL FORCES: INSERTING TROOPS

Special Forces teams take the battle to the enemy on his own ground. Working behind the lines, their missions can vary from intelligence gathering to sabotage and organising guerrilla resistance movements against the enemy. It is a war without rules. The Special Forces soldier can expect no mercy from the enemy if he is caught: it is kill or be killed.

Many of the operational techniques are made up on the spur of the moment, to take advantage of a special piece of intelligence or some unexpected opportunity, but that doesn't mean there's no formal training. The military forces of the United States of America all have their special detachments, and they all take as their guide FM 31-20, the US Special Forces Operational Techniques field manual, on which this article is based.

Because they are 'Special Forces', their job is impossible to describe without listing all the possibilities. It's safer to say that as a member of a Special Forces team, you have to be prepared to tackle just about anything that comes up. You may be able to get back-up from technical specialists, but perhaps only in the form of a hurried, whispered radio conversation with a faceless person back at the operational base.

Most of the time, it will be impossible to say whether you're in attack or defence. You'll be conducting a guerrilla war. No front lines, no organised advance from one place to another, no start and finish lines.

Much of the Special Forces' job is taken up

INFILTRATING SPECIAL FORCES TEAMS

When preparing a team for infiltration by parachute, remember the following:

1. **Aircraft load capacity may limit the equipment and personnel you can take.**
2. **The presence of a reception committee on the drop zone makes 'sterilizing' the area and hiding your parachutes less of a problem.**
3. **You must ensure you take the equipment needed for your initial tasks.**
4. **The detachment commander places himself in the best position within the stick for controlling the team.**
5. **Team recognition signals and signals for contacting the reception committee must be decided in advance.**
6. **The primary assembly point should be 100 to 200 metres from the drop zone and you should have a secondary point 5 to 10 km from the DZ for use in an emergency.**

with intelligence gathering and instruction, providing a 'cadre' of experienced leaders who pass on their knowledge to people recruited locally. Not that all of that knowledge is military. It can just as well be about personal hygiene or farming methods – anything, in fact, that proves to the local population that you and your country have their best interests at heart.

Winning the battle for the hearts and minds of the people is really much more important than taking an objective by armed force, but you can't win either of them until you get to the battlefield itself. Inserting agents into hostile territory has been a

A US Special Forces detachment is dropped into the sea by a low-flying helicopter. They will swim ashore with all their equipment, leaving no trace of their secret arrival.

front-line intelligence task for hundreds of years, and there are two main methods:
1 False identities and disguise
2 Covert operations

Even in time of war, it is usually possible to gain access to the enemy's territory from a neighbouring country. The success of this method depends on the quality of your cover and documentation.

The biggest advantage of this approach is that once you have got

through the identity checks, searches and interrogation, you will be able to live quite openly in enemy territory, not having to run and hide every time there's an unexpected knock on the door. Of course, you'll be living a double life and this will be stressful in itself, but then no-one ever said that Special Forces work would be easy, and certainly not safe!

Clandestine insertion means entering the enemy's territory without his knowledge. It could mean trekking across a border in a remote and difficult part of the country, or para jumping from an aircraft from almost seven miles up, and waiting until you're just a hundred or so metres above the ground before opening your parachute.

Or it may be struggling with all your equipment through the 64-cm diameter access hatch of a fleet submarine and swimming five miles through the dark to land on a deserted beach.

Air infiltration

Insertion from an airborne operation is popular because no area is inaccessible by air; it's quick; and, when organised properly, minimises the risk both to the carrier and to the passenger and his reception committee. There are three normal variants:
1 Low and normal altitude parachute
2 High altitude low opening (HALO) parachute
3 Air landing operations

The object of the exercise is to insert

Special Forces troops set explosives to destroy a bridge: part of the team sets the charges while a third man keeps watch in the background. Note the mixture of US and Soviet rifles. Special Forces soldiers must be trained in all types of infantry weapons.

CLANDESTINE PENETRATION

HALO (High Altitude Low Opening) is a parachute technique used by Special Forces to arrive behind enemy lines without being detected. The aircraft flies at up to 8,000 metres; so high that it cannot be seen or heard from the ground. The troops free-fall most of the way down, linking up mid-air so they land in a tight group and only deploying their chutes when they are within 300 metres of the ground.

Keith Fretwell

Fast exit
All jumpers must exit the aircraft quickly and together so they can manoeuvre and free fall in a tight group and land without undue dispersion.

Reserve parachute
Guard your reserve parachute very carefully while you are on board the aircraft: if it deploys accidentally before you jump it could stall the aircraft or try to pull you out through the side of the plane. A mistake here could spell body bags all round.

Reduced vulnerability
The idea behind HALO is to minimise the time that you spend floating slowly down on your parachute, which is your period of maximum danger from enemy fire and observation.

Tree jumping
As a technique for insertion into a jungle environment, this has been abandoned due to excessive casualties in Borneo and Malaya. You cannot expect to be able to jump directly into a tropical jungle without a lot of injuries.

Altimeter
Positioned on top of the reserve chute, this indicates your height above ground. At all costs check that this is in working order before you jump: at night it is your only means of knowing when to pull your chute.

Rifle protection
Tape over the muzzle to prevent dirt getting into the barrel when you land, and tape the handguards together to make sure they stay up. Cover all sharp edges to prevent personal injury in case of a bad landing.

Rucksack
The rucksack is rigged below your main parachute and is released on a lowering line when you are on your final approach to the drop zone.

Waiting for the Viet Cong; in Vietnam US Special Forces played the enemy at his own game by inserting small teams into the jungle and ambushing the guerrillas.

agents without the enemy's knowledge, so his capabilities as well as your own have to be taken into consideration. How good are his radar and air traffic control systems? Do adequate drop and landing zones exist? Are there personnel on the ground who can act as a reception committee, and help to transport people and supplies to safe locations and 'sterilize'

the DZ after use? Are suitable aircraft available? Helicopter or fixed wing?

Landing from the sea

You must consider many of the factors that affect airborne insertions when planning an infiltration operation from the sea. First of all, what sort of coastal areas are available and what is the depth and efficiency of coastal defences? Do you have the right sort of marine craft to hand? Do you have the facilities to make sure that sea water can't effect vital pieces of equipment?

Submarines, because they are very difficult to detect when used properly, are very attractive as delivery vehicles, especially when the agents to be delivered can exit underwater and stay that way right up to the beach.

Land operations

Infiltration overland is very similar to a long-range patrol in enemy-held territory, and can be the most secure way of all of getting the Special Forces team into place, especially if time is not all-important. Distance is not necessarily a problem to fit, well-equipped Special Forces personnel, trained to use all their skills, wits and resources.

Where you can get help and assistance from 'friendlies' already in place, to provide food, shelter and intelligence, overland infiltration is

A utility boat brings Special Forces soldiers near the coastline in an inflatable dinghy. Once ashore they must deflate and conceal the dinghy before moving inland.

often the most effective of all. Because drop zones and landing zones are unlikely to be right next door to the area of operations, both air- and seaborne insertions will probably end up as overland journeys anyway. So there's a lot to be said for relying on your own two feet rather than on technology: man can escape detection a lot more easily than a machine.

One factor is common to all three methods of insertion that we've looked at so far – the availability of people on the ground to act as porters and guides and to provide security for the infiltrators. But it may not always be that way. In some cases the mem-

AREA DROP ZONE

An area Drop Zone is used by long range patrols who cannot guarantee their exact location when a pre-planned supply drop is due. The aircraft arrives at point A and proceeds to point B, looking for DZ markings on the way. The distance between the two points should not exceed 25 km and sites should be within 1 km of the line of flight.

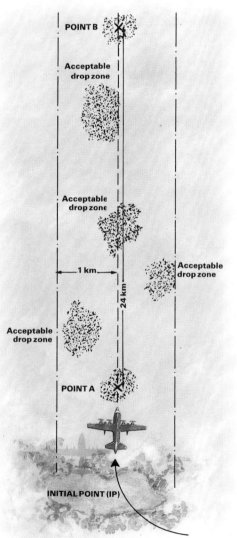

Aerial re-supply for an isolated Special Forces camp deep in the central highlands of South Vietnam. By arming and leading native tribesmen, the Special Forces inflicted serious damage on the Viet Cong.

bers of your team will have to go in blind, relying exclusively on your own skills and resources – not to mention a degree of luck!

Blind drops

These 'blind drops' are obviously very risky affairs, though probably not through exposure to enemy intelligence. After all, no-one will know you're coming, so there won't be a hostile reception committee at the DZ, either.

Blind drops are usually only made into areas that are known to contain a fair number of possible recruits – unarmed and untrained, probably, but providing the raw material for a strong indigenous operation. It may also be necessary to drop blind into areas where enemy security is tight and locals find it difficult to move around at will.

Staying behind

There is a fourth way of getting members of a Special Forces team into enemy-held territory – install them before the enemy moves in and takes over. Long-range planning and intelligence will dictate whether this is a real possibility

Keeping security will be the most

difficult part of the whole operation. Safe houses and refuges will need to be set up, communications established, caches of rations, arms and equipment made, and all without anyone outside the organisation having the faintest idea of what is going on. Members of Special Forces are trained to camouflage and conceal themselves superbly; to move silently; to live in the countryside without giving

themselves away. In towns and cities this is impossible, and so you must rely on the local people to provide security and communications, and probably rations and other supplies too – and that's all before you attempt any sort of operation!

Members of the US 7th Airborne Special Forces Group: demolitions experts, communications specialists and instructors in guerrilla warfare techniques.

RAIDS AND AMBUSHES

Special Forces units operate deep in the heart of enemy-occupied territory, undertaking both active and passive missions. A typical passive operation involves moving into position in the utmost secrecy, setting up a concealed and secure observation post, and then passing information about enemy troop strengths and movements back to HQ.

It may be months before the observers can be extracted or even re-supplied, so their training has to make them self-sufficient, allowing them to operate in the most hostile environments where one false move, day or night, could give the whole thing away.

Active operations such as raids and ambushes call for a different sort of courage. Daring instead of patience, decisiveness instead of caution. This second section on Special Forces Operational Techniques looks at the way active clandestine operations are planned and executed, and takes FM 31-20, the US Army's field manual for Special Forces, as its source.

A Special Forces raid is a surprise attack on enemy force or installation. It breaks down into four parts:

1 Clandestine insertion
2 Brief, violent combat
3 Rapid disengagement
4 Swift, deceptive withdrawal

Raids may be mounted to destroy enemy equipment and installations such as command posts, communications centres, and supply dumps; to capture enemy supplies and personnel; or simply to kill and wound as many of the enemy as possible. They may be used to rescue friendly forces or partisans, too, and can also serve to distract attention away from other operations.

Organizing the raid

The purpose of the mission, the type of target and the enemy situation will all have a bearing on the size of the raiding party. But whatever its size it will always have two basic elements — an assault group and a security group.

The assault group conducts the operation itself. They are the troops who go in and demolish installations, rescue the prisoners, steal the plans and code books or whatever the objective may be. As well as out-and-out fighting men, the group may include demolitions experts, electronics tech-

In the Vietnam war, Special Forces troops were used to play the guerrillas at their own game, small units of picked US troops raiding areas where the Viet Cong thought they were safe. Here, a US Navy SEAL takes cover by a VC bunker.

5 POINTS FOR A SUCCESSFUL AMBUSH

1. **Set the ambush in a site you can move into and out of unobserved.**
2. **Use a night ambush if the mission can be accomplished by a short, intensive burst of fire.**
3. **Use a daytime ambush if a follow-up is required.**
4. **Choose a site where the terrain forces the enemy to bunch up.**
5. **Bear in mind that you may need a secondary ambush if enemy reinforcements can reach the scene quickly.**

nicians, and whatever specialists may be needed – pilot, for example, if the object of the operation were to steal a specific enemy aircraft.

The security group is there to protect them, to secure the area and stop enemy reinforcements from becoming involved in the action, to stop any would-be escapers and to cover the withdrawal of the assault group.

Special Forces units have a well-deserved reputation for aggressiveness. Not one man amongst them will want to be idling away his time, and so they are always on the look-out for potential targets. Before operational planning can begin, each one is assessed for importance, accessibility and recoverability, taking into account distance and terrain and the strength of raiding party required.

Local repercussions

Another important factor is the likely effect on friendly natives and others as a result of the raid. There are countless examples of tens of local people being executed for every one occupying soldier killed. Planning for this possibility always forms part of the back-up organisation to the raid, and psychological operations experts (psyops) will also be ready to exploit any successes to the full.

Keep it simple

Although it should be accurate down to the last detail, the plan must be essentially simple. If success depends on a large number of factors coming together at the right time, any one of them going wrong will probably blow the entire operation.

Time – of day and of year – is a crucial factor in the plan. When the operation is straightforward and the physical layout of the target is well

US Navy SEALS (Sea-Air-Land) prepare to go ashore in the Mekong Delta and set up a night ambush. Their Tiger Stripe uniforms were developed from a North Vietnamese camouflage design.

known, it's probably better to operate during the hours of darkness. Where intelligence is less complete, go for dawn or dusk.

Withdrawal

Dusk is the best time for withdrawal; it gives you the advantage of the last minutes of daylight to exit the immediate area of the operation, and darkness to slow the enemy down during any follow-up. But in any event, choose the time very carefully to give yourself the greatest possible advantage.

It may seem obvious, but it's im-

possible to over-stress the value of accurate intelligence. There are three main sources:
1 Local agents
2 Reconnaissance
3 Satellite and high-level flights

Local knowledge is of the utmost importance. Whenever possible, friendly locals should be recruited to act as guides, and may even be employed in the raiding party itself if security considerations permit.

In the movement towards the objective, take every precaution so as not to alert hostile troops to your presence. Avoid contact, but make sure that the enemy suffers one hundred percent casualties if the worst does happen.

Test your weapons

Where conditions allow, conduct a weapons and equipment test before the assault phase, replacing any pieces of kit that may be faulty. Personal belongings should be 'sanitized' at the same time, even down to removing clothing labels if necessary.

Well defended objectives sometimes demand large raiding parties, perhaps in battalion strength or greater. Surprise is just as important as in a smaller raid, but will be much more difficult to achieve. A large raiding party will usually split into small groups and move towards the objective over a number of different routes. That way, even if some components are detected, the enemy may still be in the dark as to the real target.

Control and co-ordination of a large raiding party is more difficult, too, especially with regard to timing. Only

LAUNCHING A RAID

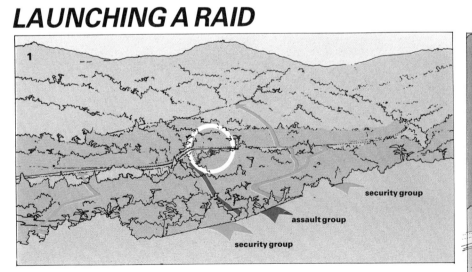

1 Whatever the mission and whatever the size of the raiding party, the principles of a guerrilla-style raid are the same. The actual assault team must be protected by security elements who will prevent enemy interference with the operation.

2 As the explosive specialist lays charges underneath the railway, on-the-spot security is provided by a small team of Special Forces soldiers. This team will take out any sentries on the objective, breach or demolish obstacles, and provide close protection for the main mission.

By taking out bridges, Special Forces raids block or delay the movement of enemy personnel or supplies, and by making certain routes useless they channel enemy movement on to a small number of major roads where it is more vulnerable to attack by other forces.

a high degree of training and excellent standards of equipment operation can make it easier.

Withdrawal after a large raid can be conducted with the party split up into small groups. This denies the enemy a large target for an air- or ground strike, but an alert and aggressive enemy may be able to mop up the force one unit at a time.

In some circumstances it is safer for the entire party to stay together and operate as a fighting column, but it will all depend on the situation of enemy forces, the terrain and the dis-

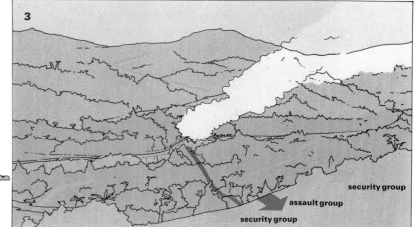

3 After the target has been destroyed the security groups provide cover on the flanks for the assault team to retreat. If the enemy follow the raiders, one security group should try to draw them away from the main assault force.

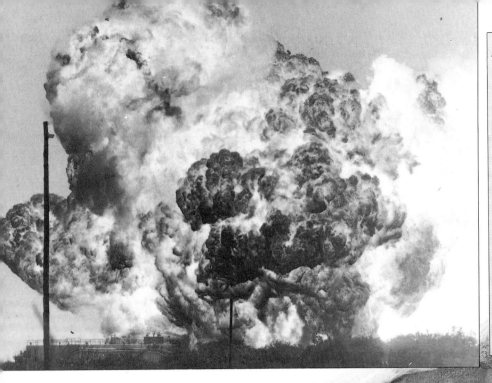

A NIGHT RAID

This is a typical night raid: blowing up the enemy's railway lines. Raids, especially if conducted at night, require meticulous planning and thorough rehearsal. Every member of the team should know exactly what he has to do where and when, and the 'O' Group (Orders Group, or briefing) should cover all eventualities. Rehearse everything, in the kit you will use on the job, preferably over similar terrain in a safe area. When planning the attack use all the available intelligence (INF), maps, air photographs, previous patrol reports and any locally-obtained INF. Practise in daylight, using the 'walk through talk through' technique; then do the whole thing again in silence.

Mission accomplished! A small team of commandos equipped with explosives can often strike strategic enemy targets more effectively than multi-million dollar airstrikes.

Cover group
While the demolition team is about its task, cover groups should provide flank, forward and rear protection.

Random frequency hazard
If you decide to electrically detonate the changes, be aware of RF hazard: your charges could be prematurely detonated by a radio transmission near your demolition circuit. You could avoid the problem altogether by using safety fuses, but this is not always tactically appropriate, so minimise the risk of keeping the radio well away from the demolition circuit.

tances to be covered. An overt withdrawal, with no attempt at secrecy, will require a great deal of external support. There's very little chance that the extraction force, if there is one, will escape enemy attention.

Ambush

An ambush is a raid on a moving target. The only real difference is that the timetable of the operation becomes much sketchier and unreliable. Even excellent intelligence sources can't really predict the enemy's operational delays, and so the raiding party will often be in position for some time before the target comes along, considerably increasing the chances of detection.

Ambushes are conducted to destroy or capture enemy personnel and supplies or block their movement. A systematic approach can channel the enemy's communications and re-supply operations, and force him to concentrate his movements on to main roads and railway lines, where they are more vulnerable to attack, especially from air strikes.

Railways themselves are always relatively open targets. Just removing the rails will bring the system to a halt. The attacking force tries to derail as many wagons and carriages as possible, and leave the wreckage blocking the track. This maximises the damage to stock, passengers and material, and slows down the work of repairing and reopening the permanent way.

Destroying the track

If the attack party is large enough they assault the train with automatic weapons and grenades. Part of the raiding party's security element will remove sections of track in both directions, some way away from the scene of the ambush. Explosive charges should be used to destroy the level rail-bed itself. This will prevent any possibility of reinforcements arriving unexpectedly.

Traffic on inland waterways – barges and smaller craft – can be disrupted in much the same way as railway trains, and the same technique is used against columns of vehicles on roads.

SPECIAL FORCES AIRBORNE OPERATIONS

The air is cold at 10,000 metres, with the hatch of the aircraft open and the wind strong enough to break the toughest grip. In the body of the aircraft the six-man HALO team crouch, every nerve tight. Suddenly the darkness is split by the red signal light on the bulkhead and the loadmaster taps the squad leader on the shoulder, sticking a thumb up in the universal sign for good luck.

The light pulses three times, goes out and is immediately replaced by

HIGH ALTITUDE LOW OPENING (HALO)

Use a visual ground marking system when there is good visibility.

1. In HALO operations the Drop Zone markings show the impact point, not the release point.
2. The ground party must indicate wind direction and speed with flares or gas pots at night and panel markings in daylight, all formed as an arrow pointed into the wind.
3. Place markers at 25-metre intervals behind the arrowhead: one if the wind speed is 5-10 knots, two if it is 10-15 knots, and three if it is 15-20 knots.
4. The jump must be aborted if the wind speed is over 20 knots.

green. All six men exit the plane as fast as they can.

For three minutes that feel like forever they dive through the night sky, each one searching the blackness below for the signal lights. Slowly they come into view, and each man traverses through the air until he's aiming at them.

The ground is close and coming up fast before they pull their cords, and the headlong rush gives way to a gentle glide into the landing site. Helping

Helicopters are an excellent means of inserting Special Forces troops and recovering them. Able to ascend and descend almost vertically, land on small plots of ground and to fly safely at low altitudes they are particularly valuable in jungle operations. On the other hand they are very noisy and have limited range.

In Vietnam, **US Special Forces teams led groups of tribal guerrilla fighters against the Viet Cong and were supplied by aircraft like the Caribou, which needs little room to take off and land.**

hands release their harnesses and silent greetings are exchanged, and then they're off about their secret, deadly business.

Airborne operations are the arteries and veins of Special Forces operations in enemy-occupied territory. In most cases, it's just not possible to get men and supplies in and out of operational areas by any other means, and so a great deal of effort goes into making them as safe, secure and simple as possible. This section, taken from the US Army's handbook, introduces you to the methods that are used.

The first stage of any airborne operation is the identification and selection of Drop Zones (DZs) or Landing Zones (LZs).

Local intelligence

Before Special Forces teams are on the ground, they have to depend on local intelligence and information, maps, and aerial or satellite reconnaissance. As many sites as possible are ear-marked for further investigation after teams have been infiltrated, and everything that's known about them is filed away for future use.

One of the first tasks for the infiltration team is a survey of all the possible zones. Because as much detail as possible has been compiled previously, only small corrections will need to be transmitted by radio, to keep traffic to a minimum and maintain security. Any site that shows up badly will just be crossed off the list. More important still, it won't be necessary to transmit even coded map references; sites will always be identified by code names or

numbers, agreed in advance in the security of the operating base.

This cloak of secrecy, by no means unusual in Special Forces operations, is to ensure the security of DZs and LZs, by sites that are very vulnerable to enemy infiltration and surveillance or attack. If the zones' locations fall into enemy hands, not only is the im-

mediate operation compromised, but it may lead to other friendly agents and sympathisers being captured too.

Air delivery operations

While the Special Forces Operations Commander has responsibility for selecting DZs and LZs, it's the air unit carrying out the mission that decides whether to use them or not. The aircrew are at a great deal of risk during these missions, and not just directly from enemy activity.

These air delivery operations are normally carried out by a single aircraft, flying at low level over difficult terrain, in conditions of poor visibility and making frequent changes of course – doing all the things that pilots normally go to any lengths to avoid, in fact. To make matters worse, they have to be pin-point accurate first time around – there's no chance for a second attempt.

The helicopter's ability to hover close to the ground allows troops to be inserted in forested areas where no landing zone can be found.

Selection of delivery zones

Drop Zones and Landing Zones must please both the aircrew who are to fly the mission, and the reception committee who will be there to meet the consignment and passengers. From the aircrew's point of view the zone should be easy to identify from above, and the countryside around it relatively free of obstacles.

Flat or rolling countryside is best, but if the Special Forces operation being supported is located in mountainous country, this may not be possible. In that case it's best to choose sites on broad ridges or plateaux. Small enclosed valleys or hollows, completely surrounded by hills, should be avoided whenever possible.

Open approaches

To give the aircrew as much flexibility as possible in the route they will take to the zone, it should be accessible from all directions. If an approach can only be made from one direction, then the area should be free of obstacles for five km on each side, to give the aircraft space to perform a 'flat turn'.

Hills more than 300 metres higher than the elevation of the zone itself shouldn't be closer than 16 km away when the site is to be used for night operations. In exceptional circum-

stances, where this sort of obstacle can't be avoided, the aircraft may be forced to fly higher than normal, and this may mean the consignment landing a long way from the DZ itself as a result of wind drift.

High wind is only one of the weather conditions that can affect the operation. Low cloud; mist and fog patches; still air where smoke may be present; and even heavy rain or snow – all these can interfere with the aircrew's ability to pick up visual ground signals.

Even particularly tall trees can be a potential danger to an aircraft doing a low-level drop. Where the operation is to take place at 130 metres or less, the safety requirements are that there should be no obstacle higher than 30 metres within 8 km, if possible. Where the aircrew have no choice but to put up with such obstacles in the immediate area of the DZ, their location must be well known.

The drop zone

The DZ should be equally accessible from all directions, so the best shape is round or square, even though the various packages that make up the consignment will land in a line parallel to the course of the aircraft. Dispersion – the distance between the points where each component will hit the ground – is mostly controlled by

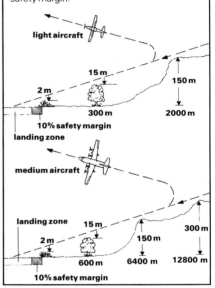

Take-off and approach clearances for fixed-wing aircraft

Minimum landing zone sizes
Light aircraft: 305 m × 15 m
Medium aircraft: 920 m × 30 m
Add a 15-metre cleared strip each side as a safety margin.

LEVEL TURNING RADIUS

1 The general area surrounding the drop zone must be relatively free from obstacles which might endanger the aircraft. Flat or rolling terrain is the best, but plateaux in hilly country can be suitable.

2 Small valleys surrounded by hills should not be used for drop zones.

3 For night operations you must avoid using drop zones with ground rising to 300 metres within 16 km of the site level.

Drop zones with a single, clear line of approach are acceptable if there is a level turning radius of 5 km each side (1.5 km for light aircraft). Remember that these are minimum distances, and if you reduce them the aircraft may be endangered or may fly higher than desirable when making the drop, leaving your supplies drifting on the wind away from the DZ.

LANDMARKS AND WAY-POINTS

The further an aircraft has to fly on a compass course, without way-points (visual checks on position), the more likely it is to be off the correct course. The main causes are tiny inaccuracies in the compass and other instruments, and external factors such as wind.

Special Forces re-supply missions rely on being pinpoint accurate first time: the pilot hasn't time to fly around the countryside looking for the drop zone.

The usual procedure is to select an easily identified landmark somewhere between eight and 24 km away from the DZ itself. The pilot then takes his bearings from this point and flies on a compass heading for a predetermined time to bring the aircraft over the zone.

Features that stand out from the ground may well not make good landmarks from the air, especially at night. These are the sort of things you should be looking for:

1 Coastline in distinctive stretches, especially with breaking surf or white sand beaches, river mouths over 50 metres wide, or sharp promontories or inlets.
2 Rivers more than 30 metres wide. Heavily wooded banks will reduce their visibility.
3 Canals. Their straight course and consistent width make them easy to spot, except where the surrounding countryside follows a uniform pattern.
4 Lakes at least a square kilometre in area with a distinctive shape or feature.
5 Woods and forests a square kilometre and more in size, with clear-cut boundaries or some special identifying feature.
6 Major road and highway intersections
7 Railways, especially when there is snow on the ground.

Drop zone

Requested track

The initial Point must be easily visible from the air

Initial Point

River

Above: Special Forces landings demand manoeuvrable parachutes. This rectangular aerofoil canopy enables you to keep a tight control on your direction and rate of descent.

Below: Securing the drop zone ready to receive air dropped supplies, US troops fan out across the selected site. Note their weak personal camouflage and the giveaway gold watch strap!

the speed of the aircraft over the ground, and the time it takes to get the whole consignment out through the hatch.

Dispersion
The rule of thumb for low-level operations is that half the speed of the aircraft in knots (nautical miles per hour; 100 knots 115 mph), multiplied by the time it takes to get the whole consignment out of the aircraft, will give the dispersion in metres on the ground.

This is the critical distance, because it determines how long the zone needs to be. If possible, add at least 100 metres at each end as a safety factor. Sometimes it may be impossible to find a potential DZ as wide as it is long that meets all the other requirements.

Drop zone axis
If you have to use an oblong DZ, it must have its long axis in absolutely the right direction to allow the pilot of the aircraft the best possible chance of completing his mission safely and delivering the consignment into the right hands. It must make some allo-

HOW TO SEND AN AIRDROP MESSAGE

Whenever you use a radio, keep the three principles of use in mind: **Security, Accuracy**, and **Discipline** (SAD).

Security
Remember the eternal triangle of sender, receiver – and enemy monitor. Keep your transmissions as short as possible, always encode your own and enemy grid references, and be careful not to use names or appointment titles on the radio. If in doubt, encode it into battle code (BATCO). Watch your speech mannerisms; these can also give you away and are a valuable source of long-term intelligence.

Accuracy
You must encode and decode accurately; BATCO leaves no room for mistakes. Corrections take up valuable seconds that could lead to a message being intercepted and a traumatic experience: for example, in a 40-second fire mission a battalion of Soviet BM-21 multi-barrelled rocket-launchers can deliver 14 tonnes of HE (high explosive) or chemical agent onto your position.

Discipline
You must obey radio net discipline, provide constant radio watch, and answer calls correctly and quickly. Use correct voice procedure, apply the rules of BATCO and this will help prevent enemy electronic warfare units from breaking in on your net.

You must be aware of your radio voice. It should differ from normal speech in the following respects: **Rhythm, Speed, Volume** and **Pitch** (RSVP).
1 Rhythm
Divide the message up into logical portions, and deliver it at an even rhythm with pauses; remember the recipient has to write it down.
2 Speed
BATCO delivered too quickly will lead to mistakes; delivery must be slightly slower than normal speech.
3 Volume
Speack slightly louder than normal, but don't shout; this just distorts the message.
4 Pitch
Try to pitch your voice slightly higher than normal; this enhances clarity.

A typical drop zone report

Your report might look like this:

Code name:
DZ HAIRY
Location:
THREE TWO TANGO PAPA TANGO SIX FOUR ONE TWO FOUR THREE
Open quadrants:
OPEN ONE THREE ZERO DEG TO TWO TWO ZERO DEG AND THREE THREE ZERO DEG TO ZERO ONE TWO DEG
Recommended track:
TRACK THREE SIX ZERO DEG

Obstacles:
RADIO TOWER ZERO EIGHT SIX DEG SIX KM

1 The **code name** would have been decided on and briefed prior to the mission.
2 The **location** of the centre of the drop zone is given as a partially encoded six-figure grid reference.
3 The **open quadrants** gives the boundaries of the drop zone. Note

these are in degrees, not mils.
4 The **recommended track** is the approach route, again in degrees.
5 The aircraft would be warned of any potential **obstacles** and their position on or near the track.

Concealed in a treeline, a US Ranger team talks to circling American aircraft near the Cambodian border in 1970.

---

wance for sidewinds, because this will dictate how far to the side of the aircraft's track the drops will land. It's not sufficient to expect the pilot to compensate completely for sidewinds by 'aiming off'.

The surface of the drop zone should be level and free from obstructions such as rocks, fences, trees and powerlines. Where personnel are to be dropped at high altitude (15,000 metres and higher), try to locate DZs in soft snow or grassland. Parachutes fall faster in the thin high air, and so the passenger will hit the ground harder.

Dangerous drop zones
Swamps and marshy ground, including paddy fields, are suitable both for personnel and bundles of goods in the wet season, and for bundles when they are dry or frozen. Water-covered DZs are particularly dangerous to heavily-laden personnel: in the airborne landings on D-Day in Normandy, for example, on 6 June 1944, the American 82nd and 101st Airborne Divisions lost so many men drowned in flooded fields that their combat

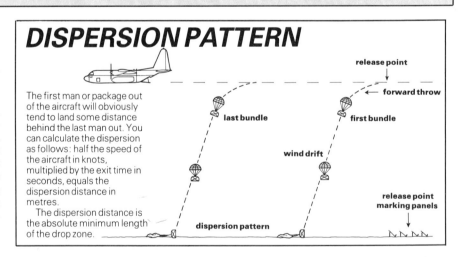

DISPERSION PATTERN

The first man or package out of the aircraft will obviously tend to land some distance behind the last man out. You can calculate the dispersion as follows: half the speed of the aircraft in knots, multiplied by the exit time in seconds, equals the dispersion distance in metres.
The dispersion distance is the absolute minimum length of the drop zone.

release point

forward throw

last bundle

first bundle

wind drift

release point marking panels

dispersion pattern

---

efficiency was badly reduced. They were carrying more than a normal equipment load.

It is possible to drop into water, providing special precautions are taken. The water should be at least 1.5 metres deep; it should be cleared of all obstructions both on and below the surface; it must be 10°C or warmer; it must be free of swift currents and shallow areas and there must be a foolproof recovery system that en-

sures that personnel don't stay long in the water and so cold that their fighting ability is affected.

One particular problem that dropping into water minimises is that of cleaning up the DZ after use, so that no tell-tale signs of the operation are left. Be particularly careful when dropping on to agricultural land. If the fields in question are cultivated, it will be next to impossible to eradicate all traces of the drop.

SECURING THE LANDING ZONE

By the time he'd struggled to get the equipment out on to the ground he was glad he'd been able to get the car so close to the Drop Zone. And God help those three if they'd brought more than the bare minimum of kit — they'd bloody well have to carry it themselves! He kept on looking up at the low grey racing clouds as he put the reflective panels into their frames and arranged them into the letter of the day. An L: L for Larry. It was his name. A good omen? He hoped so.

He hated these minimum personnel drops. He'd not only have to mark the whole DZ himself, but charge around picking everything up afterwards, too. And no security team. He loosened the Colt Centennial Airweight in the shoulder holster for the twentieth time, and then settled down to wait for the reassuring drone of the low-flying aircraft, and the parachutes flowering in the early morning sky....

Marking drop zones

Even if his navigation is excellent and his instruments spot-on, the pilot should still be helped in the final stages of the approach by signals from the ground. At night these can be made by electric torches, flares, small fires or vehicle headlights.

In daylight, the best DZ marking method is the square panels that are supplied as sets to Special Forces units. If they're not available, use bed-sheets or strips of coloured cloth, but make sure they stand out against the background. The squares or strips are used to make up distinctive shapes or letters which are changed every day according to the unit's Standard Operating Instructions.

Smoke grenades or simple smudge pots of burning oil aid identification considerably.

Radio homing devices become more and more popular as the technology that supports them improves, but remember that they need to emit a radio signal to operate. Any signal that you can pick up, the enemy can pick up too.

Ground release points

The ground party has a much better chance of computing the Wind Drift Factor (the distance that bundles and personnel will be carried by the wind) than the pilot does, so they allow for it when marking the Ground Release Point.

The wind doesn't start to act on the load immediately it leaves the air-

REPORTING DROP ZONES

The minimum amount of information required to establish a Drop Zone comprises the following:

1. Code Name and type of DZ — primary, secondary or water.
2. Location and map grid co-ordinates.
3. Open quadrants measured from the centre of the DZ and reported clockwise from the north.
4. Course for incoming aircraft, measured from the centre of the DZ.
5. Obstacles within the reporting radius.
6. Reference point, such as a landmark that can be identified by name alone on issue maps.
7. Special instructions.

Leaping into the blue on exercise: Special Forces parachuting techniques are used to deliver combat teams and military equipment to secret locations deep in hostile territory. Special Forces units stand ready to organise guerrilla armies behind the lines, forcing the enemy to divert forces from the front line to guard installations and strategic roads and railways.

Altitude and temperature
Remember that at high altitudes and high temperatures the density of the air is sharply reduced. This means the helicopter cannot carry as much cargo and will need a longer distance to take off and land.

Approach path
Helicopters need at least one approach path 75 metres wide. For a night landing a helicopter requires a minimum space 90 metres in diameter.

Weapons storage
While you are inside the helicopter and strapped in, hold your rifle with the muzzle pointed to the floor so that, if you accidentally fire your weapon, the bullet goes through the floor and not up towards the vital parts of the aircraft.

Secure camouflage
You should remove all the local vegetation, bits of scrim etc that you are using as personal camouflage when you are entering or exiting the helicopter. Loose bits of camouflage can be sucked into the air intakes and do serious damage to the helicopter.

Fast Attack Vehicle
This armed off the road racer has an excellent cross-country performance and enables Special Forces teams to operate over a much larger area. Weighing just over half a tonne, it can be armed with a Chain Gun, a .50-cal machine-gun or a TOW anti-tank missile launcher.

Avoid the jetwash
When exiting a CH-47 Chinook you must keep going in a straight line after you hit the ground. If you turn to either side you will be caught in the ferocious jetwash from its engines. This is hot enough to set fire to your personal equipment!

craft. The rule of thumb is that the load will travel in the same direction as the aircraft for around a hundred metres before starting to slip off to the side.

Drift is calculated by a simple formula: aircraft height in feet times wind velocity in knots times a constant – three for bundles, four for personnel.

Release Point Markers can then be offset according to the likely wind drift. Obstacles along the flight path might prevent the pilot from seeing

Vital cargo can be dropped without landing with a technique known as Low Level Parachute Extraction Resupply System (LOLEX). The aircraft flies a couple of metres above the ground and a parachute fitted to the cargo pulls it out of the rear door.

HELICOPTER LANDING

For maximum effective use of the helicopter you should position the landing zone to allow take-off and landing into the wind. At night the helicopter will usually have to land to transfer personnel or cargo, but during daylight hours it can fly a couple of metres off the ground and the team can leap out of the back.

Noise

The noise of a large helicopter such as the Chinook coming in to land will reveal your position to any enemy forces nearby. For this reason, helicopter landings must be conducted in remote sites away from the enemy unless you have a powerful security detail in position.

Surface and slope

The surface chosen for the landing zone must be relatively level and free from obstructions such as logs, rocks, ditches or fences. The maximum ground slope permitted is 15°. In dry conditions it is a good idea to dampen the area to reduce the tell-tale dustcloud which also hampers the pilot's visibility.

Water landings

Helicopters like the Chinook can land in a water course provided the bottom is firm and the water no more than 46 cm deep.

STERILISATION PROCEDURES

The reception committee will clean up the drop zone after the operation. Here's a basic checklist:

1 Collect cigarette ends and food wrappers; mislaid equipment; human waste.
2 Collect rigging straps and parachute line.
3 Count all items of equipment, out and in.
4 Bury any waste or unwanted equipment, preferably in a number of different places, at the base of large bushes.
5 Erase drag marks, footprints and impact marks. Use a leafy branch and disguise the freshly-cut end on the tree with mud.
6 Avoid trampling vegetation, especially in cultivated areas.
7 Maintain security on the way in and out of the DZ.

the markers, and to reduce this possibility there must be a clearance on the ground of 15 metres for every metre of the aircraft's height above ground. An obstacle 30 metres high mustn't be closer than 450 metres from the ground markings.

Markers should be sited in such a way as to be visible only from the direction from which the aircraft is approaching. This may mean screening them on three sides, placing them in pits with the appropriate side sloping, or, in the case of panels, mounting them at an angle of 45 degrees.

Unmarked drop zones

In particularly sensitive operations, it may be necessary to make deliveries of personnel and equipment to unmarked drop zones. This usually means a daylight or full-moon drop into a zone that has a particularly well marked geographical feature to identify it.

Because of the need for security, the ground party will have no way of communicating with the aircrew. The pilot will have to calculate wind drift for himself, using the latest available weather reports as a guide, and make allowances accordingly.

Electronic homing devices should be used whenever possible to help the aircrew recognise the DZ, but very careful arrangements are necessary to keep transmissions to a bare minimum.

High Altitude Low Opening

Precision skydiving, an increasingly popular sport, grew out of a Special Forces infiltration technique known as HALO - High Altitude Low Opening – parachute infiltration. Dropping from around 10,000 metres, the parachutists fall free, controlling their direction with hand and arm movements that act in the same way as the control surfaces of an aircraft.

DZ markings indicate the landing point itself in this technique, because the parachutist is able to make correc-

WIND DIRECTION

Arrowhead points in direction of wind. If the wind speed is 5 knots or less, do not add any 'shaft' behind the arrowhead.

Markers 25 metres apart

Put one marker behind the arrowhead if the wind speed is 5-10 knots.

Put a second marker behind if the wind speed is 10-16 knots.

Place a third marker if the wind speed is 15-20 knots.

If the wind speed is over 20 knots the jump should be aborted.

By laying out this arrow pattern on the ground you tell the pilot and parachutists the direction and strength of the wind, which enables them to judge the timing of the jump.

tions for windage. In the last few hundred metres of the descent, however, he will be subject to the same forces that act during a normal descent, and so it is necessary to show wind speed and direction by arranging the target marker in the shape of an arrow pointing into the wind. Up to five knots of wind are indicated by an arrow head, adding one additional marker, to form

a tail, for every further five knots of wind speed.

Using sophisticated electronics, it is not necessary for the target area to be visible from the aircraft, so the HALO jump can be made from above cloud or at night. Equipment can be free fall jumped too, using altimeter-triggered or timed parachute release and the same aiming techniques used in high altitude precision bombing.

The ultimate headbanger! A member of US Special Forces free-falls from 8,000 metres with a Claymore mine strapped to his helmet.

The reception committee

The reception committee is split into five parts, but a single person may, of course, take on more than one role. The five functions are
1 Command party, to control and co-ordinate the operation and provide medical support.
2 Marking party, which sets out and collects markers and assists in recovering equipment and personnel and sterilizing the site.
3 Security party, which ensures that unfriendly elements don't interfere in the operation.
4 Recovery party, ideally two men for each bundle or parachute. They should be spread out along the drop axis at the same interval as the drops are expected. Any back-up should be stationed at the far end of the drop track, because the drop is more likely to overshoot than undershoot. The recovery party is also responsible for the clean-up 'sanitisation' of the drop site, and that includes briefing all members of the reception committee on proper procedures. A surveillance team should keep watch over the DZ for 48 hours after the operation to warn of enemy activity.
5 Transportation party, responsible for getting personnel and equipment

away from the DZ according to a pre-arranged system. The transportation party will usually include all members of the command, marking and recovery parties.

Security

Because security and concealment is so important to Special Forces operations, you must pay a lot of attention to those considerations when selecting reception zones. Three factors are important: freedom from enemy interference on the ground; accessibility by means of concealed or secure routes for the reception committee; and proximity to areas suitable for hiding supplies and equipment.

Avoiding the enemy

It goes almost without saying that the aircraft's route into and out of the DZ must avoid enemy troop installations. There must be a very high level of patrol activity around the DZ for some time before the operation is due to take place. When the aircraft is actually scheduled to land, rather than merely drop a consignment from the air, vehicles with mounted automatic weapons should be available, to keep pace with the aircraft on both sides during landing and take-off (bear in mind that the vehicles will have to be moving and up to speed at the point where the aircraft will touch down.) If oncoming fire is received, the crews of these vehicles must be in a position to suppress it immediately.

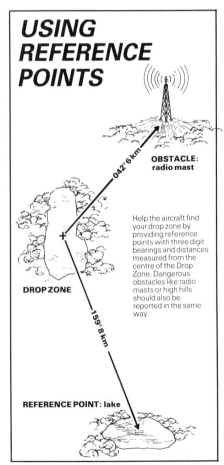

USING REFERENCE POINTS

OBSTACLE: radio mast

042° 6 km

159° 8 km

Help the aircraft find your drop zone by providing reference points with three digit bearings and distances measured from the centre of the Drop Zone. Dangerous obstacles like radio masts or high hills should also be reported in the same way.

DROP ZONE

REFERENCE POINT: lake

A C-130 Hercules equipped with a skyhook for covert operations; the yoke used to guide the lift line to the centre is folded back. Inside the aircraft is an electric or hydraulic winch to haul up the man or cargo.

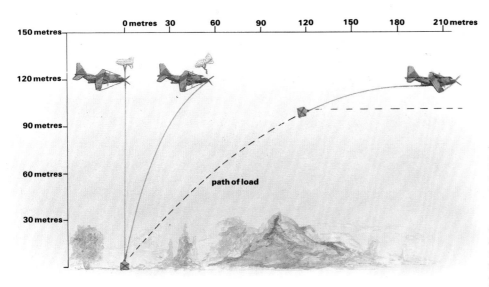

Skyhook is used to extract a single person or small package by aircraft without the plane having to land. Gas bottles inflate the balloon with helium and attach the other end of the line to a harness fitted to you or the cargo. The aircraft's yoke catches the line and snatches the person or cargo into the air.

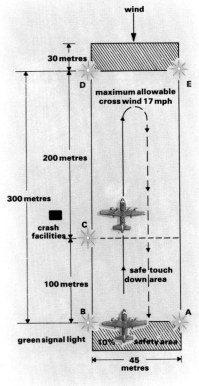

Above: Minimum dimensions of a night landing zone for light aircraft. The area at the side for crash facilities is not essential, but it is worth clearing if you have the time and space.

Aircraft are actually brought in to land only if there's no other way to complete the mission, and that usually means when people or equipment are to be evacuated. Purpose-built light aircraft are able to land and take off in very short spaces, but their range is extremely limited.

In general, medium aircraft need a flat, cleared space 1,000 metres long and 30 metres wide. Even light aircraft need 350 metres to land and take off in safety. 'Flat and cleared' in this context means no ditches, ruts, logs, fences, hedges, bushes or rocks bigger than a man's fist – quite an undertaking! It's clear from this that construct-ing a landing strip will be a major operation, and one that won't be undertaken for just a single mission.

There are field expedients, though – ice, for example. Twenty cm of ice will support a light aircraft, and 60 cm of ice – quite common enough in high latitudes – will take the weight of a medium sized transport plane. Wide, sandy beaches can also be used without further preparation. The stretch of sand between high and low water marks is usually firm and even.

Skyhooks

One of the most dramatic of all Spe-cial Forces airborne operations is the skyhook – a method of picking up pas-sengers and cargo without touching down. Put simply, skyhook opera-tions require an aircraft fitted with a yoke - a horizontal 8-metre wide fork – on the nose, and an 18 cubic metre helium-filled balloon fitted with 150 metres of lifting line.

The skyhook kit, in two containers, is dropped to evacuees – wounded US personnel, downed aircrew, guides, even corpses where it is politically advisable to recover them. It consists of the balloon and two containers of gas to inflate it, lifting line, protective clothing and a harness. An amphi-bious version also includes an inflat-able boat.

The skyhook kit is dropped on the first pass over the DZ. The person to be extracted puts on the suit and harness, attaches the lift line and inflates the balloon. As it rises, he sits facing the approaching aircraft and composes himself. On the aircraft's second pass it catches up the lift line, releases the balloon, and the evacuee is hauled up into the aircraft.

Gurkhas on an upriver recce vehicle on patrol, Malaysia, 1985.

STRIKE FROM THE SEA

A moonless night, a deserted stretch of coastline. A periscope breaks the surface of the silent sea for a moment, sweeps round once, then disappears beneath the waves again. A lone swimmer, dressed in black from head to foot, emerges from the surf and creeps up the beach, buries his equipment and disappears into the trees. Another US Special Forces operation is under way, and the enemy doesn't know the first thing about it.

Special Forces operations often start and finish on a beach. Even though airborne insertion is faster and more flexible, when safety and secrecy are the first considerations the unit commander will often opt to go in by submarine, landing his men from inflatable boats or getting them to swim. This is how US Special Forces set about landing men and equipment from the sea.

Submarines are self-contained, safe from prying eyes. This means that amphibious Special Forces missions can be mounted at extremely long range – from the other side of the world if necessary. The long journey time can often be an advantage in itself, because it allows the operational plan to be studied, pulled apart and put back together again until it is foolproof.

The first consideration is the type of boat available to carry the team to the landing site. Where security comes first, this will usually be a submarine, but that will put a severe limitation on the amount of equipment that can be carried, which may mean that a re-supply mission will be necessary. However, for infiltrating small groups of people into existing operations, or for mounting raids, the submarine is ideal.

The team leader's first job is to familiarise himself with the characteristics of the vessel assigned to the operation. Amongst other things this will determine how the team's equipment is to be packed, because everything must be in secure waterproof bundles.

The US Navy SEALs are the equivalent of the SBS and specialize in clandestine operations along enemy-held coastlines. Coming ashore from submarines or special assault craft, they recce ahead of amphibious assaults or take out targets from shore-based missile sites to enemy ships in harbour.

6 points for leaving a surfaced submarine

1. Crew members and troops should be fully briefed on the debarkation plan.
2. Inspect all your kit before the debarkation.
3. Wait for the crew to man their debarkation stations first before going to yours.
4. Swimmers debark in pairs from the conning tower of the submarine, which will surface with its decks awash.
5. Form up in the control room with all your kit. If there is space the first pair can be in the conning tower ready for the submarine to surface.
6. If possible, rehearse the whole debarkation procedure before you do it in a tactical situation.

Space is very limited in submarines, but there is room in the flooding compartments for kit such as inflatable boats, and that's where they are carried.

The mission can be split down into four stages.

1 Movement to the disembarkation point. This part of the operation is normally under the control and charge of regular navy personnel.

2 Transfer from the ocean-going vessel to the landing craft, and movement to the landing site.

Left: Submarines enable you to approach close to the enemy coast without being detected and reduce the amount of time you spend in or on the water.

Underwater infiltration

As radar and anti-aircraft weapons become increasingly effective, underwater infiltration has become an increasingly important method of infiltrating Special Forces troops. The key to any successful infiltration may be summed up as Short, Simple and Secure. Underwater operations using SCUBA equipment provide an extremely secure method of infiltrating short distances by water.

Shallow depth

Try to make your approach at the shallowest possible depth so that your air supplies last longer, and you and your equipment do not suffer the problems associated with sustained diving at great depths. There is another reason: swimmer detection systems find it harder to detect people at shallow depths.

Facemask

You can test whether a facemask fits you properly in two ways: (**1**) Hold it gently in place with one hand, inhale through the nose and let go of the mask. It should stay in place, held by the suction. (**2**) Put the mask on and adjust the headstrap, inhale through the nose and, if the mask seals, it should provide a good seal in the water. Get one with a shatterproof safety glass faceplate; the plastic ones fog up quickly and are easily scratched.

Security

Part of the team should land ahead of the main body to check that the beach is clear. Surfacing and removing their masks outside the surf zone, the security team goes ashore and signals 'Clear' to the rest of the troops when it has examined the beach area.

3 Disposal of the landing craft. This may mean destroying it, hiding it, or naval personnel ferrying it back to the mother ship.

4 Sanitization of the landing site and movement to the operational area.

The only common variation on this theme involves the use of indigenous craft – fishing boats, for example – which rendezvous with the mother ship some considerable distance off shore. Men and material can then be transferred, and infiltrated under cover of the boat's normal day-to-day activities.

Small boat handling is a specialised technique, and though it is part of general Special Forces training the unit commander will use the sea voyage to the disembarkation point to

Combat loads
Combat loads must be light and small and should include only equipment, weapons, and ammunition needed for the mission. You must have a proper equipment unloading plan and preferably have it rehearsed before landing.

Fins
A safety line can be attached to each swim fin and secured to your ankles to prevent you losing the fins if a strap breaks or if they are pulled from your feet by water action. Avoid fins with small or soft blades.

Knives
All swimmers should carry a knife with a corrosion-resistant blade such as stainless steel, and a rubber or plastic handle. Wooden handles have to be painted, oiled or waxed to waterproof them, which makes them fairly pointless, and cork or bone handles deteriorate rapidly when immersed in salt water.

Swimmer delivery vehicle
The furthest reasonable distance the swimming team should have to cover is 1,500 metres. If the submarine cannot approach this close to the target area, then swimmer delivery vehicles should be used to reduce fatigue.

go over boat drill: transferring men and materials into the landing craft while underway, personnel recovery, communications drill and the use of special equipment such as the submarine escape trunk.

Physical exercise plays a big part in the shipboard life too, to ensure that the team is in top condition for the operation. This is a particular problem when the mother ship is a submarine making a completely submerged passage. The modern generation of submarines routinely cross oceans without ever surfacing, and there's not a lot of spare space on board for calisthenics and aerobic exercises!

Transferring at sea

From a surface ship, the transfer procedure is quite simple. The landing craft are inflated and sent over the side. A scrambling net is let down, and the operational team instal themselves in the inflatables, stow their equipment, and set off on their long journey to the beach.

And it will be a long journey. To maintain security, the mother ship will never come above the horizon, as seen from the shore – maybe a distance of more than 20 miles.

Outboard engines are notoriously noisy. There are electric versions which are almost silent, but they have a very limited range. To get around this problem the landing craft may be towed in close to shore by a purpose-built tug – low to the water and fitted with a heavily-silenced inboard engine. The landing craft then make their way the last two or three miles to

Some Special Forces equipment might seem to belong more on a James Bond movie set than with a real military unit, but mini-submarines and submersible dinghies are vital to undersea raiders like the SEALs.

UNDERWATER SEARCHING

An underwater search is normally conducted secretly, and is usually done to locate a lost object – e.g. a missile dropped by an aircraft that NATO does not want to fall into Soviet hands. The procedure for an underwater search is:

1 All kit must be totally prepared before entering the water.

2 All personnel must be fully briefed on the part they are to play in the search.

3 If water conditions are not ideal (good visibility, clear weather and current under 1 knot), rehearsals should be conducted if possible.

4 If the area has a muddy or loose sandy bottom, divers should take care to avoid stirring up the silt. They should remain more than 1 metre above the bottom if possible so that their fin movements do not disturb the bottom.

The creature from the Black Lagoon: a US Navy SEAL floats himself on to the beach armed with a 12-gauge pump-action shotgun for combat at point-blank range.

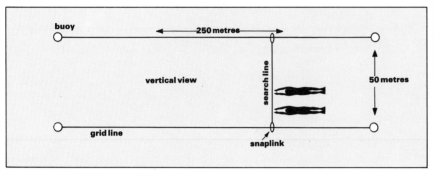

RUNNING JACK-STAY SEARCH

This is a fairly quick search technique used to find medium-sized or brightly coloured objects.

1 Only use in clear water

2 Use only experienced personnel

3 Requires one diver per 5 metres of line

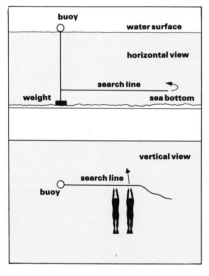

CIRCLE LINE SEARCH

This is another quick search technique, depending on the number of divers involved, and is useful in murky water or at night when searching for small objects. Inexperienced personnel can be used.

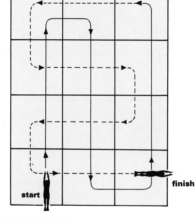

CHECKERBOARD JACK-STAY SEARCH

This is a variation of the jack-stay search used to locate small objects. In this method, the basic jack-stay system shown above is completed as normal, then the lines are taken up and placed perpendicular to the original lines and the search process repeated over the same area.

SHIPBOTTOM SEARCHES

When searching a friendly ship for mines:

1 Get a diagram of the hull from the ship's engineer.

2 Ensure that each diver knows the search procedure and objective before the dive.

3 Take a headcount of divers before starting.

4 Notify the ship's captain and harbour master before starting.

5 Wait for all machinery on the ship that might affect the dive to be shut down, especially vents, exhaust ports and engines.

6 Make sure that the sonar is turned off.

7 Once the vessel is ready, announce **"Divers underwater"**.

8 Start at the stern and work toward the bow, paying close attention to all hatches and vents. Be careful when in the vicinity of screws and salt water intakes.

9 If enemy mines are found, do not tamper with them but inform Navy Explosive Ordnance Disposal (EOD) personnel, who will deal with them.

10 Sweep the vessel several times if possible. Conduct a headcount of divers afterwards.

the beach under their own steam – or, rather, by the muscle power of the Special Forces team who are paddling.

Transferring from a submarine to the landing craft is either a lot easier, or a lot more difficult, depending on which one of the three methods is chosen. If the submarine can come to the surface, the inflatables can be dropped over the side, the landing party boards, and away they go. In one interesting variation to this method the boats are placed on the deck of the submarine and the crew get aboard, then the submarine submerges gently beneath them.

Submarine landing

Alternatively, the submarine commander comes up to just below the surface, exposing only the very tip of the conning tower and presenting a very small picture, even to enemy radar. The landing party exits and either swims to the landing point, on a compass bearing, or inflates the boats in the water and paddles in.

The most secure technique of all requires the landing party to exit the submarine underwater, usually with the ship completely stationary and sitting on the bottom. Team members wearing SCUBA (Self-Contained Underwater Breathing Apparatus) then emerge from a hatch connected to an air-lock and swim under water to the landing place.

Special Forces personnel who undertake missions like this have to be highly trained and very, very fit. If it's necessary to use this 'locking out' technique with technicians or mission specialists of any kind, who are not professional divers, then the lead pair will exit with inflatable boats and set them up on the surface. The rest of the team can then make 'free ascents' using the submarine's ordinary escape hatch, join up with the divers, and make their way to the beach in the normal way.

On the way in

In anything but a flat calm it will be impossible to see the shore for most of the journey in, except when you get up on to the crest of a wave. Even then, you probably won't have time to get a fix on your objective. You have to navigate by compass, and that's satisfactory as long as you know where you are.

Unfortunately, the seas and oceans never stand still. Except for a very short period at high and low tide (called 'slack water'), they are constantly in motion – and not just straight in to the beach and out again, either. On top of that there are coastal currents to contend with, and though they may run in the same direction all the time they certainly don't always run at the same speed.

These factors are much worse in some parts of the world than in others. The Mediterranean, for example, has no tides to speak of, while the Bay of Fundy and the Bristol Channel have up to 15 metres between low and high water. And around the Channel Islands they have four tides a day instead of two!

It's possible to compensate for all this, and the commander of the mother ship will have calculated the

transfer point to take account of all the known factors. Even so, the landing party will have to work hard to keep on course, and will be grateful for all the help they can get.

Find the beach

If there's no reception committee on the beach, the landing party will navigate for themselves, using the compass, sun or star sights and shoreline observation, and will be rather lucky to hit the beach at precisely the right place except in the easiest possible conditions.

If there is a beach party they can help with visible light, well shielded and only allowed to shine out to sea; infra-red beacons, which the boat party can pick up using special goggles; underwater sound, and radio.

The surf zone doesn't stretch very far out from the shore. When the landing party is close to its outer limit they

US Navy SEALs cling to their rubber dinghy as it is towed away from the coast at high speed by a cutter. You must minimise the time spent in transit between friendly vessel and enemy coast.

stop and maintain position. Scout swimmers get into the water, approach the beach and check it out. When they are sure there's no enemy activity they signal the rest of the party to come in.

There are no exceptions to this procedure. Even though there may be a reception committee waiting, with established perimeter security and reconnaissance patrols, the landing party still performs its own reconnaissance.

When searching for mines, lost missiles or equipment, you divide the area into manageable units using lengths of nylon rope. A systematic search can then begin, carefully examining each unit in turn. If time allows, search each one twice.

INDEX